Charles Johnson's *General History of the Pyrates* and Global Commerce

TRANSITS

LITERATURE, THOUGHT & CULTURE, 1650–1850

Series editors:
Miriam L. Wallace, University of Illinois Springfield
Mona Narain, Texas Christian University

A landmark series in long-eighteenth-century studies, *Transits* publishes monographs and edited volumes that are timely, transformative in their approach, and global in their engagement with arts, literature, culture, and history. Books in the series have engaged with visual arts, environment, politics, material culture, travel, theater and performance, embodiment, connections between the natural sciences and medical humanities, writing and book history, sexuality, gender, disability, race, and colonialism from Britain and Europe to the Americas, the Far East, the Middle/Near East, Africa, and Oceania. Works that make provocative connections across time, space, geography, or intellectual history, or that develop new modes of critical imagining are particularly welcome.

Recent titles in the series:

Charles Johnson's "General History of the Pyrates" and Global Commerce
Noel Chevalier

Revisiting Richardson
Rebecca Anne Barr and Bonnie Latimer, eds.

British Romanticism and Prison Reform
Jonas Cope

Prolific Ground: Landscape and British Women's Writing, 1690–1790
Nicolle Jordan

Consuming Anxieties: Alcohol, Tobacco, and Trade in British Satire, 1660–1751
Dayne C. Riley

The Part and the Whole in Early American Literature, Print Culture, and Art
Matthew Pethers and Daniel Diez Couch, eds.

Teaching the Eighteenth Century Now: Pedagogy as Ethical Engagement
Kate Parker and Miriam L. Wallace, eds.

Women and Music in the Age of Austen
Linda Zionkowski with Miriam F. Hart, eds.

For more information about the series, please visit bucknelluniversitypress.org.

Charles Johnson's *General History of the Pyrates* and Global Commerce

NOEL CHEVALIER

BUCKNELL UNIVERSITY PRESS
LEWISBURG, PENNSYLVANIA

Library of Congress Cataloging-in-Publication Data

Names: Chevalier, Noel, 1963– author.
Title: Charles Johnson's "General history of the pyrates" and global commerce / Noel Chevalier.
Description: Lewisburg, Pennsylvania : Bucknell University Press, 2025. | Series: Transits: literature, thought & culture, 1650–1850 | Includes bibliographical references and index.
Identifiers: LCCN 2024041361 | ISBN 9781684485536 (paperback) | ISBN 9781684485543 (hardcover) | ISBN 9781684485550 (ebook)
Subjects: LCSH: Defoe, Daniel, 1661?–1731. General history of the robberies and murders of the most notorious pyrates. | International trade—History.
Classification: LCC F2161 .J6434 2025 | DDC 972.9—dc23/eng/20251209
LC record available at https://lccn.loc.gov/2024041361

A British Cataloging-in-Publication record for this book is available from the British Library.

∞ The paper used in this publication meets the requirements of the American National Standard for Information Sciences—Permanence of Paper for Printed Library Materials, ANSI Z39.48-1992.

bucknelluniversitypress.org

Distributed worldwide by Rutgers University Press

For Heather

CONTENTS

ILLUSTRATIONS

PREFACE

At the end of August, 1881, Robert Louis Stevenson confessed to his friend William Ernest Henley that he was in the middle of writing a book for boys "about Buccaneers," passing it off as "quite silly and horrid fun," although a project that had "more coin in it than any amount of crawlers."[1] Yet Stevenson also wanted to ground his book in some historical reality; in the letter, he begs Henley to find him "the *best* book about the Buccaneers that can be had."[2] Henley's choice (the "correct choice," as the editor of the Broadview edition, John Sutherland, has it) was Captain Charles Johnson's *General History of the Pyrates*.[3] What Stevenson produced with the help of Johnson's book was, of course, the most enduring and iconic pirate narrative ever written, *Treasure Island*.

Stevenson's almost blushing reference to a pirate story as "silly and horrid fun," yet also a story that could be potentially quite lucrative—he snorted to Henley that "if this don't fetch the kids, why, they have gone rotten since my day"[4]—curiously reflects the way Johnson's *General History* has been received since its first publication in 1724. Stevenson may have thought he was writing a simple entertaining potboiler for some much-needed cash, but *Treasure Island* has proven itself quite worthy of serious literary study. So, too, the *General History* has been dismissed even by sympathetic scholars as, in Arne Bialuschewski's words, "above all . . . designed to fill [its author's] purse."[5] Yet, looking past the book as merely a collection of hair-raising crime stories designed to cash in on a vogue for pirate tales in the 1720s, it is possible to detect something much more in this highly unusual and surprisingly complex book.

At first glance, it has all the hallmarks of a Grub Street production: it is frustratingly organized and sometimes sloppily printed; its writing is highly uneven, even in its revisions; it freely blends history and fiction, which therefore makes it both invaluable as an historical source and unfortunately responsible for much of the misinformation about piracy that went unchecked until the end of the twentieth century. Its publication history is complex, even if one ignores the plagiarized versions it spawned and its second life as part of comprehensive anthology of crime narratives after 1730. Its title is almost deliberately misleading: *General History* is neither especially general, focusing as it does almost exclusively on pirates who were active between 1716 and 1726, nor much of a history, being mainly a collection of discrete, albeit related, biographies. Even its authorship is shrouded in mystery and controversy: John Robert Moore's confident attribution to Daniel Defoe has been irrevocably challenged, but no one has been able to provide a definitive substitute, and much sound scholarship has already been done on the book under the assumption of Defoe's authorship.

Underneath its surface, however, the text reveals itself to be surprisingly aware of, and frequently engages in, social, political, and economic issues of the 1720s. From references to the South Sea Bubble and remarks on colonial trade, to moral and political issues that echo *Cato's Letters* and Mandeville's *Fable of the Bees*, Johnson's *General History* uses its pirate subject as mirrors of the age, ultimately suggesting that, odious as they are, pirates differ from better-placed criminals only in class, and in the harsh punishments meted out to them that their betters almost always escaped: an observation John Gay would make a major theme in 1728 in *The Beggar's Opera*. We have, I think, only begun to understand how to read the *General History*, and to understand its place as an important text of its own time. This book, I hope, will open a fuller exploration of *General History* and its complexities.

This book owes a great deal to many people who helped create it. Special thanks are due to Arne Bialuschewski, Fraser Easton, Manuel Schonhorn, and Max Novak, who all generously shared their expertise with me and willingly listened to my ideas and commented on early versions of these chapters as they took shape. An extra vote of thanks belongs to my friend and coeditor, Manushag Powell, whose enthusiasm for and belief in Johnson's book helped keep up my own spirit to see this project through to completion. The students of my undergraduate course, the Literature of Pirates, eagerly engage in discussions of some of the issues I wrestle with here, and ask many insightful questions. The honors and graduate students of my course on the Golden Age of Piracy accepted my own anxieties and ambiguities, and turned them into fascinating, fruitful, and lively discussions: a tot of rum is due to Laetitia Adams, Sara Donovan, Destiny Kaus, Tomi Oyegoke, Kate Spencer, Cassandra Virgin, and Aysha Yaqoob for all their ideas and their perceptions. I am grateful for the support provided by Luther College, especially for two sabbatical semesters to complete the bulk of the research and writing. Finally, I am grateful every day for the love and support of my wife, Heather McKerracher, who embarked on this voyage with me, and weathered the storms and waited out the calms with endless patience and encouragement, seasoned with her keen, pragmatic mind and quick wit. She is the best shipmate I could ever have asked for.

Portions of chapter 3 have been previously published as "Treasures of the Imagination: Rethinking Pirate Booty in Pirate Narratives," *Lumen* 37 (2018): 17–33, https://doi.org/10.7202/1042221ar. An early version of chapter 4 was published as "'Pirate Vices, Public Benefits': The Social Ethics of Piracy in the 1720s," *Studies in Eighteenth-Century Culture* 51, no. 1 (2022): 147–162, https://doi.org/10.1353/sec.2022.0009.

NOTE ON CITATIONS

The edition of *General History of the Pyrates* by Manuel Schonhorn, first published in London by J. M. Dent in 1972 and updated and lightly corrected in the edition published in New York by Dover in 1999, has become the standard edition for scholarly citations. However, since much of the present book is concerned with the publication history of *General History* and the various textual revisions between its four major editions, Schonhorn's edition is inadequate as a text. Citations in this book will be made from the earliest appearance of the passage in question. The four editions of *General History* published between 1724 and 1728 are designated thus:

1724a: First edition, Charles Rivington.
  Published Wednesday, 13 May 1724. Price 4s.
1724b: Second edition, Thomas Warner
  Advertised as "just published" Saturday, 29 August 1724. Price 5s.
1725: Third edition, Thomas Warner (= 1724b with one addition)
  Published Thursday, 10 June 1725. Price 5s.
1728: Fourth edition: Thomas Woodward (2 vols.)
  Published Saturday, 27 July 1728 (4th ed. of vol 1 with the addition of vol. 2).

For the benefit of scholars, all citations will contain references to the Schonhorn's 1999 Dover edition. Thus, "1724a, 293–294 [328]" means that the passage appeared in the first edition, pages 293–294, and can be found in Schonhorn's edition on page 328. If a passage appears in both 1724a and 1724b, I cite the earlier. Substantive differences between editions will be noted in footnotes. By using this system, I hope to alert readers to the fact that *General History* exists in multiple versions, while at the same time I want to retain continuity between my work and other scholarship. At present, a new edition of *General History* is in preparation under the editorship of myself and Manushag Powell: we hope that edition, to be published by Hackett, will become the new standard scholarly text for Johnson's book.

Charles Johnson's *General History of the Pyrates* and Global Commerce

INTRODUCTION

Monstrous Business

IN JANUARY 2014, THE STARZ CABLE network launched *Black Sails*, a drama series that revisits the familiar world of eighteenth-century pirates, retrofitted this time to accommodate twenty-first-century sensibilities. The series takes some of Robert Louis Stevenson's *Treasure Island* characters—Captain Flint, Billy Bones, and, of course, Long John Silver—and recontextualizes them with real early-eighteenth-century pirates and pirate catchers: Charles Vane, John Rackam, Anne Bonny, Blackbeard, and Woodes Rogers. Like many contemporary cable shows, it features plenty of graphic violence and explicit nudity and sex, along with generous amounts of coarse language and hard booze, but it also attempts some degree of historical accuracy, and tries, despite its attractive, well-toned bodies and twenty-first-century speech idioms, to present the world of the pirates of the so-called Golden Age much as it might have been—or, at least, as it might have been without straying too far from our received ideas of pirates.

Like all pirate narratives, *Black Sails* resides within a fantasy space. The series portrays the colony of New Providence in 1715 as little more than a dumping ground for Britain's social detritus: drunks, thieves, whores, and, of course, pirates. Legitimate commerce struggles to survive in such an environment, if it even exists. The most successful business in the town is the brothel; most of the rest of the commerce is controlled by a former prostitute who also happens to have been the lover of the historical pirate Charles Vane.

Black Sails' use of many well-worn stereotypes of the colonial Caribbean satisfies its audience's expectation of what one should find in a pirate story. Everybody knows what pirates are supposed to look like. Pirates even have an immediately recognizable vernacular, celebrated every 19 September on "Talk Like a Pirate Day."[1] After nearly 300 years of image making, the pirate has come to occupy what Neil Rennie has called a "Treasure Neverland," a series of tropes that evoke a sense of the so-called Golden Age of Piracy,[2] forever obscuring the fact that pirates existed long before the late seventeenth- and early eighteenth-century world in which many pirate stories are set, and they continue existing to this day. These tropes—universally fixed as the de facto image of the pirate—serve both to mark the pirate as an eternal "other" and to decontextualize pirates from the eighteenth-century maritime and colonial culture out of which they came. In popular culture, the pirate is more a costume than a person; like the cowboy, the pirate forever exists in a lawless frontier setting, in real places long since tamed, urbanized, and converted into tourist attractions. The pirates of popular imagination are a fiction; Treasure Neverland is a perpetual fantasy space, a series of easily adaptable signifiers.

Black Sails, moreover, veers between two images that exemplify the "Treasure Neverland" pirate. As one might expect, we almost immediately are presented with the pirates as brutal, hard-drinking, oversexed, rapacious sociopaths—the monsters of the Caribbean. As we shall see, literary pirates occupy roughly the same ontological space as monsters; like werewolves, vampires, and zombies, pirates are both human and not-human, possessing useful skills necessary to survive in a new economic climate, but transformed by greed, violence, blasphemy, and sexual indecency into something repellent and inherently antisocial, the very antithesis of good capitalism.

At the same time, famous pirates, such as Blackbeard or even, in the series, Charles Vane, exhibit a kind of greatness that elevates them beyond mere brutes. Pirate captains are leaders, the underworld counterpart of "respectable" political figures—who themselves are satirically portrayed in *Black Sails* as the same as the underworld pirate captains. Anxiety and ambiguity, then, form the heart of eighteenth-century pirate narratives. Somewhere between the "Monster" and the "Great Man," we find the pirate.

The setting of *Black Sails*, therefore, exemplifies the concept of Treasure Neverland, but the defining features of this space were largely created centuries earlier by antipirate (and anticolonial) writing during the period when these pirates were most active. Only recently have scholars begun to define this space apart from the historical reality of these colonies, and the Treasure Neverland motif persists well into the twenty-first century, in shows such as *Black Sails*, in video games such as *Sid Meier's Pirates* and one installment of the *Assassin's Creed* series, and, of course, in the popular *Pirates of the Caribbean* films. Treasure Neverland has enjoyed a healthy existence since the eighteenth century, but its greatest expression can be seen in the popular fiction of the nineteenth: the *Treasure Island* characters in *Black Sails* remind us that the basic tropes of pirate fiction even now owe a huge debt to Stevenson, but Stevenson's own conception of pirates ultimately derives from a book that appeared pseudonymously in the first decades of the eighteenth century that was single-handedly responsible for fixing pirates and pirate narratives forever: Captain Charles Johnson's *A General History of the Pyrates*.[3]

It is hard to overstate the importance of Johnson's *General History* in providing the historical and narrative grounding for the pirate literature that followed it. At the same time, it is easy to dismiss *General History* as simply a source book of facts about eighteenth-century piracy. *General History* certainly is a source book, and there is no doubt that Stevenson saw it as such, but it is much more than that. As the puffs that appeared in *Mist's Weekly Journal* around the time of the first edition suggest, the book is to be of interest to readers beyond its bloody and salacious stories; it is an attempt to understand the pirates of the Golden Age as a social and political, as well as an economic, phenomenon. *General History* is the most comprehensive treatment of piracy as a distinct culture from the period, and that fact, more than anything, is what led to the pirates who were active between 1713 and 1726 becoming the archetype of all pirates in popular culture.

The popular pirate image, as Rennie and others have adequately traced, embodies contradictions one might expect of a figure that veers between Monster and Great Man. In popular imagination, the pirate is a relatively safe, self-contained icon of rogue masculinity, at once transgressive and wholly normative; sexy enough to serve as a mascot for a brand of rum, yet sanitized enough to be entirely suitable for children. The pirate's best-known contemporary incarnation, Captain Jack Sparrow, borrows elements of the rock star and the drag queen, and yet even his delightful outrageousness is brought into line by the taming hand of Disney. These kinds of contradictions have been explored before. For example, Hans Turley has analyzed the ambiguity of piracy in *Rum, Sodomy, and the Lash* (1999), applying queer theory to show how the pirate and the "sodomite" occupy a similar theoretical space in eighteenth-century discourse.[4] Both transgress heteronormative rules, especially in terms of domestic life: the sodomite rejects heterosexual norms in favor of an "unnatural" union with other men, while the pirate rejects the domestic norms of economics that define, as Nancy Armstrong puts it, the husband as "earner and producer, with [the wife] as a wise spender and tasteful consumer."[5] For pirates, domestic life happens at sea, in the company of other men. Despite *Black Sails'* attempts to portray its pirates as vigorously heterosexual men, so hungry for regular sexual activity that they erect a "fuck tent" on the beach for the men to use with local prostitutes while the ship is being careened, the show also reinscribes the idea that pirate life is innately homosocial, and that pirates must reject the regular company of women, except for sexual purposes. *Black Sails*, in fact, at times goes out of its way to emphasize that the pirates of Charles Vane's crew are as obsessed with sex almost as much as they are with plunder. Clearly, the pirate is a mass of ambiguous signifiers, and *General History* both contains and nurtures those ambiguities in its pages.[6]

The ambiguity of pirates is related to another feature routinely associated with them: their inherent fearsomeness. While Joel H. Baer has suggested that historical pirates were mainly common sailors who were desperately trying to improve a harsh and unrewarding existence, literary pirates are at once jolly, free-wheeling anarchists and ruthless, sadistic murderers. This image, not entirely created out of thin air, nevertheless plays to a considerable anxiety about piracy that is reflected in their legal definition, *hostis humani generis*—"the enemy of all humanity." The main argument for wiping out piracy is the fear that pirates, in their jolly anarchy, would destabilize all commerce and bring the whole enterprise of empire building to a crashing halt. There is little evidence that pirates, even during the height of the Golden Age, were ever that powerful, but the fear that they could gain such power was enough to generate the anxiety that pervades the pages of pirate narratives.

I am not interested here in either relieving the anxiety or clearing up the ambiguity. If anything, what follows assumes that the term "pirate" is perpetually polysemous and multifaceted, and was so even at the time the pirates themselves were active. Writers on piracy published in the 1720s—and, in particular, the writer or writers of *General History*—made pirates into whatever they needed them to be: sometimes mere criminals, sometimes criminals with a strain of misguided heroism inherent in them. At times, they even appear as renegade versions of *Homo economicus*, both an example and a warning to a nation that had positioned itself to become a leader in a nascent global economy. Pirates were, of course, quite real, but it was important that, in the 1720s, they also be quite symbolic.

BRITAIN AND COLONIAL ECONOMY IN THE 1720S

In the preface of the *General History*, Johnson feels compelled to mention that "no Apology" is needed for recording "nothing but the Actions of a Parcel of Robbers." In fact, a book about criminal activity was, in many ways, quite fitting for the decade in which it appeared. Clement Hawes has suggested that "the decade of the 1720s is a cultural moment in Britain that seems particularly marked, above all, by a pervasive and disorienting sense of criminality."[7] The South Sea Bubble and its aftermath, the notorious Black Act of 1723, the rise and fall of Jonathan Wild, the seeming increase in criminal gangs around London, and, of course, the proliferation of piracy: whether or not crime was greater after the War of the Spanish Succession (1701–1714), there certainly was the perception that the 1720s were an especially crime-ridden and dangerous decade. Such a perception was helped in no small part by John Trenchard and Thomas Gordon's *Cato's Letters*, which examined moral conduct in the months following the collapse of the South Sea Bubble; by Daniel Defoe's fiction, which elevated common criminals such as Moll Flanders and Colonel Jacque to the status of heroic figures; by Bernard Mandeville's *Fable of the Bees*, whose reissue in 1723 set off a storm of debate about the "proper" use of vice and luxury; and, at the end of the decade, by John Gay's phenomenal *Beggar's Opera*, which reveled in the irony of thieves and prostitutes aping the conventions of opera seria even as it offered pointed commentary on the leniency shown to wealthy and influential criminals, while the poor ones were sentenced to hang. In *Polly*, the suppressed sequel to *The Beggar's Opera*, Gay resurrects his highwayman antihero, Macheath, this time disguised as a Black pirate, and moves the focus of corruption from London to the plantation owners of the American colonies.[8]

General History's focus on the pirates who appeared after the War of the Spanish Succession is also a focus on the pirates who rose under George I and the Whig ministry he supported. That Britain should have looked all the way to Germany for a monarch who would successfully resist the Jacobite claims to the throne is some indication of how anxious the country was to avoid a Catholic monarch, and the fear of Jacobitism pervaded a good deal of the politics of the age. George I's ascension meant the end of the power the Tories had enjoyed under the last Stuart monarch. Although, as Julian Hoppit notes, some Tories undoubtedly sympathized with the Jacobite cause, either because they actually did want to see the restoration of the Stuart dynasty or because they saw it as the only force capable of resisting the Whigs, most Tories were probably not ardent Jacobites.[9]

Once we begin to see piracy as a more loosely defined phenomenon than pirate narratives have allowed, we can also locate pirates more neatly within the power structures of the decade. At the top, of course, was Whig power, especially consolidated in the figure of Sir Robert Walpole. Walpole's figure, sometimes portrayed accurately, sometimes quite distorted, runs through the pages of the present book. To Tory satirists, such as Gay and Jonathan Swift, Walpole was indeed a monster, an unstoppable force committed primarily to his own self-interest, and dedicated to obliterating Tory power permanently. Walpole was notorious for his patronage appointments, his blatant disregard for anyone or anything that was of no use to him, and his thin-skinned intolerance for any criticism or opposition. Small wonder, then, that he attracted considerable commentary in the writing of the time.

Walpole's larger-than-life status also inevitably meant that he could not be seen as anything other than a Great Man, even if that designation was intended ironically. So great was Walpole's importance, both politically and culturally, during this period that his rule was referred to as the "Robinocracy," a term coined to refer to Walpole's unchallenged dominance in British politics between 1721 and 1741. On the one hand, Walpole represents the modern ideal of a politician: he consolidated power, both for himself and his party; he handily defeated opponents and promised considerable rewards for his supporters; his power and influence made him virtually unimpeachable, and he maintained a public persona as an able and decisive leader, even though his dealings behind the scenes were not always completely above-board. Walpole's "greatness" could be measured by his wealth and influence. But, on the other hand, as his critics were quick to point out, greatness by these definitions need not equal moral goodness, and Walpole achieved power as much by subterfuge, patronage, luck, and sheer plain bullying as by some inherently superior quality.

Walpole is remembered today, especially by literary scholars, in terms of the brilliant satires that attacked him—he is Swift's Flimnap, Gay's Peachum, and Fielding's Jonathan Wild. These characters, of course, are the creations of Tory writers, but the extent to which Walpole disturbed and outraged many observers went beyond simple partisan sniping: Walpole was deeply unsettling because, in a universe that makes sense, Walpole should have been answerable for his crimes, should have been disgraced even when his crimes were exposed, and yet he flourished. Such freedom from accountability was possible because of Walpole's money and influence, but the fact that money and influence could insulate someone from justice, while not a new idea, seemed acutely disturbing to writers on both sides of the political fence. To moralists of the period, Walpole's "greatness" represented a significant challenge to any moral system. As we shall see, some of the same moral ambiguity was applied to pirates, especially those who were noteworthy or successful.

Walpole's problematic status had as much to do with the events of the times in which he rose to power as it did with the personality of the man himself. The years following the Jacobite uprising did represent a consolidation of Whig power, which also coincided with the rise of Britain's overseas economy. In "the languages of empire," as Jack P. Greene notes, "empire and trade were far more commonly associated than empire and war." Greene also notes that, "Before the British military successes in America and in India in the late 1750s, the central figure in imperial thought was . . . not the general or the admiral, but the overseas merchant."[10] *General History* is, in part, a book about colonialism and imperialism; in particular, it is a dissertation on the beneficiaries of empire and a reflection on the moral implication of Britain's dependence on colonial commerce and its role in shaping a national British identity.

It should be noted that, at this period, such concepts as "national British identity," and even "British Empire" were still largely undefined, especially when compared to their nineteenth-century iterations. When Edward Said explores the relationship between empire and literature in *Culture and Imperialism*, he focuses on an understanding of "empire" that is reasonably well established: Britain's dominions and possessions, united under a stable monarchy and partaking of a carefully constructed literary culture.[11] One can easily perceive Britain in this state as a monolithic culture, a robust and solidly constructed center to which the colonized dominions, as peripheral possessions, must invariably turn, even for their own identity. Eighteenth-century Britain was hardly the same animal: even the British Isles themselves, as Julian Hoppit has noted, appeared as a tenuously united entity, having only recently become Great Britain by the formal union of England with Scotland in 1707; the term United Kingdom would not even exist until 1800. Britain's relationship with its colonies, therefore, was equally tenuous; the American colonies' declaration of their own autonomy in 1776 was simply the culmination of well over a century of tensions between the center and the peripheries.

Some of these tensions revealed themselves during the decade or so covered by *General History*. Politically, the Hanoverian succession was challenged by the continued support for the sidelined Stuarts, especially in Scotland. While official discourse denounced the Jacobites for their efforts to destabilize a country that had bloodlessly avoided another succession crisis, outside of official discourse support for the Jacobites was more vocal, especially among the lower echelons of society. Jacobitism directly related to the socioeconomic realities of the majority of people in the years following the war. High food prices, combined with a large number of now-unemployed soldiers and sailors, led to a rise in both petty thefts and highway robberies.

Some resistance to the Hanoverian succession can be traced even in the pirates who form the main subjects of *General History*. In his 1984 essay "Radical Pirates?," Christopher Hill shows that the pirates of *General History* have an ideology that seems to have derived from radical Puritanism.[12] Hill draws parallels between the egalitarian codes of Bartholomew Roberts and the egalitarian tenets of the Levellers and the Diggers. Hill also analyzes the life of the fictional Captain Misson, whose story occupies the same narrative place in volume 2 of the *General History* as Henry Avery's did in volume 1, to show how the Libertatia of Misson's ideal community is rooted in the radical communities of the 1650s. Arne Bialuschewski, building on Hill's seminal essay, has noted that a number of the pirates who appeared after 1715 consciously adopted Jacobite symbols, although he is cautious to point out that one cannot draw broader conclusions about pirates' political loyalties from their supposed Jacobitism.[13] Jacobites were seen as rebels, hostile to the primarily Whig government, so it seems fitting that pirate-rebels should align themselves with another antigovernment group. While that may be true, I think that Captain Johnson could not have been unaware of the political significance of pirates' associating themselves with Jacobitism, and *General History* itself stands, in part, as an indictment against Walpole's government and of Walpole's failure to address the issues of colonial economics that allowed piracy to flourish in the first place. Although the Whigs did not specifically create pirates, piracy itself—especially in the form it took after 1714—was a kind of commentary on the colonial economy that was sustaining Britain. At the same time, Walpole's eventual crackdown on piracy, and the government's high-handed moral judgments against pirates as "enemies of all mankind," must be seen as ironic in light of such disasters as the South Sea Bubble, in which Walpole certainly had a hand. It would not be too much of a stretch to suggest that *General History* positions itself as a critique of colonial economy, and of the Whig government that was growing wealthy on it.

Even though many of these crimes were driven by desperate poverty, the government preferred a "tough on crime" approach, and prosecuted—and in a number of cases executed—those who had been caught. Despite all this criminal activity, Walpole's government celebrated Britain's increased commercial activity, especially across the Atlantic, as a sign of the country's overall prosperity. In particular, the Whig government could boast of having secured the *Asiento de Negros* at the end of war, which allowed Britain to transport up to 4,800 slaves per year from Africa to the American colonies, in addition to one large ship containing trade goods. From 1714 onward, Britain ramped up its colonial economic activity, much of it dependent on the slave trade. At the same time, an increase in colonial commerce also meant an increase in piracy: the coasts of North America, the islands of the Caribbean, and the ports of West Africa were the natural homes of pirates, as was the vast ocean that lay between. The relationship between pirates and slavery is complex, as we shall see, in no small part because the relentless pursuit of piracy as the destroyer of all commerce, and the portrayal of pirates in published accounts, including *General History*, drew some of the attention away from ethical issues surrounding colonial trade.

In that way, *General History* helped to frame the moral debate for mercantile readers, in part by constructing the figure of the pirate as a monstrous, inhuman Other, filling a niche that might well be occupied by, say, slave traders or plantation owners, or even navy captains. The definition of the pirate as *hostis humani generis*, while derived from law, actually begins to be seen as somewhat severe given the lives of the people featured in the pages of *General History*. They are, to be sure, the enemies of trade—but throughout the text there is a nagging sense that it is not always clear what, specifically, pirates do to make themselves so thoroughly despised. Violence? Sure, but the merchant navy was well known to indulge in harsh, even sadistic violence in the name of "discipline." Robbery? Yes, but they are by no means the only ones to transgress against property. Moreover, the nature of trade itself, especially colonial trade, suggests that, while theft of mercantile goods may be harmful to the livelihood of some merchants, the free circulation of stolen commodities in colonial centers actually contributed to a robust economy, and was even encouraged by many colonial governors.

The designation of pirates as the enemies of all humanity therefore serves to endorse a narrative of progress, expansion, and economic determinism that is part of the larger project of defining nationalism. In this narrative, colonial trade contributes to the economic health of the nation, which in turn contributes to the social and political well-being of colonizer and colonized alike. The centrality of the plantation in the colonial economy, entirely dependent on slave labor to maintain itself, is asserted as an obvious good, which can therefore mitigate or even obscure the moral atrocity of slavery it perpetuates. Voltaire's reminder "C'est à ce prix que vous mangez du sucre en Europe"[14] isn't read as the admonition it seems to be; it is merely a bald statement of cost. The pirates of the legal imagination seek to undermine this good, and, by extension, to undermine the stability of commerce itself. By contrast, the piracy that we read in *General History* undermines and destabilizes only the legal fiction, and introduces from the margins a counternarrative that challenges the universality of what Jürgen Habermas calls the "project of Enlightenment."[15] Instead of a public sphere guided by rational discourse and trust in the institutions of democracy, piracy, for the writers of the 1720s, represents an anarchic dismissal of reason and structure in favor of a libertarian free-for-all. Some contemporary scholars of piracy, particularly Marcus Rediker and Peter Linebaugh, have attempted to assert that, far from undermining the Enlightenment project, the pirates of the 1720s constructed a progressive space that, in fact, moved that project forward into a protomodernity. There is some validity in this idea: pirate life was defined by an egalitarian share system, an elected captain (who received only one share more than the lowest member of the crew), insurance for injuries received, and even a modern-seeming sensitivity toward escaped slaves, dramatically signified by Rediker's description of White and Black pirates lifting their shirts and comparing the scars on their backs, made by the same instrument of punishment, doled out by the same cruel masters. It is a compelling but somewhat distorted vision, as we shall see: a suggestion of egalitarianism between pirates and slaves that really did not exist.

In fact, it is helpful to keep in mind that, despite official attempts to portray it otherwise, "piracy" during this period was not a monolithic culture: about all that most pirates had in common was that they were sailors and that they plundered ships. The notion that pirates themselves subscribed to some kind of universal code of conduct, or even that a sharp line designated "pirate" from "merchant," must be understood as primarily a product of publications like *General History*. The attempt to delineate and define a specific pirate culture was the work of piracy's victims, not the pirates themselves.

Given the interest in crime and criminality, pirates in the 1720s were as much an ideological phenomenon as anything else. In the final decade of the Golden Age, the years covered by *General History*, a sea-change had come about from the time of Henry Morgan and Henry Avery. With a greater reliance on colonial revenue to sustain it, Britain sought to tighten the regulation of colonial economies, including cracking down on illegal trade. During the War of the Spanish Succession, maritime conflicts along the eastern coast of North American and in the Caribbean islands allowed licensed private marauders, or privateers, to raid enemy ships on behalf of Great Britain in exchange for a percentage of plunder. These privateers, as Mark Hanna has shown, were more than just legalized pirates, they were an essential part of colonial economics, in their ability both to support the fledgling colonies in North America and the Caribbean and to keep the power of Spanish maritime trade in check.[16] Far from being simply tolerated, privateers truly were colonial heroes. Tim Beattie has noted that, during the early part of the eighteenth century at least, privateers were lauded in print at the expense of the navy itself, which was seen as a refuge for incompetent, avaricious, and sadistic officers.[17]

Johnson's pirates, on the other hand, are often portrayed as drunken, blasphemous, bloodthirsty outlaws, fighting against authority, although they are still carrying on the work of the privateers a generation earlier, only this time without government sanction. By the early 1720s, as Hanna notes, "No longer could a successful pirate cruise into the Delaware Bay, dine with the governor, marry his daughter, and settle down into a pleasant life on land."[18] *General History* reflects a change in attitude consistent with the pirate's change in status. For example, Johnson presents the brutal Edward Low as being "designed" by Nature "for a Pyrate from his Childhood" (1724a, 282 [318]). His reported actions include some of the most horrific and stomach-turning acts of sadism in the entire book. Hanna, on the other hand, argues that Low's conduct was not a result of his "nature," but that he turned "vengeful, then sadistic" after seeing the very town that formerly had supported pirate activity stage a harsh crackdown on pirates.[19] Low's uncontrollable rage against New Englanders, which Johnson mentions but never explains, now seems at least to have some identifiable cause. In Hanna's reading, Low did not start out as *hostis humani generis*, but rather became so after the colonial government attempted to suppress him.

Anarchy and order, liberty and control, legitimacy and rebellion: the way pirates move between these two binaries forms much of the way they are presented in *General History*. Johnson understands that pirates are criminals, that they are "Desperadoes, who [are] the Terror of the trading Part of the World" (1724a, 17 [26]). At the same time, he understands that, beyond their criminality, they are central to an important conversation about the role of both the individual and the corporate body within the larger body politic. The pirate redefines the relationship between the individual and the state, and in so doing redefines the relationship between the individual and economics. The Golden Age pirate is an aberration of modern commerce, while also being a product of it.

THE PIRATES OF *GENERAL HISTORY*: CONSTRUCTING PIRATE CULTURE

Pirates do not write their own histories. Except in very crude ways, they are not in charge of their own image. Yet, as Blackbeard certainly understood, the pirate *is* an image, a brand, a figure whose reputation for fearsomeness is of paramount importance, since the more fearsome a pirate was said to be, the less likely the crew of a captured vessel would be to engage in combat. The need to distinguish piracy as a distinct culture seems to be present in all pirate narratives: in Alexandre Exquemelin's *Buccaneers of America*, Henry Morgan becomes an archetypal pirate, although Exquemelin distorts Morgan's monstrousness, and evades the issue of Morgan's legal status as a privateer.[20] In both of these aspects, Exquemelin's portrayal of Morgan sets the pattern for subsequent pirate narratives. However, while Exquemelin focuses mainly on a single individual, Johnson goes further than anyone had before in presenting the pirate as a member of a distinct, recognizable group. *General History*, as we have already noted, in turn provided the springboard for fictional pirate narratives and, ultimately, the pirates of twentieth- and twenty-first-century popular culture.

We can start by asking who, exactly, is meant by "Johnson's pirates" and what it meant to be a pirate in the early decades of the eighteenth century. To begin with, the image of "the pirate" as it has appeared in popular culture from the eighteenth century to the present is derived chiefly from the brief period—roughly the decade between 1716 and 1726—that forms the bulk of the pirate narratives in *General History*. To put it another way: while, as Johnson reminds us, piracy existed in antiquity, and while piracy, in the sense of robbery at sea, still exists today, Johnson's decision to focus primarily on this decade of pirate activity forever fixed the pirate as a phenomenon of the Hanoverian period—a decision that, as we shall see, has important implications for the way we still read pirates today.

As we have seen, the economic and social conditions at the end of the War of the Spanish Succession in 1714 contributed greatly to the rise of Caribbean piracy. Some former privateers, whose activities had been legalized during wartime, simply continued their activities after the Treaty of Utrecht rescinded their legal status. At the same time, an increase in overseas trade, combined with a relative scarcity of naval authority in the waters of the Atlantic or the Caribbean, provided exactly the right conditions for piracy to flourish. The Atlantic is vast, and the hundreds of islands in the Caribbean offered numerous safe hideouts for vessels on the run from the law. Marcus Rediker estimates that, between 1718 and 1722, some 1,800 to 2,400 men were involved in piracy, deployed in about thirty or so vessels.[21] That number had declined sharply to about 500 by 1724, the year *General History* was published, thanks mainly to the efforts of Woodes Rogers to eradicate pirates and their land-based supporters. Rediker further suggests that pirates during this period did manage to have a significant impact on trade, seizing an estimated 2,400 vessels in all, and significantly stagnating growth in England from overseas trade, even as colonial ports flourished. The crisis in commerce that nearly all antipirate writing from the period warns about seems not to have been entirely rhetorical, even if it was not the immanent collapse of all trade that it was made out to be.

At the same time, making a cumulative impact on trade is not necessarily the same thing as having a monolithic pirate culture. Many of the so-called pirate stereotypes, such as their distinctive linguistic habits or their keeping parrots or other exotic pets, were common also to other sailors: the vast majority of pirates, of course, were sailors first, and so drew their identities from a long-established maritime culture.[22] The switch from sailor to pirate, therefore, did not entail a change of culture, merely a change in legal status. In fact, it is this very fluidity of legal status, from sailor to privateer to pirate, that made eliminating piracy so difficult before the general War on Pirates after 1718. In order to justify eradication of pirates, it was therefore first necessary to define and isolate pirates as a distinctive group. *General History*, to a large degree, helped in shaping and delineating a distinctive pirate culture, but it also has tended to mislead us into thinking of unusual, aberrant figures, such as Blackbeard, as the norm.

The first indication that Johnson's book is designed to construct a pirate culture can be found in its title. *General History* is, in fact, neither particularly general nor entirely historical. As a comprehensive survey, even of English piracy—even of *eighteenth-century* English piracy—the book falls quite short. Captain Kidd, arguably, with Edward Thatch, the most famous pirate of the Golden Age, receives a chapter only in volume 2, suggesting he was something of an afterthought. Johnson especially ignores two celebrated early eighteenth-century pirates, John Quelch, hanged in Boston in 1704, and Thomas Green, tried in Scotland the following year. Both men had accounts of their trials published, which could easily have furnished Johnson with material for chapters in *General History*. Green's case is particularly significant, since his trial and conviction were controversial even at the time, and a pamphlet, *Remarks upon the Tryal of Thomas Green*, forcefully argues for the innocence of Green and his crew, on the grounds that very little evidence existed that they ever engaged in any piracy at all.[23] In addition, there were several important pirates operating in the late seventeenth century; among them George Cusack, J. Golden, Thomas Vaughan, and Joseph Dawson. Even in the period that primarily concerns Johnson, there were other pirate crews operating within Caribbean and African waters, whose stories could comprise a more comprehensive history than *General History* presents us with. What kind of history, exactly, is *General History*?

The first edition may provide some explanation. The book is a series of vignettes, short narratives designed more as portraits than as parts of a large chronicle. It may be useful to think of *General History* as a kind of rogues' gallery, especially since some of the figures in 1724a were still active at the time of publication. As if to highlight this feature, the life story of Henry Avery stands isolated, outside of the main hall, but clearly given pride of place as the "ideal" pirate of the Golden Age. In 1724a, Avery's narrative precedes a short narrative passage, "Of the Growth of the Pyrates in the *West-Indies*, their Settlement in *Providence*, and the Arrival of Governor *Rogers* at that Island" (1724a, 43–54). This short chapter introduces the reader to Thatch, Vane, and Bonnet, and so serves as an introduction to the main part of the book.

In 1724b and subsequent editions, this arrangement is abandoned, and the section on the rise of piracy in the Caribbean is revised, slightly expanded, and inserted at the end of the introduction proper. The change is, on the one hand, seemingly more logical, since it gathers all of the introductory material in one place and establishes some of the context for the chapters that follow. However, the revised sequencing detracts from the assertion that *General History* is, in fact, not general at all, but a very specific set of views of contemporary British pirates, primarily operating in the Caribbean between 1717 and 1724. In light of the fact that *General History* established the iconography of piracy that persists even today, its focus on this narrow strip of pirate history is especially significant. What is easy to miss, however, is the point that the selected portraits in this very select rogues' gallery have been chosen to make a particular argument about the state of commerce and colonialism in the post-Hanoverian world.

Part of maritime culture, of course, included emphasizing the class divisions between career naval men and the common sailors who were generally more attracted to piracy. Similarly, social status features in the pirate biographies recorded in *General History*. Many of the pirates we encounter in *General History* are simply able sailors, and it is common for mutineers to eliminate officers. At the same time, some mates, frustrated with having to serve under an incompetent captain, were known to have willingly participated in mutinies, and became captains primarily on their navigational abilities. Walter Kennedy, we are told, was chosen captain despite being unable to read or write—a direct violation of the usual principle that a ship's captain needs to be an educated gentleman.

General History makes clear that the usual direction of class mobility for pirates was upward only: anyone of sufficient status who might be attracted to piracy is considered highly irregular. For example, Stede Bonnet's status as a gentleman stands out as unusual, to the extent that the first edition suggests that his decision to turn pirate proceeded from "a Disorder in his Mind" (1724a, 60 [95]). It was almost inconceivable that a "Gentleman of good Reputation . . . Master of a plentiful Fortune, and [having] the Advantage of a liberal Education" (1724a, 60 [95]), should be attracted to a life of piracy. Bonnet, in effect, did not need to achieve status this way. On the other hand, *General History* uniquely suggests that John Gow's motivation for turning pirate was that he had been prevented from marrying the woman he loved back in Scotland because he was not a ship's captain. In this reading, Gow is driven by a deluded belief that his status as a pirate captain would count as a mark of newfound respectability; as a result, he carries his crew to his home in the Orkneys and certain capture. Gow seems to have misunderstood the point of achieving a captaincy by legitimate means: for pirates, one became a captain either by simply seizing a vessel or by a majority vote from the crew, thereby subverting class distinction and the system of patronage that ensured that all naval officers, and especially captains, should come from respectable families. A pirate captain's first act of piracy, therefore, was to plunder a title and an authority that would have been otherwise denied him on any other vessel.[24]

It is important to note that, by citing examples of individual pirate captains, we are already distorting the reality of pirate activity in order to fit pirates into a specific narrative paradigm. The "lives of the pirates," which selects particular individuals as representative of the entire group of pirates, and delineates particular characteristics and defining features of these individuals, is a narrative mode the much better suits land-based highwaymen. In fact, it is a narrative mode that is quite familiar to criminal biographers; an important compendium of criminal biographies, ascribed to "Captain Alexander Smith" and published in 1713, establishes the mode that Captain Charles Johnson would follow in *General History*.

This difference, however, is that whereas highwaymen often did work alone, or at most in small groups, piracy was never an individual activity. The nature of sailing vessels demands a substantial, tightly knight group, capable of handling the daily demands of deep-sea navigation. The question of whether all crew members of a pirate vessel were, in fact, pirates, became extremely important during pirate trials. Philip Ashton, whose capture at the hand of Edward Low and whose subsequent escape from Low's crew and remarkable survival on a desert island became a celebrated account in his own time, repeatedly made a point of refusing to sign the articles that would have made him an official member of Low's crew, even though he was forced to work alongside crew members to sail the ship. Ashton rightly believed that it was his skill as a sailor that had kept him alive: Low, for all his sadism, was reportedly unwilling to harm a useful able seaman, and so insisted on keeping Ashton alive. In numerous pirate trials, crew members who could swear that they were held against their will, or forced to participate as crew members without fighting or plundering other vessels, were often pardoned.

Whether or not the collective nature of pirate vessels made pirates protosocialists, my point here is that the tales in *General History* often veer unsteadily between two narrative modes. In the case of strong characters, such as Blackbeard, or Stede Bonnet, or the two celebrated female pirates, Mary Read and Anne Bonny, the focus is primarily on the characters of the pirates themselves. At other times, however, the particular captain's name is merely a convenient shorthand for the crew who sailed under them: the events recorded therein could just as easily have happened to any captain and crew. But by constructing his book as accounts of individual pirates, Johnson obscures the fundamental difference between land and sea criminals, and thereby also obscures the uniquely problematic nature of pirating, namely, that large pirate crews tended to be a valuable economic driver for the small North American colonies who harbored and often encouraged them.

It should be clear that the complex relationship *General History* has with both the historical pirates who form its subject and the readers who form its audience demands further exploration. John Robert Moore, as we shall see, based his case for Daniel Defoe's authorship of *General History* in part on the phenomenal success of *Robinson Crusoe*. In *Defoe in the Pillory and Other Studies*, Moore argues that writing *Crusoe* whetted Defoe's appetite to explore pirate narratives (as evidenced by *Captain Singleton* the following year), and so began the trend of incorporating pirates into adventure fiction that continues to this day.[25] Moore, however, takes *General History* as journalism, and ignores the strong thread of fiction that runs through *General History* itself.

John Richetti was among the first to recognize that the book elevates the pirate to "a compelling mythical figure who combines the attractions of the merchant-traveller with the seductive vigor of the criminal, a legendary figure at last rather than a historical figure of common dimensions."[26] For Richetti, it is precisely how the book deviates from its journalistic details that has allowed it to endure. He cites as examples both the heavily documented careers of Blackbeard and Bartholomew Roberts and the highly romanticized career of Henry Avery. He even includes a lengthy discussion of the biography of Captain Misson, now recognized as a purely fictional creation. That *General History* freely blends fact and fictions seems not to matter; what does matter is how the narratives transform what Richetti sees as "dull and cautious entrepreneurs" (65) into the dazzling characters of fiction.

More recently, Richard Frohock has questioned historians' use of *General History* as a reliable source for actual pirate life. Frohock cautions against "insisting on too much consistency" in *General History* "to support a monologic view of pirate life."[27] At the same time, however, Frohock notes that the book "offers ample opportunity to consider the textualization of factual events and persons, the creation of viewpoints about governance and criminality, and the possibilities of political commentary opened by means of the figure of the pirate." Frohock's essay is an excellent start at rereading *General History* as a literary rather than a purely historical document. Frohock also helpfully leads us away from the often-made suggestion that *General History* was written purely as a money maker for its author, a way of cashing in on the early 1720s vogue for pirate stories. The present book expands Frohock's view further, to consider the book within a wider intellectual context.

PLAN OF THE PRESENT BOOK

This book is the first extensive study of *General History of the Pyrates*, which Hans Turley laments has been "unacknowledged or underestimated by both historians and literary critics in English studies," an especially sad state of affairs "given the ways it constructs and mythologizes the pirates as we know them."[28] While some considerable work has been done on the literature of pirates since Turley published his book in 1999, there is still no comprehensive study of *General History* that treats it as an intellectual product of the 1720s—the same decade that saw the publication of Defoe's great novels, the final edition of *The Fable of the Bees*, the rise and fall of the South Sea Company and the anxious attempts to analyze and understand what happened, and, later in the decade, Swift's *Gulliver's Travels* and Gay's *Beggar's Opera*, two texts that also have something to say about the economic and political cultures that helped to produce Blackbeard and Anne Bonny. The decade also saw Robert Walpole's consolidation of power as First Lord of the Treasury—Walpole himself, it must be remembered, was associated by his Tory critics with the successful Jonathan Wild—Wild's biography, published in 1724, was often advertised along with *General History* as appealing to the same readership. Not merely a source of stories about colorful sea bandits, *General History of the Pyrates* is very much a part of the intellectual climate of its time.

The overall design of this book is to examine how *General History* constructs the pirate as both Monster and Great Man, taking its cue in part from the ambivalence expressed elsewhere about the after-effects of the South Sea Bubble, the consolidation of Whig power, and the rise of the colonial—and particularly the slave-based—economy, and, in general, a perception that the present time made heroes out of villains and scapegoats out of common folk. *General History*, therefore, engages in a larger conversation about the state of Britain in the 1720s, and the effects of the changes mentioned above on the British nation. While *General History*'s value as an historical source book appears increasingly dubious, its value as a measure of the time that saw the final wave of the Golden Age of Piracy is immeasurable.

Part of the problem with using *General History* as a source book is that it is the product of several editions, including one version clearly pirated from that published by Thomas Warner. Books and articles on pirates that treat *General History* as an historical source frequently confuse the various versions in which this material was published. Moreover, the attribution of authorship to Daniel Defoe has been seriously questioned, although Defoe's presence still hangs over much discussion of *General History*; his ideas permeate portions of the book, even if he had nothing to do with it. A proper consideration of *General History* must first examine this unusual, even mysterious, publication history: this is the subject of chapter 1. *General History* ran through four editions in as many years, but was also bounced between three different publishers. Nathaniel Mist's obvious interest in the book adds another level of intrigue to its publication history, as does the timing of the various editions when they appeared. The book was translated into French, German, and Dutch; Scottish and Irish editions also appeared. Most important, the pirate history was itself pirated—or, at least, heavily plagiarized—in a version that enjoyed its own audience and its own multiple editions quite independent of Johnson's original. In fact, in some studies, the two editions are confused, and the crude woodcuts from the plagiarized edition are sometimes thought to be from *General History* itself.[29] After 1728, as pirate historian Philip Gosse has outlined, *General History* took on a new life, paired with a series of stories about highwaymen and other land criminals: it is likely in this format that Stevenson first read Johnson's text. It is clear that *General History* was popular, but why exactly it became so influential, and how it almost single-handedly shaped the perception of piracy that lingers even today remain issues to be discussed in more detail.

Part of the perception developed in *General History* starts from the legal definition of pirates as *hostis humani generis*: the universal adversary. The next section, "Monsters," examines the meaning behind this legal definition, taking at face value for the moment the extreme vilification of piracy one encounters in official discourses related to piracy. Chapter 2 looks at the *hostis humani generis* definition in greater detail, tracing similarities between the pirate and other monstrous figures who, as Jeffrey Jerome Cohen argues, embody the anxieties of the age in which they appear.[30] Because the so-called Golden Age of the Caribbean pirates coincided with Britain's expansion into global economics, the Caribbean pirate—the specific focus of *General History*—acts as a fitting "monster" for this new activity. Reading the pirate in terms of Cohen's monster theory helps explain how the much-maligned common seaman could be easily transformed into not simply a criminal or a social adversary, but a *universal* adversary, a threat to all commerce and, by extension, to the very stability of Britain as a nation.

Chapter 3 places the pirate within the wider context of Britain's colonial activity, and attempts to place the monster within the peripheries of Britain's growing empire. This chapter examines colonial commerce in general and how casting the pirate as monster helps to clarify Britain's own role as a nation involved in colonial expansion. For the revised, second edition (1724b), *General History* added two lengthy descriptions that have little or nothing to do with any of the pirate narratives, but which are fascinating in their own right. The first of these, "A Description of São Thomé and Principe," appears in the chapter on Howell Davis, prompted by a note that Davis and his crew spent some time on the island of Principe. The second, "A Description of Brazil," adds another ten or so pages to the already lengthy narrative of Bartholomew Roberts, again, prompted by little more than a mention that Roberts and his crew happened to sail to Brazil at one point. Both of these descriptions are explicitly not the work of Charles Johnson, but are said to be by John Atkins, ship's surgeon. São Tomé and Brazil were centers of the slave trade on either side of the Atlantic. These descriptions, then, offer us a window into the transatlantic world that the pirates inhabited. By shifting the focus away from the primarily Caribbean world, we can gain some insight into British attitudes toward colonialism and global trade. Certainly, there is an overwhelming emphasis on these places as receptacles for commodities, especially in the descriptions of São Tomé and Brazil. Lands are worth exploring and colonizing for what they can supply economically; here we get some idea of the richness of global commodities European colonizers were scrambling to control.

In the wake of the South Sea Bubble, a vigorous intellectual debate crystallized concerns that had already been voiced in the previous decade about the right use of money and the growing power of both the Whigs and credit-based economics. Chapter 4 takes a step back and considers the larger debate in the 1720s over the ethical parameters of wealth, especially wealth derived from global commerce. Bernard Mandeville's *Fable of the Bees,* Defoe's tracts against stockjobbing, even Steele's journal *The Theatre* all debated the ethics of speculation, national debt, and the power of the South Sea Company. John Trenchard and Thomas Gordon's *Cato's Letters,* begun in the aftermath of the bubble, reiterated some of these arguments, and dared to speculate on the fitness of the Walpole government to deliver a sound judgement on the bubble. Although none of these publications deals directly with pirates and piracy, echoes of them find their way into *General History,* and Johnson's presentation of pirates both as important actors in the colonial economy and—as we shall see later—reflections of Great Men such as Walpole. Chapter 5, therefore, will focus on *General History* as a text that engages in the ethics of the 1720s, specifically as it relates to the figure of the pirate as a fitting reflection of the time.

If *General History* were simply interested in presented gory and salacious tales of pirate activity, it would barely rise above its seeming Grub Street origins. In fact, the abridged and rewritten version published by Edward Midwinter, *History and Lives of All the Most Notorious Pirates and their Crews,* often goes out of its way to emphasize the notoriety and bloodthirstiness of pirates, being careful, of course to remind its readers that such activity invariably leads to the gallows and to eternal damnation. In *General History,* however, the "monstrous" pirate has a place in a much larger debate about the ethics required of a burgeoning market economy. The next section, "Great Men," explores how *General History* expands from its narrow focus on tales of crime and punishment, to consider the pirate as a phenomenon enmeshed in its own time.

General History occasionally displays a grudging respect for its criminal subjects. References to Plutarch, for example, direct the reader to consider the pirate as an exemplum, a model for the time. While these references may no doubt be read ironically, they also serve to prompt the reader to consider the nature of "greatness," and to ask—as others certainly do—whether criminality is simply a matter of class rather than actual ethics. Chapter 5 explores the presentation of pirates as "great," especially the pirate whose biography is by far the longest in the book, Bartholomew Roberts. Roberts, in many ways, embodies a different sensibility than Henry Avery, in that he is presented as one who regards piracy as a kind of business, and brings to his pirate activities a level of what could only be called "professionalism" not seen in earlier pirates. He is, therefore, granted a significant, fold-out portrait in the book, a kind of apotheosis, as he appears, dressed as a gentleman, standing in front of his impressive fleet of ship. Here is no grubby sea-robber: Roberts is all that a pirate should be.

If the pirate is a monster in the eyes of the law, then it is the prerogative of the law to capture and exterminate the monster whenever possible. More importantly, however, the law must be *seen* to be capturing and exterminating the monster, to maintain its authority and to assert that the law is, in fact, in control. However, not all pirates did face capture and execution; many of the pirates featured in *General History* were either still active when the book was first published or had suffered an unknown fate. Moreover, the publicly executed criminal also enjoyed a kind of fleeting celebrity, an acknowledgment of a kind of ironic "greatness" that also resonated with critics of the "greatness" of those involved in mercantile and colonial enterprises. In a sense, then, the spectacle of law in the eighteenth century, as much as it depicted the pirate as a monster, also had a hand in creating the idea of the pirate as a Great Man. As a kind of hinge between the two depictions, chapter 6 will examine how *General History* presents the legal consequences of pirating as a kind of myth building. The chapter looks at the roots of such legal spectacles and at how the form of public execution, rather than acting as a deterrent to crime, actually helped perpetuate the mystique of the famous criminal, a figure as iconic and as spectacular as, say, a Lord Mayor, as William Hogarth's famous *Industry and Idleness* prints reveal. While *General History* suggests, as it must, that the proper punishment for piracy is hanging, and occasionally indulges in reprinting trial transcripts, it also undermines the ultimate authority of the law, both by commenting on the inequities in the application of the law and by demonstrating, largely sympathetically, pirates' own contempt for a set of laws they know are stacked against them.

General History's presentation of the pirate as both Monster and Great Man accurately captures, I believe, the general anxiety and ambivalence towards global commerce in the 1720s. While the understanding of this period has traditionally focused on the political leanings of the main authors in the debates about the place of global commerce in the life of Britain during this period—including, of course, Defoe—that anxiety and ambivalence extend well beyond simple partisan lines. *General History* is neither obviously a Whig book, nor obviously a Tory one. It defends commercial activity against its attackers—the pirates who are the main subject of the book—and condemns piracy's violent excesses and ruthless plundering; yet it also critiques global commerce itself, and, in its seemingly ironic portrayals of figures such as Henry Avery, Blackbeard, Bartholomew Roberts, or even the fictional Captain Misson as Great Men, echoes the satirical treatment of the whole great man idea, as embodied in Robert Walpole, that Tory writers such as Jonathan Swift and John Gay explored later in the century. Were they inspired to see a connection between successful criminals and Walpole, or to underline the inequity of the law as meted out to the wealthy criminal and the poor one, from the pages of Johnson's book? To say so definitively is, I think, too much of a stretch. Johnson's comments on the inequities of law, even put in the mouths of his pirate subjects, are hardly unique to him. In many ways, *General History* is, as I hope to show in the following pages, very much a product of its time. And yet, to read *General History* as a critique of global commerce and the pirates who were caught up in it is to read it as more than just a simple source book of stories. *General History*, for all its clumsiness, its strange composition, and its odd place in both the literary and historical canons of the eighteenth century, is an important piece in the intellectual history of the early years of the Whig ascendency.

1

A GENERAL HISTORY OF *GENERAL HISTORY*

ONE OF THE MOST UNUSUAL literary bibliographies ever prepared is the slim volume compiled by Philip Gosse in 1927 for the "Works of Capt. Charles Johnson." Gosse (1879–1959), son of Edmund and grandson of naturalist Philip Henry, was a physician by profession and, like his grandfather, keenly interested in what the Victorians called "natural history." However, he maintained a secondary interest in piracy, and produced a comprehensive *History of Piracy* (1932), a *Who's Who of Piracy*, and the aforementioned *Bibliography of the Works of Capt. Charles Johnson*. Gosse acknowledges that Johnson is a pseudonym, although he does seem to think that Johnson himself was responsible for the hybrid *History of the Highwaymen*, first published in 1734, which combines parts of *General History* with Captain Alexander Smith's *History of the Lives of the Most Noted Highway Men*, first published in 1714. However, he does not seem to think that Smith and Johnson might have been the same person; more importantly, he neither offers any suggestion of nor even seems overly concerned about whom he thinks Johnson might have been.

Gosse's bibliography is invaluable for tracing the publication of *General History*, and yet it is also frustrating at times. He mentions, for example, that a New York edition of *General History*, dated 1723, is described in Isaiah Thomas's *The History of Printing in America*, but the book is otherwise untraced. He also is guilty of a few (understandable) errors: he mentions a 1735 "fifth edition," which is actually the fifth edition of the 1725 plagiarized or rival volume *History and Lives* (about which, more later). Gosse seems unaware that *History and Lives* went into so many (and more) editions; he also misspells the publisher "A. Bettesworth" as "Betteswood." The most annoying discrepancy occurs in his description of the fourth edition, since he suggests that volume 2 was issued in 1726, along with the reissue (and revision) of volume 1. However, the third edition alone was advertised for sale throughout 1726, with absolutely no mention of a fourth edition. It seems reasonable to assume that, despite the date on the title page, both volumes of the fourth edition appeared in 1728. Likewise, Gosse lists the German translation, *Schauplatz der Englischen See-Räuber* (literally, "Theater of English sea robbers"—an interesting distinction) under versions published in 1725, even though the title page is clearly dated 1728. If there is a reason for this discrepancy, Gosse does not provide one. For the most part, however, Gosse's bibliography is a valuable survey of this most unusual publication; it also provides a quick overview of the remarkable history of the work itself.

Gosse's bibliography is also significant as a reminder of an important feature of *General History* that is often overlooked: its publication history. Publication histories can tell us much about both the genesis and the immediate reception of a literary work; place of publication, choice of publisher, even specifics of printing can all contribute to our understanding of how a text emerges. In the case of this work, in the absence of a definitive author, the publication history raises significant questions about authorship and authority that are especially vital for a text that is so important as an historical source.

Even a quick a study of the publication history of *General History* reveals that, despite its importance as a source for narratives about the lives of pirates of what is considered the Golden Age of Piracy, it is an obscure, mysterious volume. Its value as history, as we have seen, is problematic, since it is sometimes difficult to determine whether the unique information it contains is the result of Charles Johnson's own independent research or whether it has simply been fabricated for the sake of the book. While the chronology of the various pirate crews and their relationships to each other can be worked out, most readers coming to the book will derive only a vague idea of when the events described in the narratives have taken place. The original 1724 volume does follow a roughly linear chronology, but pirate narratives are so closely interrelated that virtually every major pirate captain had some connection with every other captain.[1]

Moreover, as Arne Bialuschewski has demonstrated in his article on Blackbeard, the information in the *History* is sometimes contradictory: 1724a lists Blackbeard's birthplace as Jamaica, while all later editions make him a native of Bristol (Bialuschewski asserts that the historical record proves Jamaica to be correct).[2] Additional material in later editions blurs distinctions between fact and fiction. Volume 2 opens with an account of a fictional Captain Misson, who sails with the historical Captain Tew.[3] Misson founds a colony, Libertatia,[4] on the island of Madagascar, much as Henry Avery is said to have done. The story places Misson and Tew during the War of the Spanish Succession, while in fact Tew had sailed with Avery himself in the mid-1690s, more than a decade earlier. Misson himself seems to have been invented so that *General History* could include the account of the utopian colony of Libertatia; nevertheless, he has somehow acquired a first name, James, and an alternate spelling of his surname as Mission. Such inconsistencies make *General History* more a series of discrete biographies than a comprehensive history, an aggregate collection of pirate narratives rather than a study of why pirates flourished when they did.

A good deal of the commentary that exists on *General History* has paid little attention to the complexities of its own history. Modern editions, such as the 1927 edition recently reprinted by Routledge, or Manuel Schonhorn's 1972 scholarly edition, reprinted by Dover in 1999 and now the standard scholarly edition, have tended to use the 1728 fourth edition as the copy-text, following an assumption that this fourth edition not only represents final authorial intentions (Schonhorn, following widespread acceptance of John Robert Moore's attribution, also assumes the author to be Daniel Defoe), but also offers the most accurate and factually sound narratives of its pirate subjects. *General History*, therefore, has been read as an historical document, whose narratives offer information useful to the modern historian of pirates, and whose revisions were made primarily in the interest of correcting errors and providing accurate information. As we shall see, neither of these assumptions is necessarily true; to approach *General History*, especially in its fourth edition, as an uncomplicated, transparent document is to ignore its particular complexities. What are we to make, for example, of the fact that the book had three different publishers between 1724 and 1728? Who was responsible for the extensive rewriting of some sections of the book, even as other sections were not even reset as the book changed publishers between the first and second editions? Can we consider the book to have a single "author," given that some sections have been reprinted verbatim from previously printed trial records? On the other hand, how much of what cannot be corroborated by external sources was simply invented? Who added the chapter on John Gow, which was the sole revision made for the third edition in 1725? Who then substantially rewrote the Gow chapter for the fourth edition? Was the same person responsible for the shoddily produced volume 2? Finally, how do we read these various editions alongside other pirate and criminal narratives of the time, especially since there is evidence that the author(s) and/or publisher(s) of *General History* were competing directly with rival pirate narratives?

Once we begin to consider even these basic questions, we can quickly see that *General History* was not, like a modern work of journalism, adapted from "sources," either firsthand or print, then shaped by a single hand into the book we now have; rather, it was cobbled together out of a hodgepodge of sources and perspectives, and is a text that changed substantially in its first four editions and then took on a new, somewhat bizarre, life after 1734. With each new version of *General History*, both its audience and its focus changed somewhat, so that the history of the book is, in part, also a history of its reception. Since *General History* is so crucial in forming our understanding of pirate culture, any analysis of its text must take its textual history into account.

DANIEL DEFOE AS CHARLES JOHNSON

The true identity of the author of *A General History of the Pyrates* may always remain inconclusive. All scholars agree that the "Captain Charles Johnson" whose name appears on the title page is a pseudonym, and that there seems to be no connection between this Charles Johnson and the Charles Johnson whose play *The Successful Pyrate* (1712), loosely based on the Henry Avery legend, enjoyed a moderate success at Drury Lane Theatre.[5] Beyond that, there is no firm evidence to attribute the book to anyone else. In 1939, John Robert Moore confidently ascribed the work to Daniel Defoe, based on internal evidence and perceived connections with other works that Defoe is also supposed to have written, particularly *The Four Years' Voyage of Captain George Roberts* and *Robert Drury's Journal*. Defoe, claimed Moore, had set out to become an expert in piracy while he was writing *Captain Singleton* (1720), and the fruits of his extensive research led him to publish *General History* in 1724. Moore's attribution was accepted unquestioningly, and not without reason. Moore argued that the author needed to be someone who had extensive knowledge of maritime life and culture, but who also had the literary skills to endow these narratives with a novelist's sense of drama and characterization, coupled with enough of an education to account for the few classical references that pop up occasionally. Defoe seemed to fit the bill perfectly; that is, if one accepts that Defoe had access to an extensive research library and was able to conduct interviews with convicted pirates as they were held in the Marshalsea prison. In Moore's reading, *General History* is a masterpiece of journalism: Defoe weaves information from newspaper and trial accounts but supplies original details that could only have come from the pirates themselves. Whatever cannot be verified in printed sources must, in Moore's view, have derived from first-hand knowledge. Moore accepts *General History* as a work of nonfiction, and never considers the possibility that Defoe the novelist might have indulged in creative license in crafting his pirate stories.

The assumption of Defoe's authorship has colored not only *General History* itself, but many texts from the period that mention pirates. For example, in his introduction, Schonhorn includes a reference to John Atkins, surgeon aboard the

Weymouth, which was part of Chaloner Ogle's fleet that eventually captured Bartholomew Roberts. In an article in *Notes and Queries*, Moore asserts that Atkins and Defoe were in close contact, because Atkins had been shipmates with Alexander Selkirk, the supposed model for Robinson Crusoe.[6] Selkirk had, in fact, died on the 1722 voyage to Africa which resulted in Roberts's capture. Moore's point is that Atkins "suppl[ied] Defoe with some rather long passages for the great 'History of the Pirates' and with a vast number of details which can be traced in various parts of that work."[7] However, Moore seems to be misconstruing the nature of Atkins' contribution: Johnson's preface specifically mentions the lengthy interpolated descriptions of São Tomé and Brazil found in 1724b. These interpolations have little or nothing to do with pirates, being primarily geographical descriptions added, Johnson explains, to improve merchant traders' knowledge of foreign coasts. On the other hand, Atkins is a tantalizing phantom presence in *General History*: Atkins may possibly have contributed heavily to the chapter on Bartholomew Roberts, which is the longest and one of the most carefully revised of any of the chapters. Moreover, 1724b contains an advertisement for Atkins's book *Notes on several Chyrurgical Subjects*, to be published "Next Week" by T. Warner: a somewhat odd choice to appeal to readers of pirate stories. However, neither the passages in Atkins's book, the advertisement in 1724b, nor a notice in an issue of *Mist's Weekly Journal* (*MWJ*) that Schonhorn references does anything to prove any kind of "collaboration"—all that can be gleaned is that both the author of the notice in *MWJ* and Atkins were aware of a book called *General History of the Pyrates*—the *MWJ* notice (from 3 April 1725) may even be little more than a puff for the book, to help lagging sales of 1724b. However, from this rather shaky assertion by Moore, for which no hard evidence exists, a reasonably plausible narrative emerges of Defoe the journalist receiving valuable first-hand information from an actual eyewitness to the capture of the pirate whose narrative forms a substantial part of the book.[8]

In *The Canonisation of Daniel Defoe* (1988), P. N. Furbank and W. R. Owens challenge Moore's attribution and set out clear reasons why it was based on faulty methodology. Much of their criticism of Moore stems from his conviction that Defoe wrote not only *General History*, but *George Roberts* and *Robert Drury's Journal* as well. Since these other narratives were also published anonymously, Moore had to rely on internal, stylistic evidence to prove his claim, although he bolstered his arguments with the assertion that no one else had the right combination of journalistic and narrative skills to write *any* of these texts. Furbank and Owens carefully sort through Moore's methods, and find both glaring problems that Moore simply ignored and new evidence that challenges Moore's confident ascription of supporting texts to Defoe.[9] The evidence they provide does not prove definitively that Defoe is not the author of *General History*, but it does prove that Moore's scholarship is questionable enough to leave room for reasonable doubt.

Defoe's authorship has been sufficiently challenged that recent scholarship that engages with *General History* simply mentions Johnson as the pseudonymous author, and leaves the issue at that.[10] However, while this book follows the same practice of referring to Johnson as author, and while I have no wish to assert my own candidate for authorship, I would like to modify Furbank and Owens's arguments somewhat, in order to challenge the all-or-nothing sensibility that seems to characterize the authorship question. When we consider Defoe's authorship, therefore, we are left with several possibilities:

1. Defoe is, as Moore claimed, the sole author from start to finish, even of the revisions and additions.
2. Defoe had absolutely nothing to do with the book, and Moore's attribution, as Furbank and Owens have argued, is entirely spurious.
3. Defoe was responsible for the first and possibly the second editions, but the book was subsequently added to and revised by additional hands.
4. The book is the product of multiple hands, of which Defoe's may well be one.

The last option has a certain attractiveness to it. It is curious, for instance, that Moore's most convincing evidence for Defoe's hand is not necessarily found in the chapters of the first edition. The life of Gow, of which Moore makes a great deal, was, as I have said, hastily inserted in order to compete with a pamphlet life of Gow advertised as being in press eleven days before the third edition of *General History* was published. Manuel Schonhorn, while acknowledging the great contributions of Furbank and Owens, maintained that he was "still inclined to see Defoe's hand in the *Pyrates* of 1724–26."[11] But even if certain chapters can be proven to be Defoe's, it does not follow that Defoe was responsible for the entire work.

The authorship question has broader implications for further study of *General History*. Attribution to Defoe entirely means reading the book according to Defoe's concerns and principles. In so doing, however, we run the risk of misrepresenting Defoe's status within the intellectual and literary milieu of his own time, and of obscuring how much *General History* owes to that milieu. There is no doubt that Defoe is a towering genius, and the variety and quality of his published output, even accounting for all the deattributions, is nothing short of staggering. But to claim him as the *only* person who could have written a particular book or pamphlet is to deny others a voice in the scholarly conversation of the 1720s.

One example of the danger of assuming Defoe's authorship can be found in the opening pages of the preface. Johnson, in a rather curious aside, mentions his belief that the creation of a national fishery, such as existed in the Netherlands, would provide demobilized sailors with a ready income and would thus stem the attraction to piracy. William Graves, introducing the 1972 Garland reprint of 1724a, sees this proposal of a national fishery as an idea characteristic of Defoe, as indeed it is. However, a pamphlet on that very subject, *The Interest of Great Britain Consider'd; or, The Herring Fishery Propos'd, as the Most Rational Expedient for Paying Our National Debts*, had been published in 1723, written by one Henry Elking. Elking (ca. 1670–1740) had earlier proposed to the directors of the South Sea Company a plan for setting up a Greenland whale fishery that, Elking believed, would also generate considerable revenue. In *The Interest of Great Britain Consider'd*, Elking praises the Dutch in general, and their fisheries in particular, arguing that

> [a] People that have no native Materials for Trade, are, of a sudden, become Masters of the Art, and, but for *England*, would probably monopolize all the Trade in the World. Since they have been inspir'd with the Spirit of Commerce, their growth has been admirable, and if permanent, old *Rome* must submit to the Comparison: Poverty made 'em Industrious, Industry render'd 'em opulent and powerful. *Holland*, once an uncultivated Marsh, is now, for its Dimensions, the richest Spot of Ground in the World; fuller of People, Cities, Towns, Castles and Forts, than any Country in Europe.[12]

For Elking, commerce—in this case the commercial exploitation of an abundant natural resource—in an integral part of national identity. Elking's argument runs roughly thus: If the Dutch can successfully use other people's resources to become a great and powerful nation, how much more great and powerful could Britain be with her own resources. Much of Elking's attitude reappears in *General History*'s remarks about the Dutch national fishery, proving that, at the very least, Defoe's was not the sole voice in the public discussion of Britain's commercial future.[13]

It would be irresponsible to suggest that Henry Elking was anything more than a minor voice in this larger debate. Although nothing more of a national fishery is mentioned in the remainder of the book, the economic chord sounded in the preface resounds throughout all of the pirate biographies that follow. The primary focus in *General History* is not simply a salacious interest in criminal behavior for its own sake, neither is it a treatise on the morality of theft delineated in a series of object lessons designed to prove that crime does not pay. Rather, it is a study of the phenomenon of piracy as it has manifested itself in Britain between

1714 and 1724—specifically, the years following the War of the Spanish Succession, the arrival of the Hanoverian monarchy, and the ascendancy of the Whig government. It is imperative, then, that the pirate be constructed as a representation of the challenges and dangers of participating in a global economy, as opposed to developing domestic resource industries.

Despite its brief mention, the connection between piracy and the need for a national fishery did not entirely go unnoticed. A puff piece for the book, published in Mist's *Weekly Journal* for 6 June 1724, quotes the relevant passage from the preface as a "reasonable" solution to the problem of piracy.[14] Piracy was something more than a crime against individuals; it was a crime against the state. It was also a universal problem, since the fortunes and misfortunes of the merchant contribute to the fortunes and misfortunes of the country as a whole. What matters here is that *General History* explores piracy and crime from a new perspective. Whereas accounts of land criminals, and even earlier accounts of piracy, focused on the moral deficiency of following a life of crime, *General History*, as these puff pieces make clear, direct the reader to consider the pirate as a figure within the particular economic and political context of the 1720s—a figure who is not an aberration of the times, but very much a part of them.

Such an innovative approach might lead one to assume that Charles Johnson must be a professional writer, someone whose name must surely be known to us already—which naturally leads us to consider Defoe. We are used to thinking of Defoe as a deeply read expert on all subjects he turned his hand to; we are also used to granting to Defoe a level of journalistic integrity that far outstrips that of his contemporaries. In effect, Defoe becomes the author we want him to be. For example, more than one commentator has assumed that Defoe, in his "research" for *General History*, somehow had access to pirates who were being held in the Marshalsea prison awaiting their trial, and that he was willing to conduct, and they were willing to provide, interviews for the book. There is, of course, no firm evidence that any such research was undertaken or that modern standards of journalistic integrity and accuracy can be applied to *General History*. In the absence of such evidence, there is nothing to confirm that anything a pirate is alleged to have said and done while at sea is the truth. Dialogue provided in the book should not be understood as a verbatim transcript of words actually spoken, but a dramatic reconstruction to help the narrative along. This fact may help explain why some of the chapters indulge frequently in pirates' colorful, foul-mouthed talk, while others stick to a more neutral authorial voice. What matters, of course, is not what pirates actually said and did, but that what they are reported to have said and done conforms to our expectations about them. The more outrageous the pirate's behavior, the more memorable he is as a genuine pirate.

NATHANIEL MIST AND *GENERAL HISTORY*

Ruling out Defoe's authorship, of course, means proposing another name in his place. Arne Bialuschewski has proposed Nathaniel Mist as a possible author, an attribution that has some merit, and a fair bit of evidence—albeit much of it circumstantial—to support it.[15] Bialuschewski's argument starts as an answer to Moore's assertion that no one but Defoe possessed the maritime knowledge and the literary ability to produce *General History*. Mist, Bialuschewski offers, actually possessed both of those qualities even more than Defoe, since Mist had actually served as a merchant sailor in the Caribbean, and so would have had firsthand knowledge of many of the places described in these chapters. He counters the claim that, while Mist was undoubtedly a capable editor, he himself did not demonstrate the literary quality one finds in *General History*. He points to a series of letters on the state of the exiled Stuart court, written pseudonymously from France between 1730 and 1734. Bialuschewski describes these letters as "written in a vigorous style," using "articulate, explicit, and succinct" prose.[16] Clearly, then, Mist appears to satisfy Moore's criteria for authorship.

There are, to be sure, stronger connections that would allow us to link Mist to *General History*. The first edition was published by Charles Rivington, who, Bialuschewski asserts, had close ties to Mist. Mist's name appears in the Stationers' Register entry for *General History* on 24 June 1724—a compelling, though not necessarily definitive, piece of evidence. In addition, a bizarre 1728 pamphlet attack on Mist, *Mist's Closet Broken Open*, features two references to a "Captain Johnson" corresponding with Mist. Mist's *Weekly Journal* certainly advertised the book extensively; Mist's location is even listed as one of the places where purchasers may find stock of the third edition, indicating that Mist was definitely selling the book himself by 1725. I think it is fair to say that Mist, if not the actual author, certainly had a keen interest in the success of *General History*. That fact alone might at least definitively rule out Defoe's involvement in the project, since Defoe had severed ties with Mist by the time *General History* was published. Why, then, would Mist be interested in promoting an anonymous volume from an author with whom he had fallen out? Mist's self-imposed exile to France after 1728 may also help explain *General History*'s changing fortune after that time.

Despite these compelling pieces of evidence, however, Bialuschewski must still resort to speculation to establish Mist's authorship more definitively. He suggests, for example, that during Mist's imprisonment in the King's Bench prison, he "could have easily" consulted with Walter Kennedy, whose own story is somewhat awkwardly wedged in with the chapter on Bartholomew Roberts. Perhaps he could have, but there is no firm evidence that he did, any more than Defoe consulted with imprisoned pirates. Bialuschewski also ignores the complicated nature of "authorship" of the book, since some parts have been simply cribbed from other sources: the chapter on Stede Bonnet is almost entirely lifted verbatim from *The Tryals of Stede Bonnet*, published in 1719. Furthermore, Bialuschewski tends to simplify the complicated relationship between the various editions published between 1724 and 1728. He states, for instance, that volume 1 of the fourth edition "contained no further alterations beyond some minor corrections on the last pages of the text," ignoring the almost wholly rewritten chapter on John Gow that had first appeared in 1725. Is this new chapter Mist's work, assuming he wrote the version that appeared in the third edition? It's impossible to say—especially considering that a good many of the revisions incorporate information found in the rival *Conduct and Lives* pamphlet published by Applebee. In short, while it is undoubtedly true that Mist had a much more direct concern with *General History* than Defoe, and while it is possible that some of the book did indeed come from his pen, the entirety of the book in all its parts cannot be attributed to Mist, or anyone else, beyond a reasonable doubt. Indeed, it is reasonable to suggest that his role in the project was that of a general editor, commissioning chapters from various writers, cribbing from various sources, and welding all of that material into a unified whole. It is also quite possible that something similar was attempted for the ill-fated Volume II, but without Mist himself at the helm, with the result being a much clumsier editorial effort.

It may be most useful, then, absent any firm external evidence to support any single author, to adopt Max Novak's suggestion that "if [*General History*] is not by Defoe, it might, in the manner of a painting, be said to belong to the 'school of Defoe.'"[17] Hal Gladfelder offers a similar perspective when he suggests that even the deattribution of the criminal biographies of the 1720s "might also suggest . . . that Defoe's nuanced, elaborate representations of criminal subjectivities had observable influence on subsequent authors."[18] Gladfelder is "content to let the name Defoe—a name that, in any case, Daniel Foe invented for himself—stand for an indeterminately plural author, a multiply embodied voice."[19] I certainly take that as my assumption about Johnson throughout this book. "Charles Johnson" may indeed be a pseudonym, but whether it is Defoe's, Mist's, or someone else's entirely, the work of single or multiple hands, the book itself by and large displays some coherence of thought, and is certainly distinct enough to set it apart from other accounts of piracy, both fiction and fact. Until concrete evidence emerges to point to one definitive author, I am content to let Johnson stand in for a variety of voices, to contradict himself, to be large, to contain multitudes.

THE FIRST EDITION (1724A)

The first volume, published by Charles Rivington on 13 May 1724, appeared in an octavo of 320 pages, embellished with three engravings of particularly noteworthy pirates: a portrait each of Blackbeard and Bartholomew Roberts, and a double portrait of Mary Read and Anne Bonney. Its price, 4 shillings, and its relatively careful production, signify that the market for this book included, somewhat in keeping with the market for other criminal biographies, relatively affluent readers.[20]

Johnson makes little direct reference to his audience, although he suggests that the book "may fall into the Hands of some Masters of Ships" (1724b, A2r [3]), and that they would find the book useful. At the same time, he hints that the book has already been seen by

> some Gentlemen, who have rais'd an Objection against the Truth of its Contents, viz. that it seems calculated to entertain and divert.—If the Facts are related with some Agreeableness and Life, we hope it will not be imputed as a Fault; but as to its Credit, we can assure them that the Sea-faring Men, that is all that know the Nature of these Things, have not been able to make the least Objection to its Credit:—And he will be bold to affirm, that there is not a Fact or Circumstance in the whole Book, but he is able to prove by credible Witnesses. (1724b, A5r–A5v [8]).

Johnson, therefore, does not deny the value of the book as "entertainment," and freely admits to having embellished and even invented some material, while sticking, when necessary, to the facts.

Ten days after the publication of the first edition, a puff piece for the book appeared in Mist's *Weekly Journal* (23 May 1724).[21] Not merely a review of the book, however, this essay is both a short discourse on the book's audience and a broader guide to the political implications of a history of pirates. I return to the political discussion of the essay in a later chapter, but the remarks on readership are worth noting as a hint for the intended reception of this unusual volume. The essay begins with a discussion of the pleasure of reading in general, and specifically suggests that "Men of Fortune," with too much time on their hands may . . . both for their Health and Diversion . . . fill up those empty Spaces in reading good books." The author is careful to note, however, that while what he means by "good books" certainly includes edifying classical authors—he particularly name-checks Livy and Tacitus—it may also include entertainment:

> I would not have any Readers fancy by this, that I am a Cynick in my Studies, and am always acting the Wise-Man, will admit no Book into my Study, where the Subject is not handled in a grave Manner; on the contrary, I can laugh with *Martial* and *Rabelais*; and when I see a new Book advertised with a promising Title, my Expectation is raised as high as a Girl's of fifteen, at her going to her first Masquerade.

The reference to masquerades is not casual, as a few paragraphs later the author mentions that the price of *General History* is "not the tenth Part of the Price of a Masquerade," and therefore better value as entertainment. The implication seems clear: the piece is situating *General History* as a book worthy of consideration by "Men of Fortune," yet valuable as much as entertainment as erudition.

THE SECOND EDITION (1724B) AND THE THIRD EDITION (1725)

A second edition was advertised at the end of August of the same year, this time published by Thomas Warner. The second edition includes some revisions of and additions to the existing lives, plus some additional lives, most notably that of Thomas Anstis. There is also some rearrangement of chapters, so that that the historical, background material is all placed in the opening chapter and the chronologies of the captains is somewhat regularized. The effect of this rearrangement, however, is to distort what might be seen as the specific plan of the book, which is a study of British pirates primarily active in the Americas between 1718 and 1724. The opening chapter on Captain Avery, who belongs to an earlier generation, appears in the first edition more as part of the general introductory material, a prologue to the main body of pirate narratives that follow. Avery is legendary—the most successful pirate of his age, the subject of a play, and the standard for all pirates to reach. Although Johnson is careful to note that Avery died penniless, he also died free, and the loss of his fortune was not by his own profligacy, but by the treachery of English merchants. Many of the pirates whose lives form the bulk of the book could do worse than follow his example.

The revisions in the second edition are worth considering in some detail. Bialuschewski helpfully documents which pages were revised and which remained substantially unchanged between the two editions—a practice which, as he notes, allowed the printer to use as much of the first edition as possible. However, the second edition did not simply reuse sheets from the first, as there is evidence of correction, and some change of ornaments between the two editions. A more curious question, however, concerns the change in publisher. If the first edition had been successful, it is unlikely that Rivington would have relinquished copyright; on the other hand, it is unclear how or why Warner would have been persuaded to accept a revised edition of a book whose sales had not been promising. It is possible that Mist, if Mist indeed was involved in its publication, managed to persuade Warner that a revised edition would meet with greater favor.

The third edition introduced a major new pirate, John Gow, whom Johnson, for some reason, prefers to call by his less memorable alias of Smith. Gow's activities had taken place too recently for either of the 1724 editions: his initial act of mutiny dates from 3 November 1724. The third edition was rushed into print specifically to include Gow: the rest of the volume simply reuses sheets from the second edition.[22] The Gow chapter was rather hastily inserted, since the gathering that should be signed Dd is instead signed cc (ignoring the fact that the Spriggs chapter concluded in the second edition on Cc8v). The pages in the third edition are also misnumbered at this point—and the proper pagination resumes after the Gow insertion, with what had been the conclusion of the Spriggs chapter now headed "A Relation of Five Men Setting Up for a Company of Pyrates." It is no surprise that a new edition of *General History* should include an account of Gow: he was one of the few pirates who operated in British waters. In fact, his capture, reported in both the *Daily Post* and the *Newcastle Courant* for 13 March 1725, took place after he had returned to the Orkney islands, where he was raised. A fuller account appeared in the *Weekly Journal, or British Gazetteer* on 3 April; while *Mist's Weekly Journal* featured an account of the trial on 29 May.[23] Two days later, the *Daily Post* is advertising the forthcoming pamphlet, *The Adventures and Proceedings of John Gow*, as being "in press." It was eventually published by John Applebee on 2 July as *An Account of the Conduct and Proceedings of the Late John Gow*. Since the third edition of *General History* was published on 10 June—the day before Gow's execution—*General History*'s account of Gow was hurriedly written and rush-released to beat the pamphlet account into print. However, the fourth edition features a completely rewritten version of the Gow chapter, this one drawing heavily on details—and even some phrases—from the Applebee pamphlet, while supplying some new information not in any of the previous published accounts. A "dying confession" pamphlet from Gow and his crew, published by Warner, appeared on 28 July, the advertisement in the *Daily Journal* for that day cautioning readers that "All the pretended Accounts hitherto publish'd, are false and spurious"—including, presumably, Warner's own published version in *General History*.[24]

1725: A DUBLIN EDITION, A DUTCH TRANSLATION, AND THE MIDWINTER VERSION

General History's success can be measured by the various other editions that appeared in 1725, including an important—though often overlooked—version. Gosse records a Dublin edition of what is actually 1724a, printed by J. Watts. It is also clear that 1724a had filtered to other areas of Europe: a Dutch version, *Historie der Engelsche Zee-Roovers*, translated by Robert Hennebo, appeared in Amsterdam, notable for the original copperplate engravings that were prepared for the volume, and that have been sometimes reproduced as belonging to the "original" editions of *General History*. Even the 1728 German edition uses 1724a as a copy-text, suggesting that the first edition sold more widely and was better known than the later revision.

But by far the most significant "edition" of *General History* is the likely unauthorized rewrite published as *History and Lives of All the Most Notorious Pirates and their Crews*. This volume was published in early August by Edward Midwinter, who had recently taken over the Looking-Glass booksellers from Josiah Blare. His specialty was chapbook and broadside publications, and *History and Lives* shows evidence of this: its most distinctive feature is the series of "Twenty Beautiful Cuts, being the Representation of each Pirate" found at the head of each chapter. Some of these woodcuts have been reproduced in both scholarly and popular studies of pirates, and have often been misattributed as having come from *General History* itself.

The English Short-Title Catalogue lists this volume as an "abridgement" of *General History*, and attributes it to Defoe. While it does follow the general outline of the second edition of *General History*, its substantial textual changes go beyond simple abridgment, and may be said to be a shorter rewrite of the Johnson original. On the whole, it adopts a more explicitly judgmental tone against its subjects, and strictly avoids any language that might ennoble either pirates or the profession of piracy itself. The frontispiece is a woodcut showing, in the upper half, the figure of Justice holding her scales in front of several gallows, from which pirate bodies may be seen hanging. The lower half depicts a sea battle between members of the Royal Navy and an unidentified pirate ship (see Figure 1.1).

The preface to the Midwinter edition is much more insistent than Johnson's original that the book has a specific didactic purpose. It is designed "to caution

Figure 1.1 Frontispiece to *History and Lives of All the Most Notorious Pirates* (1725). Library of Congress.

the unwary Mariner against the Temptations he may meet with at Sea," and "to shew the Merchant what Perils Sailors daily undergo to make them Rich and Great" (A3r). The preface concludes with a reminder that

> as Thieves of all sorts are Villanous, [there is] none to be compared to the Villany of a Pirate, who knows not what he is about till he finds himself going to be hang'd; and then usually dies in such a desponding Condition, that the last Moment of his Life sours all the Relish of his inhumane Pleasures. (*History and Lives*, A5r).

For all Johnson's acknowledgment of the criminality of piracy, there is nothing like this kind of language anywhere in *General History*.

History and Lives seems to have enjoyed its own independent audience: an "eighth edition," virtually identical to the first, appeared as late as 1765. In 1913, publishers Simpkin, Marshall, Hamilton, Kent and Co. reissued a version based on the so-called fifth edition of 1735. The editor, C. Lovat Fraser, laments that the book does not have "very much 'cut and thrust' about it," since it was "written in that uninspiring day when Pirates were a very real nuisance to such law-abiding folk as you and I" (ix–x). Fraser also acknowledges that his copy-text is, in fact, a piracy itself, but he dismisses the original as "a much larger and more pretentious work" (xiii), saying little about Johnson himself except that he "was one of those inspired folk who would be quite capable of spelling 'schooner' with three variations in as many lines" (xv): clearly, the suspicion that Johnson might have been Defoe seems not to have occurred to him.[25]

THE FOURTH EDITION

Finally, on 27 July 1728, advertisements for a "second volume" appeared, along with a fourth edition of what is now volume 1. The publisher for both of these was Thomas Woodward, although it is worth noting that the advertisements appeared almost exclusively in *Mist's Weekly Journal*, and Mist himself appears to have had copies of the third edition available for sale. The two-volume version was the one best known to later eighteenth- and nineteenth-century readers, and is the copy-text Manuel Schonhorn used in his 1972 edition. Schonhorn's edition presents the first "edited, corrected, and annotated" version of *General History* since its first appearance. However, Schonhorn's "corrections" complicate an accurate assessment of the text as it originally appeared, and certainly does not allow the reader to see the various changes and additions that followed the text from 1724 to 1728.

Volume 2, which appeared only in 1728, was an extremely haphazard and sloppy production. Its method of arrangement, as Schonhorn notes, did not follow any chronological order. In fact, the lives seem to have been printed as they were received: the fact that the chapters are not even numbered, as they are in the first volume, may suggest that the publisher might not have known how many lives were going to be included in the finished volume. The "Description of Magadoxa" is awkwardly inserted, as is the life of Captain North, which Schonhorn prints as a chapter in its own right, but which in 1728 appears among the supplementary material for the lives in volume 1 (and, curiously, a two-page addition to the life of John Bowen, which had appeared as the second chapter in volume 2). Finally, the page numbers jump from 144 to 161, a mistake that is corrected only when the volume reaches page 273.[26]

Schonhorn's rearrangement, while it lends some chronological coherence to the stories, obscures the fact that volume 2, far from being the "carefully documented record of fact" and the "completed form" of *General History*, reads in its original publication like a volume quickly thrown together to offer readers something a little more than just a reprint of a volume that had already seen three editions in as many years. Curiously, too, many of Moore's proofs for Defoe's authorship are derived either from the 1728 volume or from one of the additions to the original 1724 volume. Moore clearly assumes that Defoe had a direct hand in the revisions and additions to the original volume as published by Rivington, but there is no evidence to support this. In fact, the variety of publishers in such a short time, coupled with the generally haphazard nature of the additions, especially in 1728, does not suggest a careful reworking up to an "ideal" or "complete" two-volume form; rather, it suggests a succession of editorial intrusions at several removes from the original 1724 version. It may be that the 1726/1728 version is more historically accurate or contains updated information (which it certainly does in the case of pirates who were still at large when the 1724 version appeared), but there is nothing to show that the "completed" two-volume version represents anything like a single author's final conception of his work—any more than the 1734 reprint, which combines *General History* with stories of famous highwaymen, represents a reconsideration of the work by the author who produced the first edition a decade earlier. (Moore, in fact, points to the 1734 edition as evidence that "Charles Johnson" is a pseudonym. On the assumption that "Johnson" is Defoe, he argues that the publishers of that edition took advantage of Defoe's death to use the Johnson name freely. Defoe, Moore asserts, never would have allowed the Johnson name to be attached to anything as inferior as the 1734 volume.)

PIRATES AND HIGHWAYMEN: THE 1730S AND BEYOND

In order to trace the history of *General History* after 1728, we must briefly digress into the underworld of popular crime writing. The most important collection of early eighteenth-century crime narratives is Captain Alexander Smith's *The History of the Lives of the Most Noted Highway-Men, Foot-Pads, House-Breakers, Shop-lifts and Cheats*, first published in 1714, but extended and reissued multiple times. There is little doubt that the work of "Captain Johnson" was modeled on that of "Captain Smith"—so it is not surprising that the two fictitious writers of criminal history should be made to "collaborate" at some point. This is precisely what happened in 1734, with the appearance of *A General History of the Lives and Adventures of the Most Famous Highwaymen, Murderers, Street-Robbers, &c, To Which is Added A Genuine Account of the Voyages and Plunders of the Most Notorious Pyrates*. The whole heady soup of a volume was published by one J. Janeway, and remained the standard edition of both Smith and Johnson throughout the eighteenth century and into the nineteenth.

Smith's 1714 edition, a forerunner of the later, more popular *Newgate Calendar*, advertised itself as a compendium of negative exempla that has been assembled "that by the dreadful aspects of Vice, [readers] may be deterr'd from embracing her Illusions" (A2r). This overtly didactic purpose seems fitting for a book to justify itself as something more than a series of lurid crime stories, even if that is largely what it is. The sense that the present age—the age of highwaymen—is somehow a lost, decadent age in need of correction is underscored by the quotation from the third satire of Juvenal on the title page:

> *Foelicies proavorum atavos, foelicia dicas*
> *Secula quae quondam sub regibus atque tribunis*
> *Vedirunt uno contentam carcere Romam.* (3.312–314)
>
> (Happy, one feels, were our distant ancestors, happy the ages
> which lived of old beneath the rule of kings and tribunes
> in the days when a single jail sufficed the capital city.)

By the 1734 edition, however, "Johnson" isn't even pretending that there is anything morally instructive or uplifting about the book, except perhaps as an ironic commentary on the inherent antiheroism of the age. Instead of Juvenal, we have a quotation from Garth's *The Dispensary*, which identifies the Old Bailey as a place where "little Villains must submit to Fate / that Great Ones may enjoy the World in State" (1:9–10).[27] The sense here, reinforced by the preface, is that highwaymen and pirates are not aberrations of society, but merely different expressions of a tendency that runs through all of society, the only difference being that highwaymen and pirates, generally being of a lower socioeconomic class, receive the punishment of law, whereas those above them escape. The preface even turns the implications in *General History*'s preface on its head (or, perhaps, takes the implications in the earlier preface and follows them to their logical end), by suggesting that even supposedly "great" figures in history are little more than criminals who got away with their crimes:

> What was *Nimrod* but a successful Free-booter? and what were all the Founders of Monarchies, but Encroachers on the Properties of their Brethren and Neighbours? *Alexander* was a Plunderer of the first Magnitude; and all his extraordinary Exploits, with much Admiration, were only Robberies committed upon Men every way better than himself. *Cæsar*, that other prodigious Name, was a Plunderer of his native Country, or (as the great *Cowley* has warmly and nobly express'd it) *a Ravisher of his own Mother*. What better can we call any of his Successors who have sacrific'd the Lives and Liberties of Thousands of their Fellow-Creatures to an extravagant Passion? Whether we name it Tyranny, Ambition, or only Greatness of Soul, 'tis much the same, while the Effects of it are so very terrible. (B1r).

Johnson acknowledges that, while the book may have some didactic purpose, its main reason for existing is to be diverting—anyone who wants may also derive "instruction" from these histories, but it is entirely up to the individual reader: "Which is," Johnson remarks, "all we can promise and, we believe, all that can be expected."

As we move further away from the editions of the 1720s, and as we move further away from the historical reality of the Hanoverian pirates, the figure of piracy itself begins to seem increasingly unreal. Even by the 1734 edition, pirates had already begun to morph into fantasy figures, thanks in part to the addition of fictional characters, such as Sir John Falstaff and Defoe's own Colonel Jacque, to the roster of criminal biographies. Quasi-historical figures, such as Robin Hood and the notorious Scottish cannibal Sawney Beane, also appear among the genuinely historical criminals, further blurring the lines between historicity and fiction that were already present in these biographies. A 1742 version of the *Highwaymen* volume, printed in Birmingham, distorts history even further, by reducing the number of lives but retaining many of the most sensational ones, including Falstaff and Jacque, but also historical figures for whom accurate information is generally lacking: noted underworld figures such as Moll Cutpurse and "The Golden Farmer" (whose true identity has only recently been rediscovered).

My point in outlining all of this is not necessarily to reopen the authorship question, but to suggest that *General History* is not the unified and comprehensive work that Moore believed it to be, or even that Schonhorn's 1972 edition presents. Rather, its initial moment—the 1724 edition and its quick revision that same year—needs to be seen as a distinct incarnation in its own right, with the 1728 second volume, and its appendices, a somewhat clumsy attempt to bring the work into line with its avowed intention as a "general history" of pirating. We can situate *General History* among other books concerned with transatlantic economies, the morality of commerce, and the burgeoning wealth of the mercantile class, which piracy threatened to undermine? How do we read *General History* in terms of other economic activity of the period, especially the South Sea Bubble which, as *General History* itself reminds us, was taking place in London at the same time as the height of the Golden Age of Piracy was in full swing? While piracy, as a practice, certainly receives its share of censure in the book, in the lives of the pirate captains whose names form the titles of its various chapters, there is almost a grudging admiration, a recognition that these figures had "an eye to the Main Chance," as more legitimate entrepreneurs were being encouraged to maintain in other publications. Pirates seized goods, to be sure, but they also seized opportunities, and displayed the same kind of initiative and aggressiveness that would prove to be both the making and the unmaking of the English economy in the 1720s. Perhaps this is why the pirates of *General History* captured the imagination as they did in the 1720s, and why they continue to capture the imagination. *General History*, it must be noted, both reports facts and creates fictions. It ignores even easily-accessible documents when it wants to, and is not above reporting or even inventing incidents in order to make its accounts of pirates readable and entertaining. And yet, it is also remarkably bloodless, being careful not to present too many lurid details, and even then, presenting those that are present almost apologetically, as if they must be there for the sense of the narrative. Again, this is no cheap publication aimed at readers who might well be sympathetic to—even from the same world as—the pirates featured. Instead, it is aimed at educated readers concerned to understand the pirate world as an intrinsic part of the commercial world they also inhabit.

MONSTERS

2

"LET US MAKE A HELL OF OUR OWN"

The Pirate as Monster

IN HIS 2003 STUDY *THE PIRATE WARS*, Peter Earle begins, like many historians, by separating the fiction—or, as he terms it, the "fable"—of piracy from the facts that make up the bulk of his book.[1] He handily obliterates many of the tropes that compose the Treasure Neverland version of pirates, but he is also keen to dispel the idea advanced by scholars such as Peter Linebaugh and Marcus Rediker that pirates were egalitarian protomoderns who looked past race, gender, and even sexual orientation on board their ships, in direct contrast to the mores of their time. In Linebaugh and Rediker's view, the very term "pirate" is "highly ideological," embodying a powerful resistance figure who offered the hope that "the fortunes . . . of those who lived bitter and impoverished lives" might be reversed.[2] For Earle, however, pirates are simply bloodthirsty criminals, much more akin to football hooligans than enlightened activists. In his account, the "golden age of piracy" is suffused with "dirt, drink, disease, suppurating wounds and plebeian captains":[3] hardly the stuff of adventure fiction or Hollywood fantasy.

Whatever the reality may have been, Rediker and Earle, like everyone else, have only extant texts to work with, and these texts tend to construct the pirate as an ambiguous figure, both criminal and hero, Monster and Great Man. While Rediker favors the latter, and sees pirates as embodying a seemingly modern sense of concern for the rights of the individual, Earle argues that such a view is somewhat overstated, since it tends to ignore the pirate's remarkable capacity for violence and cruelty. What both historians tend to overlook is that their source texts, especially *General History*, are not necessarily factual records, but freely blend fact and fiction, and are governed by social and ideological prejudices that shape the way that we read pirates.

In fact, much of the recent scholarship on piracy has been concerned with navigating what are understood to be unreliable texts. Neil Rennie devotes considerable attention to separating the morally reprehensible sea robber from the attractive and sympathetic figure.[4] Margarette Lincoln surveys the construction of a pirate culture in her wide-ranging study of both familiar and obscure works.[5] Frederick Burwick and Manushag Powell, focusing on the representation of pirates in the later eighteenth and nineteenth centuries, note that the term "pirate" in these texts almost always signifies a native of the British Isles whose base of operations is generally in the Caribbean, thus obliterating the considerable discourse surrounding Muslim pirates operating in the Mediterranean in the seventeenth century and the rich history of Asian pirates.[6] Finally, Mark Hanna, in *Pirate Nests and the Rise of the British Empire*, radically shifts the focus from the sea to the land, arguing that colonial settlements were much more receptive to maritime plunderers than the merchants back in Britain: the designation of pirates as a "universal" adversary made little sense to the North American and Caribbean ports that actually depended on piracy for a good deal of their economic health.[7] As useful as all of these studies are for expanding our understanding of how the pirate figure has come to be constructed, we are only beginning to appreciate the wider implications of how pirates fit in an age that depended so heavily on trade that was itself morally reprehensible: both the plantations and the slave trade that made them possible. European incursion into Africa, an essential part of the colonial narrative, carried pirates with it, and pirates were not untouched by this activity. To consider piracy fully, then, we must consider what texts like *General History* also have to say about the monstrosity and the greatness in colonial trade itself.

With that in mind, we can begin to reconsider Johnson's *General History* and its place in the wider conversation about commerce and colonialism in the 1720s. Johnson's perspective on piracy, naturally, is shaped by his somewhat restrictive focus on Caribbean piracy from his own recent past. Hanna has suggested that *General History*'s focus on the decade between 1716 and 1726 has seriously distorted the complexity of pirate reality, and has obscured piracy's role in developing the North American colonies. Prior to 1714, Hanna argues, American colonists, from Newfoundland to the coasts of Central America, depended on piracy to keep their fledgling economy viable. Moreover, in the seventeenth century, the line between "privateer" and "pirate" was obscure and intangible: privateers who had a legal right to plunder ships of particular nations could find their status invalidated with the stroke of pen—and be unaware that anything had changed. Colonists in Massachusetts repeatedly insisted on referring to pirates as "privateers," regardless of their actual status, since the money and goods they brought to shore was an intrinsic part of the local economy. Some local governors even actively supported piracy, and heavily resisted all attempts by the Admiralty to suppress it. Until 1714, Hanna suggests, piracy was neither an exclusively maritime phenomenon, nor was it simply a matter of rogue criminals and disaffected sailors striking out against legitimate commerce. Piracy was, to a degree, *part* of legitimate commerce, and might have continued well past 1730 had it not been for a concerted effort to eradicate it.

Part of the reason for not only suppressing piracy with such vigor but also for constructing a monolithic image of the pirate in print has to do with what Hanna calls the "notions of aggressive social mobility considered dangerous to gentry readers on land."[8] Unlike Henry Morgan or William Kidd, who could legitimately call themselves privateers and who had royal assent for their activities, Hanoverian pirates operated outside the bounds of legitimacy, yet still dared to appropriate the title of "captain." At the same time, Morgan and Kidd, who styled themselves as gentlemen, both emerged from obscurity in Wales and Scotland, respectively. Little or nothing is known of either man's family; both achieved a considerable measure of respectability in their lifetimes, with Morgan even ending up governor of New Providence. Likely, too, had Kidd not overstepped himself both by turning pirate and by brutally murdering a member of his own crew, he might even have achieved the same kind of honor. In a way, both of these men embody properties of the Monster and the Great Man, the figure from the margins who ends up in the service of the center.

THE UNIVERSAL ADVERSARY

"Bourgeois modernity," Mark Neocleous asserts, "is oriented around the imagination of an Enemy." The reason for this, he suggests, is that "the fear of some kind of Enemy is a fundamental feature of the supreme concept of bourgeois society: security."[9] Britain in the 1720s, beginning to display many of the characteristics of what would come to be defined as "bourgeois," held numerous enemies before the public, all of whom were said to threaten the stability of the state: Roman Catholics, Jacobites, Dissenters, highway robbers, and—perhaps the most fearsome of all—pirates. Pirates, as we have seen, acquired the designation *hostis humani generis*—the enemy of all humanity—which fixed them in a particular legal and ontological space. The term *hostis*, as Carlo Galli reminds us, originally meant "the stranger within us"—the enemy stands outside and against the boundaries of the state, and, more importantly, stands outside and against the principal values of the state. It is the enemy's desire to transgress the physical border and to undermine the legitimacy of the state itself. To be a *universal* enemy, therefore, implies that the *hostis* does not simply seek to undermine the values of a particular state, but stands in opposition to *all* states, even to the very idea of statehood itself.

If, as Galli also suggests, "enemies are not criminals and criminals are not enemies"[10] for the simple reason that criminals are still regarded as part of the state, then pirates are stateless, outside of any political organization but their own: the pirate ship is, literally, a ship of state; the Jolly Roger, in its numerous variants, is the banner of a separate nation. Pirate statelessness needs to be considered alongside larger questions about colonialism and the destabilizing of social and political hierarchies that colonial settlements brought with them. Like other vilified colonial figures, such as the nabobs later in the century, the pirate's ability to obtain wealth and to seek social status even within a remote colony is a threat to established order, to the very notion of statehood itself.[11] In order to be constructed fully as *hostis humani generis*, the pirate must be seen to be cut off from all systems of stability: marital and familial ties, or regional and national loyalties. Pirates flourish in international waters, and their crimes are crimes against not just one state, but all states. At the same time, as Neocleous explains, the international nature of piracy also connects it with colonialism and empire building. The pirate is a kind of "'juridical nomad,' who traverse[s] the porous spaces between the lawful privateer and the pariah entrepreneur, between the law and the outlaw." Neocleous also notes that the words "peril" and "empire" share a root with the word "pirate," emphasizing that colonialism and piracy are conceptually intertwined.[12]

The designation of the pirate as *hostis humani generis* is treated somewhat ambivalently in *General History*, as Johnson resists presenting the pirate simply as an embodiment of evil. *General History* certainly does much to embody the pirate as Enemy, even as a "universal adversary." At the same time, the pirate operates within a context, not just of commerce, but global commerce, and Johnson cannot avoid portraying Britain's global economic activity as itself morally ambiguous. The enemy, therefore, emerges as a shadowy, slippery figure, a ghostly presence, one who is subject, as is much maritime lore from the period, to exaggeration and distortion, to fiction blurred with fact. The point of writing pirate biographies, then, is to give recognizable shape to these ghosts, to construct a face for these indistinct figures.

The pirate is a blank slate, a screen onto which may be projected all of the economic and political anxieties of an emerging capitalist culture. Pirates never speak for themselves, nor relate their life histories in their own words. Trial narratives ostensibly record the actual words of captured pirates, but those words are both filtered through the official discourse of the legal system, and constructed primarily with the purpose of establishing guilt or innocence, not of revealing the inner lives of those who speak them. What matters is only what a pirate is alleged to have done, not what he may have thought, or felt, or believed. Occasionally, pirates speak from the gallows, although even these speeches are deemed memorable only insofar as they help to determine the mental and spiritual state of the pirate at the point of death. If penitent, the pirate pleads for forgiveness and begs God to be merciful; if unrepentant, a pirate's last words may be a foul-mouthed rant against society, God, or the law, thus reinforcing the pirate's status as universal adversary. Even Johnson himself, who claims to reproduce faithfully pirates' own words, is an assumed voice, a fictional "captain" designed to lend verisimilitude and authority to his subject matter. *General History*, therefore, is a carefully crafted portrait of piracy that provides readers with the pirate they expect and need, if not necessarily the pirate who actually lived.

As the title *hostis humani generis* implies, piracy is considered, under the law, to be a universally deplorable phenomenon. In practice, of course, what actually constituted piracy could be difficult to pin down, especially when one considers privateering as a legally sanctioned form of piracy (a sanction that could be, and often was, rescinded without the privateer's knowledge). Despite the claim of universality, piracy itself under closer examination emerges as ambiguous and slippery, a legal designation more than anything else. Because the concept of the universal adversary is itself so amorphous, so fluid, it must be incarnated in clearly demarcated and well-defined groups. In order for a universal adversary to exist, it must be seen to exist within a specific and identifiable culture. Pirates were, first and foremost, sailors, and the culture with which they identified was the larger Atlantic maritime culture. While it is true that some pirate-specific cultural artifacts, such as the Jolly Roger flag, developed during the 1713–1730 period, for the most part the so-called pirate culture that even young children can identify today didn't exist as such in that period. It was, however, necessary to the war on piracy to create such a culture. As we shall see, the pirate's body, to paraphrase Jeffrey Jerome Cohen, is primarily a cultural body.

The specific biographical subjects of *General History* suggest that, to some degree, the book was designed to present piracy as a monolithic culture. Johnson is largely unconcerned with the overall history of piracy and is, in fact, most concerned with the generation of pirates who rose to prominence after the War of the Spanish Succession. Even then, Johnson's dedication to factual accuracy is somewhat haphazard. The pirate narratives in *General History* are all, to this degree, fictions. While there is much journalistic detail in each of the chapters—in particular the dates of various expeditions and the names, captains, and home ports of dozens of ships captured—*General History* is memorable because its narratives ultimately transcend its sometimes soporific details. What emerges from the lists and the interpolated travelogues is a set of sharply defined portraits of the men and women whose mythic status was quickly accepted and exploited in later incarnations of the book, and is still being exploited today. *General History* is a literary tour de force that captures, and to a considerable degree invents, the romance of piracy, even as it condemns its subject as lowlife thieves and murderers.

MASTERLESS MEN

The universality of the pirate adversary signifies a universal order, which pirates naturally threaten to disrupt or destroy altogether. Trial accounts repeatedly stress that pirate activity is not simply an economic nuisance, but a threat to all trade itself: it is as if an exterminator were to suggest that an infestation of mice was not just a health hazard or a source of property damage, but a scourge that would bring down one's entire house. The extreme anxiety this view displays has antecedents in the previous century, in the "masterless men" that Christopher Hill examines in *The World Turned Upside Down*. Hill suggests that these "servants to nobody" were seen as "potential dissolvents of the society."[13] Although some of these itinerants were politically unaligned beggars or vagabonds, or simple day-laborers and craftspeople seeking employments over a wide area, others, especially after the period of the Commonwealth, were members of subversive sects, and did represent at least a challenge to the established social order. While Hill suggests that none of these masterless men was ever seriously anything more than a "security problem," he also notes that there was a certain attractiveness in the freedom a life outside of society represented: "What produced alarm and anxiety in some was an opportunity for others—though not an opportunity for climbing up the normal social ladder. A masterless man was nobody's servant: this could mean freedom for those who prized independence more than security."[14] We can see the same kind of combination of anxiety and attraction in the figure of the pirate: they are the masterless men of the new global economy, a perceived threat to an economic order even more than the beggars, itinerant laborers, strolling players, quack doctors, tramps, and general misfits and dropouts that constituted the bulk of the underworld of England.

But why the pirate? The view of the sea robber as not just a threat, not just a disturbance, not even as a mere adversary, but a *universal* adversary, in part depends on the view of the common sailor in the early eighteenth century. As Marcus Rediker has noted, sailors themselves would have understood their importance in the growth of transatlantic trade, especially after the Treaty of Utrecht in 1713 had largely shifted attention in Atlantic waters from military to commercial competition.[15] Put simply, Britain depended on the activity of merchant ships, and the merchant ships depended on able seamen. At the same time, as Rediker also notes, the sailor would have understood that the phenomenal and rapid growth of transatlantic trade meant that his labor, though important, was seen as merely a small part of a much larger machine. Worse still, given the number of demobilized navy seamen now out of work since the end of the war, the common sailor was himself expendable and easily replaceable. Wages were kept low, and discipline on merchant vessels was often harsh and brutal. Captains could be virtual laws unto themselves; unless someone was willing to testify otherwise, mutilations or even deaths could easily be attributed to accident, disease, or even the sailor's own carelessness.[16] Since the essence of social control in the eighteenth century was respect for and belief in social stratification, an organized body of individuals who openly challenged such stratification, while at the same time threatening the security of commerce, would cause considerable anxiety.

Linebaugh and Rediker have explored the connection between the growth of maritime trade between 1670 and 1730 and the preservation of the radical ideas of the mid-seventeenth-century masterless man. They note, for instance, that "the ship became both an engine of capitalism in the wake of the bourgeois revolution in England *and* a setting of resistance, a place to which and in which the ideas and practices of revolutionaries defeated and repressed by Cromwell and then by King Charles escaped, reformed, circulated, and persisted."[17] Linebaugh and Rediker trace ideas found in the writings of the Levellers to some of the more antiauthoritarian practices aboard pirate ships, and note that the Golden Age pirates, unlike the gentleman adventurers of the Elizabethan period, were primarily average sailors, uneducated, illiterate, drawn from the lowest social circles. More terrifying than their plunder or their threats of violence was the threat of social upheaval that successful pirates promised.

In light of the above, it is not hard to see how the image of the sea robber—who, *General History* reminds us, has existed since classical times[18]—could be transformed from an economic nuisance to a considerable menace. Unlike beggars or day-laborers, or even highwaymen, pirates were in command of considerable technologies, both ships and heavy artillery. Moreover, pirates acted in consort, so that the adversary was not simply an individual but an entire crew. Rediker notes that pirate ships could consist of up to eighty men, more than the average merchant vessel. Since the captain was chosen by common consent, in theory any crew member could assume captaincy in battle, and so the death of one ship's captain did not necessarily mean the surrender of the entire crew.

Even if the pirates of *General History* were not the forward-thinking democratic sailors Linebaugh and Rediker would like them to be, their conception of an alternate social order, one that devalued rank, bloodline, or title in favor of merit and consent, certainly resonated with political thinkers in the 1720s, who were considering the applicability of such ideas to the larger body politic, especially in the aftermath of the South Sea Bubble. Like the masterless men of the previous century—which, in effect, pirates were—their continued existence suggested a perpetual threat to the social order. Unchecked, still free, the pirate of the imagination—the pirate of *General History*—lurked in the shadows, threatening, terrifying: in a word, monstrous.

MONSTER THEORY AND PIRATE NARRATIVE

Johnson includes some examples of the official discourse surrounding pirates, especially extracts from trial documents and legal definitions of the pirate; at the same time, he does not shy away from lurid tales of brutality and violence that always accompany pirate stories. Yet, he is also aware that the pirates he studies are products of a particular time and place; their monstrosity is always rooted in circumstance. We can, therefore, consider the pirate as a cultural hybrid, a monstrous figure who embodies the anxieties over the social, political, and economic changes brought about by the financial revolution, the consolidation of Whig power under Robert Walpole, and the growing importance of colonial commerce—all of which came together during the period covered by Johnson's *General History*.

We may use the theses Jeffrey Jerome Cohen offers in his seminal article "Monster Culture (Seven Theses)"[19] to examine how *General History* represents the pirate as a kind of monster for a readership already highly sensitive to and anxious about overseas commerce. Cohen's seven theses[20] offer as a polemical framework for "reading cultures from the monsters they engender."[21] Cohen casts the Monster in the role of universal Other, a figure at once fantastical enough to arouse our most profound fears by its strangeness, yet familiar enough to be realizable in flesh. The Monster is a cultural construct, but one that challenges the very definitions of the culture itself. The Monster lives on the fringes of society, "dwell[ing] at the gates of difference" and "polic[ing] the borders of the possible." The Monster challenges identities, especially those of nationality, gender, sexuality, and race: "the monster is transgressive, too sexual, perversely erotic, a lawbreaker; and so the monster and all that it embodies must be exiled or destroyed."[22] Johnson's pirates are precisely these marginal, terrifying, monstrous figures who nevertheless still retain some resemblances to "normal" humanity—and therein lies the fascination. Like zombies or vampires, they are both human and not human, once just like us, but now irrevocably turned and their humanity permanently lost; like exotic non-Europeans—Jews, or Muslims, African or North American "savages," "wild men" and the like—they draw us in with their resemblance to ourselves, and yet disturb us by their essential Otherness. It may be significant that Johnson concerns himself exclusively with European pirates, and so avoids racial or cultural markers of Otherness that might divert focus away from the Otherness of being pirates. There is no shortage, for example, of stories of Barbary Corsairs who can easily be slotted into Orientalist tropes of Otherness; such figures, however, are already made Other by these tropes, and their role as pirates therefore becomes merely an extension of their already essential monstrousness. They are not, as their European counterparts are, monsters by virtue of their piracy.

The pirate of popular imagination, typified in part by *Treasure Island* but also by numerous Hollywood films, is characterized by a feature shared with other monsters: the deformed and maimed body. The peg leg, the eye patch, the hook: these are universal pirate markers, as if the degradation of the body is a prerequisite for piracy. Historically, of course, maimed bodies were a common by-product of shipboard life: the daily work was dangerous, and loss of limbs or eyes was an accepted risk. How useful a maimed sailor would have been on a working ship is open to question; such men could be assigned tasks not involving heavy labor, as per Stevenson's maimed cook, Long John Silver. What is of greater interest here, however, is how the eye patch and the peg leg have become inextricably associated with piracy itself. The deformed body is a monstrous body, a transformation of a normal human body into something strange and, to use Johnson's word, "frightful." The hook that replaces the hand also endows its wearer with a ready weapon; the hint of something ghastly lurking under an eye patch suggests a body already in transition to something other than human. Moreover, as Stephen Pender has shown, early modern writers on human monstrosity linked the deformed body with an equally deformed mind.[23] In the case of pirates, the loss of body parts is a reminder of violence, of bodies torn apart in battle, and a reminder of the fragility of one's own body.[24]

With this in mind, it is all the more noteworthy that the pirates of the *General History* are not monstrous because of bodily deformity. Eye patches and peg legs simply do not feature in Johnson's accounts, and the iconography of the book, even in its *Historie den Engelsche Zee-Roovers* or Midwinter version, shows a distinct absence of such inherently piratical markers. For Johnson, as for his contemporaries, the pirate's monstrosity lay not just in his body, but in his mind: the pirate's deliberate flouting of the natural social order, the desire to act as a force threatening all commercial activity—these are the distinctive features of the 1720s pirate. As the immediate social and economic context of eighteenth-century piracy retreated further into history, the more conventional markers of physical deformity replaced those of economic or social deformity. The pirate of *General*

History is no less monstrous than the frightening maimed figures of popular imagination. At the same time, the pirate's body becomes a powerful tool for demonstrating state power, particularly in the figure of the hanged criminal, permanently left on display as a warning to others.

Even with a distinct face and shape, the pirate still inhabits the margins of human society; he is perpetually relegated to the status of outsider, a permanent exile from civilization. As Isaac Kamola puts it,

> The pirate engages in a kind of "border thinking," existing at the "intense battlefield"; between "colonial modernities" and the lived worlds of the subaltern. Existing on the violent border of capital accumulation, the vast spaces of maritime circulation, and sovereign power, the pirate is uniquely well positioned to provide an account of the modern/colonial capitalist economy.[25]

Pirates' liminal status allows them simultaneously to embody the very qualities that comprise the successful modern capitalist and to reject the desire for wider social legitimation that accompanies much capitalist activity. Aspirations to gentility, access to the centers of political or economic power, fall outside the pirates' purview: marginality is absolutely crucial to the pirate identity.

In fact, it is the pirates' very monstrosity, their seeming lack of humanity, that resonates so strongly with readers of *General History*. Even more than his land-based counterpart, the highwayman, the pirate embodies the political and economic anxieties of the early eighteenth century, in part because the pirate is such a marginal figure. Piracy is associated with Jacobitism,[26] but also with the remnants of the radicalism of the Commonwealth. Pirates embody the bold, resourceful, innovative, individualistic spirit of the entrepreneur, the Whig man of business, but they also reveal the worst corruptions—greed, ruthlessness, antisocial tendencies, disrespect for class distinctions—that can befall him. They are both a product and an aberration of the commercial revolution that had transformed Britain at the start of the century, and in their very monstrosity, they seemed to reveal the true shape of the Hanoverian age. Pirates needed a *General History*, in short, because they demanded some way of defining them and, perhaps, of controlling them.

The designation "monster" implies much more than simply a "frightful" adversary. As Cohen suggests,

> The monster is difference made flesh, come to dwell among us. In its function as a dialectical Other or third-term supplement, the monster is an incorporation of the Outside, the Beyond—of all those loci that are rhetorically placed as distant and distinct but originate Within.[27]

Part of the strategy of nation defining and empire building involves a subjection of the Other, an eradication of difference that might challenge or unsettle the Center. Cultural and linguistic suppression, geographical marginalization, a mythology of "taming" the frontier, even outright genocide: these are the hallmarks of empire building. If pirates emerges from the margins of empire, then they, like all monsters, must be seen to be kept in check by the same forces that promise a community of properly ordered subjects, identity with the imperial center, and the stability of a tightly maintained marginal space.

All of the above combined with another anxiety that was explored in the essay-journals of the day: the social and political implications of the Financial Revolution, especially after the fiasco of the South Sea Bubble. The bubble itself, as we shall see later, seemed to confirm the fear of potential social upheaval that a money-based economy could bring. Although some of the voices examining the Financial Revolution were Tories who simply wanted to preserve the traditional social structure based on land ownership, the most interesting commentaries came, in fact, from Whigs, whose anxieties were centered on the potential corruptions of what they saw as essentially a superior economic system. John Trenchard and Thomas Gordon, Bernard Mandeville, and, of course, Defoe—all focused on trying to define the proper use of trade and finance. In order to embody the evil of corrupt trade, however, it was necessary to embody that corruption inside a monster. Defoe had briefly located that monster in the stockjobber,[28] but the perils of speculation, considerable though they are, did not quite have the same reach as the monster who could dismantle all trade itself. The culture of the early eighteenth century needed the pirate as an embodiment of its fears of a growing global economy. If, as Nina Auerbach has suggested, each age embraces the vampire it needs, then the pirate is the commercial version of the vampire: the monster that must, as Marina Levina and Diem-My Bui argue, "offer a space where society can safely represent and address the anxieties of its time."[29] Britain's growing dependence on overseas trade, on its colonial holdings in the Americas, generated considerable anxiety among economic commentators, especially Defoe.

JOHNSON'S MONSTERS

It is perhaps no accident that the most famous pirates featured in *General History* are also the most notorious. In the 1720s, Henry Avery was the "king of pirates," in part because he was never caught or tried: the best outlaws are the ones who get away with their crimes. Yet, as has been noted, Avery himself belongs to a generation earlier than the pirates of *General History*: with the possible exception of

Roberts, none of the pirates discussed here comes close to matching Avery's successes or his escapes. The heroes of this new age are the villains, who embody the decadence and grotesqueness of the age. To end this chapter, then, I would like to highlight some of *General History*'s more notable "monsters," some of whom helped to furnish the iconic pirate image for generations afterward.

Blackbeard: The Pirate as Brand

Perhaps the most iconic pirate character outside of literary fiction is that of Edward Teach, better known as Blackbeard. Fearsome, hard-drinking, bold, outrageous, and yet wildly successful, Blackbeard seems to embody everything we expect from swashbuckling pirates. He even had the decency not to be captured or tried; rather, he died in battle with the authorities who sought to bring him to justice. Blackbeard's life, one of the more exciting chapters in *General History*, seems to be the model for a good amount of adventure fiction—he even merits a significant, if thoroughly fictionalized, role in the fourth *Pirates of the Caribbean* film.

Substantial information on Blackbeard's early life is hard to come by, and even Johnson is of little help: 1724a consistently spells his real surname as Thatch and asserts that he was born in Jamaica, while 1724b spells the name Teach, and calls him "a Bristol Man born."[30] Ultimately, of course, what matters in the narrative is not so much Blackbeard's origins as how he managed to recreate himself as an iconic pirate. Blackbeard, perhaps more than any other pirate of the Golden Age, understood the concept of what we would now call branding. More than his actual plunder, what mattered about Blackbeard was his reputation, and given the number of fanciful anecdotes associated with him, and his remarkable physical appearance, he seems to have been most successful at cultivating his image as something larger than life.

Johnson, of course, dutifully repeats some of the more outrageous details associated with him. He is said, for example, to have had fourteen wives, the last of which, a girl of sixteen, he basically kept as a prostitute for the enjoyment of his crew. There is a mention of buried treasure, made with the tantalizing boast: "That no Body but himself, and the Devil, knew where it was, and the longest Liver should take all" (1724a, 101 [85]). His surviving crew, we are told, reported seeing a mysterious figure who "was . . . several Days amongst them, sometimes below, and sometimes upon Deck, yet no Man in the Ship could give an account of who he was, or from whence he came . . . but, it seems, they all verily believed it was the Devil" (1724a, 101 [85–86]).[31] Finally, there is the astonishing story of Blackbeard's drink-inspired game of taking a few crew members with him into the hold, and lighting several pots of brimstone as an endurance test: "*Come*, says he, *let us make a Hell of our own, and try how long we can bear it*" (1724a, 100 [85])—Blackbeard himself, of course, held out the longest.

These stories, along with the reports of his noteworthy beard, festooned with ribbons, along with his general appearance:

> In Time of Action, he wore a Sling over his Shoulders, with three brace of Pistols, hanging in Holsters like Bandaliers; he wore a Fur-Cap, and stuck a lighted Match on each Side, under it, which appearing on each side of his Face, his Eyes naturally looking Fierce and Wild, made him altogether such a Figure, that Imagination cannot form an idea of a Fury, from Hell, to look more frightful. (1724a, 99–100 [84–85])

Few pirates in *General History* get such detailed descriptions, nor are so clearly constructed to evoke such an effect in the reader: Johnson uses the word "frightful" twice in as many pages. To cement the image in the reader's mind, Blackbeard is given one of only three engravings in both 1724a and 1724b. In this account, Blackbeard embodies all that is monstrous about the pirate.

Mary Read and Anne Bonny: Monstrous Women

If the masterless men were enough of a source of anxiety to become monsters, then it seems reasonable that the most fearsome "masterless man" should not be a man at all: hence, the inclusion of the two best-known female pirates, interpolated into the chapter on John Rackam, but significant enough to be given a special mention on the title page.[32] Marcus Rediker has noted that Mary Read and Anne Bonny were not necessarily unique in being female sailors, or even pirates: the inherent fascination in their story lies with their frustration of gender norms, and their monstrous ability to shape-shift between male and female.

Read and Bonny are granted one of the three engravings in 1724a and 1724b—a double portrait that shows both women armed and ready to fight, although both women are rendered in oddly static poses (see Figure 2.1). They are clearly dressed in men's clothes, the comfortable, loose-fitting jackets and trousers that are appropriate for a common sailor. As Sally O'Driscoll has noted, this engraving quite conceals Read and Bonny's feminine attributes; the desire to reveal the truth hidden by the clothing causes "a frisson of ambiguity [that] remains as a pleasurable tension" for the reader.[33] O'Driscoll, naturally, contrasts this image with the portraits in *Historie der Engelsche Zee-Roovers*, which show Read and Bonny in much more dynamic poses and, significantly, with their shirts wide open, clearly revealing their breasts—no ambiguity, and with their attire now "seem[ing] to the modern eye more like an erotic party costume than real clothes"

Figure 2.1 Ann[e] Bonny and Mary Read, from 1724b. HathiTrust.

(see Figures 2.2 and 2.3).[34] The Dutch image, O'Driscoll suggests, sexualizes the two pirates, and in so doing turns Bonny and Read "into glamorous, notorious, and malleable figures used to reframe and normalize excessive or problematic female behaviour."[35] By revealing their indisputable femaleness, O'Driscoll argues, the image shifts the focus away from the enigmatic, gender-fluid nature of these pirates as presented in the original portraits, to an "absolute fact" that Read and Bonny are, without question, cisgender women posing as men. We can move the focus of O'Driscoll's argument slightly to align my own remarks on the pirate-monster. As she notes, the Read and Bonny stories participate in a larger cultural discussion about the very nature of femaleness itself: "Representations of female bodies marked them as appropriate or aberrant, codifying a new way of being sexed."[36] By covering up the markers of their gender, the original British portraits of Read and Bonny actually draw greater attention to their strangeness, their inherent monstrosity, since these two women transgress gender norms and freely appropriate symbols of masculinity—in particular the phallic sword that Mary Read deftly wields—so that these figures are deeply unsettling, opening up the boundaries of the possible.

It should be noted that Read's and Bonny's monstrosity is almost completely a construction of Johnson's narrative. The original trial account of John Rackam, which provides our only definitive historical mention of Read and Bonny, presents the two women quite differently. Witness Dorothy Thomas notes that Read and Bonny "wore Mens Jackets, and long Trouzers, and Handkerchiefs tied about their Heads; and that each of them has a Machet and Pistol in their Hands, and cursed

Figure 2.2 Mary Read, from *Historie der Engelsche Zee-Rovers* (1725). KB Nationale Bibliotheek, Da Haag.

Figure 2.3 Anne Bonny, from *Historie der Engelsche Zee-Rovers* (1725). KB Nationale Bibliotheek, Da Haag.

and swore at the Men, to murther [her] . . . [and] the Reason of her known and believing them to be Women then was, by the largeness of their Breasts"[37] In the same way, John Besneck and Peter Cornelian note that "when [Read and Bonny] saw any Vessel, gave Chase, or Attacked, they wore Men's Cloaths; and, at other Times, they wore Women's Cloaths; That they did not seem to be kept, or detain'd by Force, but of their own Free-Will and Consent."[38] In both of these depositions, Read and Bonny behave pretty much like other pirates. What is especially noteworthy, however, is that the certainty of their gender is not in question, but neither does it need to be determined by either women revealing her breasts: for Dorothy Thomas, their femaleness is clearly visible even through their male attire; for Besneck and Cornelian, neither woman seems to need to hide her gender at all, and except in times of battle, could appear freely on the deck as women, and be accepted as full members of Rackam's crew.

If such was the case, what are we then to make of the narratives in *General History*? Both stories center almost exclusively on the issue of gender concealed and revealed. Read is given an elaborate backstory, wherein she is raised as a boy with the sole purpose of inheriting her wealthy grandmother's estate, in effect standing in for an older half-brother who had died in infancy. The grandmother unfortunately dies before Read has reached maturity, and the money that had been paid for Read's maintenance is no longer paid. Read is first hired out as a footboy to a wealthy French woman, but she decides instead to join as an army cadet, and is shipped off to fight in Flanders. There, the story becomes focused on Read's control over revealing or concealing her gender; the reader's interest is maintained primarily in whether anyone is allowed to see her breasts, even described as "very White" at one point (1724a, 133). In the end, Read sublimates her courage, her resourcefulness, and her intelligence for the sake of romantic love; at the same time, she is still a pirate, and so her monstrousness derives from her inability to establish herself in a normal domestic position. Her one attempt, as co-owner of an inn, is thwarted by both the death of her husband and the Peace of Ryswick, but the narrative suggests that Read would not have been the sort to have settled for long anyway.

At the point where Read is about to face sentence, Johnson invents for her a thoughtful, revealing speech, supposedly uttered to one of the witnesses at her trial—although no such speech is recorded in the official account. Asked why she would choose a life of piracy, she answers:

> As to hanging, she thought it no great Hardship, for, were it not for that, every cowardly Fellow would turn Pyrate, and so infest the Seas, that Men of Courage must starve:—That if it were put to the choice of the Pyrates, they would not have the Punishment less than Death, the Fear of which,

> kept some dastardly Rogues honest; that many of those who are now cheating Widows and Orphans, and oppressing their poor Neighbours, who have the Money to obtain Justice, would then rob at Sea, and the Ocean would be crowded with Rogues, like the Land, and no Merchant would venture out; so that the Trade, in a little Time, would not be worth following. (1724a, 125 [158–159]).

Read repeats a trope that echoes elsewhere in *General History*: for all their monstrosity, pirates are no worse than other "rogues," some of whom, with power, wealth, and a corrupt justice system on their side, would be far worse than any pirate sailing with the immanent fear of death. Monsters though they may be, pirates are still the reflection of the culture that has produced them.

Edward Low: The Pirate as Sadist

Blackbeard is, undoubtedly, both one of the most famous and the most notorious of the Golden Age pirates, but to understand exactly how *General History* shapes its narrative to underline the monstrosity of certain pirates, we might better examine an equally notorious, though far less well-known, figure whose story occurs near the end of the first volume. The version of the narrative in 1724a was carried over substantially into 1724b; in many paragraphs the typesetting is exactly the same, or with only an obvious error corrected or a minor word altered. However, 1724b also contains substantive additions and revisions, nearly all of which serve to emphasize the bloodthirstiness of both Low and his crew. At the same time, both versions omit a major incident in Low's career about which we know a great deal, and which puts Low in a substantially different light.

As told in 1724a, Low was born in Westminster, received little or no education (he is described as illiterate), and began his life of crime early on the streets of London. On reaching adulthood, however, Low sailed with his brother to Boston, and was employed in a rigging-house there. However, "being too apt to disagree with his Masters" (1724a, 283), he ended up sailing to Honduras, working as a logwood cutter. Disagreeing once again with authority, Low stole a ship, gathered a small crew, and turned pirate, teaming up for a time with George Lowther.

Low's pirate career seems to have lasted from about early 1722 to at least January 1724, during which time he developed a reputation for violence and cruelty. Johnson, in 1724a, presents a relatively straightforward account of Low's activities, reporting on some of his sadistic actions (such as mutilating the faces of particularly New England sailors) only late in the narrative, so that the reader perceives Low as a man coming unhinged with his own power. The account in 1724b both fleshes out reports of Low's cruelties and suggests on several occasions that this sadistic behavior is shared by the entire crew. For example, an account of a capture of French ship in August, 1722, concludes with this anecdote:

> The Pyrates took several of the Guns out of the *French* Ship, and mounted them aboard the *Rose,* which proved very fit for their Turn, and condemned the former to the Flames. They took all the Crew out of her, but the Cook, who, they said, being a greasy Fellow would fry well in the Fire; so the poor Man was bound to the Main-Mast, and burnt in the Ship, to the no small Diversion of *Low* and his *Mirmidons.* (1724b, 373–374 [323])[39]

Both the horrific act of burning a man alive, and the "diversion" it entails among the crew, serve to dehumanize Low, who seems in 1724b to delight merely in bloody violence for its own sake.

By contrast, something like an attempt to understand Low's psychology appears in 1724a, in a passage subsequently deleted. At the end of a short list of vessels Low and his crew have captured, Johnson mentions a pink, *Stanhope,* captained by one Andrew Delbridge, "which . . . they burnt, because of *Low*'s irreconcilable Aversion to *New-England* Men" (1724a, 290; 1724b, 377 [326]). The paragraph ends there in 1724b, but the earlier edition featured a further explanation of Low's "aversion":

> among whom [i.e., New Englanders] he had lived for some Time, as has been before taken Notice of, and who being of a vindictive Temper, could never forgive a Person from whom he imagined to have received Injuries; and as his Behaviour had merited no extraordinary Treatment in *Boston,* so he met with his Usage accordingly, and now he prosecuted his Revenge against all of that Country, where ever he met with them. (1724a, 290–291)

Low's particular violence toward New England sailors, therefore, is explained as a form of "revenge,"—an interesting insight, and one that serves, if not to vindicate, at least to offer some sort of understanding of this otherwise mentally unhinged sailor.

The narrative in 1724a concludes with the speculation that Low had been killed by his crew, "who lately grew weary of his insolent and tyrannical Government" (1724a, 302). By contrast, the crew in 1724b, far from disapproving of Low's "cruelty and inhumanity," actually work to keep it going:

> Thus these inhumane Wretches went on, who could not be contented to satisfy their Avarice only, and travel in the common Road of Wickedness; but, like their Patron, the Devil, must make Mischief their

> Sport, Cruelty their Delight, and damning of Souls their constant Employment . . . so that they almost as often murthered a Man from the Excess of good Humour, as out of Passion and Resentment; and the Unfortunate could never be assured of Safety from them, for Danger lurked in their very Smiles. (1724b, 388 [334])

As before, the monstrosity is shared among all the crew, and Low himself is but the most inhuman of the diabolical crew.

Significantly, we have one account of Low that serves to qualify all of the above. *Ashton's Memorial,* an astonishing true account of survival on a desert island, was published in Boston in 1725, and in England the following year.[40] Dictated to John Barnard, a priest in Ashton's home town of Marblehead, Massachusetts, the *Memorial* relates how in mid-June 1722, Ashton, then about nineteen or twenty, is fishing off the coast of Cape Sable when his ship is captured by Low. Ashton and his crew are taken aboard, tied up, and compelled to join Low's crew. Ashton relates how Low is particularly anxious to know whether any of the men are married—seemingly odd question, until Ashton explains that Low is, in fact, deeply grieving for a wife and daughter he has lost to illness, and so he has sworn not to separate any married men from their families. In fact, Low, through brutal, is not especially sadistic in Ashton's account: even when Ashton refuses to assent to Low's articles of piracy, Low forces him to work as a skilled sailor, and is reluctant to injure or mutilate anyone who might prove useful to him. Even Low's supposed rage against New Englanders is somewhat qualified by the Massachusetts native Ashton. If anyone is especially sadistic in the crew, Ashton suggests it is Low's first mate, John Russell, who is verbally and physically abusive to Ashton because of his refusal to become a fully-fledged pirate. Ashton's account, which is largely concerned with his escape from Low's captivity and his sixteen-month sojourn on a deserted island, presents a remarkably different picture of this pirate than the one in *General History.* Interestingly, while Ashton's version of Low forms the basis of his portrayal in the anonymous novel, *The Four Years' Voyage of Captain George Roberts* (1726),[41] the version in *General History* remained unrevised even in the fourth edition.

Johnson's monstrous pirates—justifiably the best-known of his narratives—dramatically assert the more horrific aspects of piracy. However, Johnson manages to make his point without overindulging in too many of the lurid details we might expect from a true-crime potboiler. Despite their monstrosity, there is a hint of greatness about these men and women—a point to which we will return later. What emerges from *General History* is something more than even a grudging acceptance of the remarkableness of pirates: it is a kind of respect, a recognition that the pirate, although banished to the margins of civilization, embodies the spirit of the age. Johnson's view of pirates in *General History* illustrates Cohen's point that the monster is attractive, even as it is repulsive: "We distrust and loathe the monster at the same time we envy its freedom, and perhaps its sublime despair." Cohen also suggests that the monster, dwelling as it does in "realms of happy fantasy, horizons of limitation"—for which one may easily read "Treasure Neverland"—is an icon of possibility, "through which the possibilities of other genders, other sexual practices, and other social customs can be explored."[42] That sense of possibility is also the excitement of the colonial experience: while official discourse may present other lands as mere depositories of valuable resources, the presence of monsters—pirate or otherwise—suggests that this land is also a transformational space, and no one who ventures there can remain unchanged. In the following chapters, we will explore how the monster-pirate interacts with the colonial experience, and how Johnson's narratives preserve both the horror and the attractiveness of the 1720s pirate.

3

THE "BORDERS OF THE POSSIBLE"

General History, Commerce, and Empire

THE MONSTER IS AN INCARNATION of the Other, one who inhabits marginal, border spaces and who remains an object of both fear and desire. Colonialism, in its relentless desire to penetrate these border spaces and to create margins, invariably encounters monsters—or, more properly, constructs them as necessary inhabitants of these borderlands. Cohen suggests that

> one kind of difference becomes another as the normative categories of gender, sexuality, national identity, and ethnicity slide together like the imbricated circles of a Venn diagram, abjecting from the center that which becomes the monster. This kind of violent foreclosure erects a self-validating, Hegelian master/slave dialectic that naturalizes the subjugation of one cultural body by another by writing the body excluded from personhood and agency as in every way different, monstrous.[1]

One sees this most obviously in the portrayal of indigenous peoples that European colonizers encountered: peoples who could be easily reclassed as nonhuman chattel, fit only as a supply of cheap labor or, worse, nonpersons who could be simply eradicated to pave the way for European settlement.

At the same time, however, the Monster is not simply a nonperson to be used or eliminated at the whim of the colonizer. Monsters are monsters in part because they push back from the margins, challenging and redefining both the artificial frontiers created by colonialism, and their own easy categorization. As Michael Uebel points out, "Monsters, by inhabiting the gap between exclusive zones of intellectual or social meaning, deliver a threat to the zones' integrity, or, more precisely, to the assumption that such zones can be delimited in the first place."[2] In retaliation to colonialism, especially colonial commerce, pirates emerge as the distorted, misshapen, villainous face of capitalism, yet a face that mirrors back the face of the colonial capitalist himself. The monstrous pirate thus redefines the very category of monster, by drawing attention to the overall monstrousness of colonial commerce itself. To be sure, pirates prey upon legitimate trade—but throughout the text there is a nagging sense that "legitimacy," when applied to colonial commerce, is itself a slippery concept.

The pirate is the product of the colonial margins; they are colonized subjects resisting the lopsided social and economic hierarchies that clearly favored English interests and that helped assert English nationalism. "Colonial," we need to remember, includes non-English peoples inhabiting the British Isles, and the pirates of *General History* certainly represent a healthy proportion of such people. Bartholomew Roberts, the most successful pirate of his generation, was Welsh (a plaque in his home town of Casnewydd Bach gives his nickname as Barti Ddu, or "Black Bart"); Anne Bonny was Irish, as was Walter Kennedy; Stede Bonnet and several others were raised in the Caribbean; John Gow was Scottish; Samuel Burgess was American-born. In addition, the trial lists of pirates preserved in *General History* record the names of several other Welsh, Irish, Scots, and Caribbean sailors who had gone on the account. Finally, if Marcus Rediker is right, a number of escaped African slaves also found refuge on pirate ships.

Given this colonial diversity, it is not surprising that, as Jack P. Greene has suggested, the prominent discourse in British writing on the colonies employs "the language of alterity or otherness to depict the colonies as receptacles for those who had failed at home."[3] Greene further suggests that "this widely circulated language ran as a strong undercurrent in metropolitan conceptions of empire."[4] This language of alterity was employed widely in the maritime fictions of the 1720s, but its presence here in the narratives of pirates is no less noteworthy. It is certainly likely, as Greene has shown, that the effect of colonization and the importance of empire produced a considerable anxiety and ambivalence among the British intelligentsia of the 1720s. Some of this anxiety was related to questions of national identity, as Britain's new role as a world power generated some debate about what the face of that new role would be.[5] In reaching out to the far-flung regions of the Earth, and in attempting to incorporate the different versions of humanity and human culture found in those regions, Britain encountered, and to some degree constructed, monsters. David A. Hedrich Hirsch, looking at Mary Shelley's monstrous creation in *Frankenstein*, has noted that the Creature can be read as a metaphor for the failed promise of a united humanity that fueled some of the French Revolution. Looking back from 1818, Shelley could see the "over-weening confidence" of radicals such as her own parents, whom Edmund Burke also characterized as "a species of political monster." Hirsch's point—that the grand, though ultimately unsuccessful, attempt of Enlightenment thought to delineate a more egalitarian version of humanity generated considerable political and social anxiety—can be retrofitted to the earlier part of the century as well. The intellectual debates over the limits of state power and the right use of money-driven state formation produced monstrous figures, including the pirate, whose diverse ethnicities presented a threatening alternative to the homogenous "true-born Englishman."[6]

Pirates were not, however, the only monsters. The plantation colonies in America and the Caribbean perpetuated the morally repugnant system of slavery. Plantation owners and slave traders alike were notorious for their cruelty and their utter indifference to the human suffering they inflicted, and yet, as Greene notes, the importance of slave-maintained plantations to Britain's prosperity was universally acknowledged. British merchants, profiting greatly from the products of these inhuman spaces, were seen as complicit in the degradation of slaves and slave-owners alike. Despite the moral admonitions, there was no mad rush to change the system, even if there was a strain of narrative that attempted to address the issue.[7] No one, after all, was prepared to end the prosperity that flowed to London from the plantations, even if the plantation owners could be vilified as moral reprobates. It seems to have been a case of hating the sinner, while loving—or at least tolerating—the sin.

If legitimate plantation owners and colonists could be seen as, in Greene's words, "little more than an agglomeration of social pariahs who had taken advantage of the loose texture of new societies to advance their social standing,"[8] then the criminals of these new societies must themselves be of a far worse character than that. Indeed, the notion of pirates being outcasts among the outcasts, the scum that even the scum rejects, fits in well with their portrayal in pirate narratives. However, just as the plantations and colonies have been of great economic benefit to Britain, and therefore cannot be easily dismissed, so pirates, in the boldness of their enterprise and the extremity of their villainy, must display some kind of exceptional qualities that veer close to what we might call "greatness." Such, in fact, is the difficulty that *General History* faces, and it is consistent with the difficulties that the larger intellectual world of the 1720s faced when attempting to deal with the realities of empire.

It is important, however, to distinguish at this point between the ideas of "empire" that developed later in the century—largely the focus of Greene's study—and the understanding of empire, colonialism, and commerce that existed at the time of *General History*. While the view of the North American and Caribbean colonies was largely negative in terms of its inhabitants, no one denied that these places offered opportunities for individuals to accumulate vast wealth, and that individual success somehow contributed to the success of the nation.

At the same time, between 1707 and 1754, the East India Company gradually consolidated political power in the remains of the Mughal Empire, which had begun to dissipate after the death of the emperor Aurengzeb.[9] The propaganda campaign launched in 1711 in support of the South Sea Company attempted to convince investors to support the potential for vast wealth potentially available upon completion of the peace negotiations with Spain and France. While ultimately the Treaty of Utrecht and the *Asiento de Negros* would prove disappointing and the South Sea Bubble would prove disastrous, the relative success of joint stock companies, and the fabulous wealth that continued to be derived from colonial commerce, ensured that the future of British commerce lay in overseas trade, so that, by the 1750s, Malachy Postlethwait could argue for the "civilizing" and "redemptive" aspects of commerce, as the monsters of indigenous peoples, colonial settlers, and even pirates, all had come under the steady hand of regulated commerce.

THE PIRATE AS COLONIZER

If piracy is, by definition, inseparable from colonial commercial activity, then the imaginative shift from everyday commodities to the fantasy treasures of fiction represents a shift in perception both of pirates and of commerce itself. Piracy, we should recall, was primarily an economic problem in the 1720s: anxiety around piracy centered largely on pirates' ability to disrupt trade. As the author of the *Discourse Relating to the Laws of Pirates and Piracy* has it, "Piracy and Robbery at Sea is . . . so destructive of all Commerce between Nation and Nation, that all Sovereign Princes and States have thought it their Interest, and made it their Business, to suppress the same."[10] Numerous descriptions of piracy suggest the same kind of anxiety: piracy is a threat to all commerce, important enough to involve "sovereign princes" in its suppression. Yet, at the same time, the notion of the pirate as a simple parasite, preying on legitimate commercial activity, offers too simplistic a model for the complex relationship between pirates and colonial settlements in the Caribbean. J. L. Anderson asserts that, during the 1716–1726 period, "Piracy had become a business global in its reach, with plundered assets being no less mobile than the mariners who acquired them."[11] In order to emphasize the seriousness of piracy to Britain's colonial economic interests, the pirates themselves must be transformed into larger-than-life figures. In turn, pirate plunder had to be something less mundane than sugar, oil, or ships' supplies. Part of the fantastic iconography of pirate treasure has something to do with the need to see piracy as a different sort of phenomenon than what it actually was.

Pirate treasure, imagined in terms of "elite" commodities rather than everyday possessions, reframes the parameters of discussion about the place of piracy within this nascent global economy. There is a kind of Robin Hood mentality about the pirate of fiction, in which the pirate acts as an agent against the rapacious, avaricious wealthy, presumably either recirculating that wealth in a spirit of freedom and enjoyment or, in a more twisted bit of social leveling, taking it out of circulation altogether by burying it, in theory leaving it available for anyone to discover. Pirate activity certainly focuses on "the bottom-up processes and the everyday actors which both effect change in the . . . global structural contexts,"[12] but in order to see these processes at work, we must see pirate activity for what it truly is—an attack on everyday commodities and everyday trade. Piracy certainly brings to the forefront the agency of the so-called 99 percent in effecting social change; at the same time, we must be careful to avoid the view of pirates as protoradicals or protolibertarians, free agents acting on behalf of a larger social agenda. Pirates are liminal figures, both participating in global commerce and undermining it. Narratives such as we find in the *General History* seem acutely aware of this kind of contradiction, since the book acknowledges the potential "greatness" of pirate captains, while at the same time never letting the reader forget that pirates are, in fact, guilty of serious capital crimes. With a stronger connection between piracy and everyday economic activity, piracy emerges as a much more dynamic and more intrinsic part of our understanding of the ethics of commerce.

At first, however, it is necessary to identify the monster and root it out. The severity with which piracy was treated in official discourse can be read from the opening statement by Richard Allein, attorney-general of South Carolina, at the trial of Stede Bonnet and his crew. Allein describes piracy as:

> a Crime so odious and horrid in all its Circumstances, that those who have treated on that Subject have been at a loss for Words and Terms to stamp a sufficient Ignominy upon it: Some calling them Sea-Wolfs; others Beasts of Prey, and Enemies of Mankind, with whom neither Faith nor Treaty is to be kept. And all this is but a faint Description of these Miscreants: For Beasts of Prey, tho' fierce and cruel in their Natures, yet, as has been observ'd of them, they only do it to satisfy their Hunger, and are never to be found to prey upon Creatures of the same Species with themselves.[13]

The association of pirates with "beasts of prey" is an important trope, to which we will return later. Allein goes on to explain *why* piracy, of all crimes, should be singled out for such vehement language. Although he acknowledges that pirates are violent and occasionally commit murder "for Pastime and Diversion," he saves his strongest language for the effect pirates have had on trade. Pirates, he says, "prove destructive to all Trade and Commerce in general. And if a Stop be not put to those Depredations, and our Trade no better protected, not only *Carolina*, but all the *English Plantations* in *America*, will be totally ruin'd in a very short time."[14] Even keeping in mind the context in which these remarks were made, it is easy to see how the language of alterity has come to dominate the discourse of piracy itself, and to delineate the pirate as not simply a criminal but as a kind of subhuman monster, worse than animals, whose continued existence threatens they very nature of commerce itself. Allein goes on to note that Bonnet's status as a gentleman is a great "Aggravation to his Offence," and his education "still a far greater, because [education] generally softens Mens Manners, and keeps them from becoming savage and brutish."[15]

Perhaps worse than the gentleman who turns pirate, however, is the pirate who dares to turn gentleman. In its issue for 29 July 1721, the *Weekly Journal; or, British Gazetteer* featured an "Account of the Life, Behaviour, &c." of Walter Kennedy, a pirate who had sailed with Bartholomew Roberts, but who had established his own reputation by the time of his capture. Kennedy had been executed on 21 July, so the "Account" is really a final confession and expression of repentance that also attempts to explain Kennedy's attraction to piracy. Kennedy, we are told, had "served Her Majesty Queen Anne in the Wars against France, but being told what Lords the Pirates in America were, and that they had gotten several whole Islands under their own Command, he coveted to be one of those petty Princes."[16] The "Account," therefore, directly blames tales of wealthy pirates for corrupting the impressionable young Kennedy. Kennedy did achieve some success as a pirate, but, as Kennedy himself in his final confession, notes, his pirate career "had so ill prosper'd, that he should want a Coffin to cover his Carcase in."[17] The message is clear: tales of wealthy pirates living like "petty Princes" are simply fanciful fictions, and rumors of pirate treasure should be ignored by any sensible individual.

If we look at the various account of Kennedy's ignoble life and eventual fate, what emerges is a view of an individual who got what he deserved not merely because he dared to overreach but because, even among other pirates, he seems not to have commanded much love or even respect. The *Weekly Journal* version prints the account as told by Kennedy himself; as to his capture, Kennedy mentions only that, some time after his return to England, he was "observed, apprehended, try'd, and convicted." The term "observed" is important here—the implication being that Kennedy was recognized by someone who was willing to inform on him. In Johnson's account, Kennedy heads a crew of mutineers from Roberts's command; he is not especially liked or respected by his crew and, being illiterate, is chosen captain mainly for his "courage," rather than any special nautical skill. Kennedy makes his way back to England, where he is soon captured and executed. Curiously, Johnson offers two different versions of Kennedy's capture. In 1724a, Johnson suggests that Kennedy might still be living safely in obscurity, "Had not his Sister, out of mere Malice, (provoked thereto by a Quarrel,) given an Information against him" (1724a, 168). A few months later, however, 1724b reports his betrayal quite differently: "*Kennedy* having spent all his Money, came over from *Ireland*, and kept a common B[awd]y-House on *Deptford* Road, and now and then, 'twas thought, made an Execution abroad in the Way of his former Profession, till one of his Houshold W[hore]s gave Information against him for a Robbery, for which he was soon committed to *Bridewell*" (1724b, 228 [209]). This time, Johnson also takes the opportunity to indulge in some rather half-hearted moralizing:

> Thus we see what a disastrous Fate ever attends the Wicked, and how rarely they escape the Punishment due to their Crimes, who, abandon'd to such a profligate Life, rob, spoil, and prey upon Mankind, contrary to the Light and Law of Nature, as well as the Law of God. It might have been hoped, that the Examples of these Deaths, would have been as Marks to the Remainder of this Gang, how to shun the Rocks their Companions had split on; that they would have surrendered to Mercy, or divided themselves, for ever from such Pursuits, as in the End they might be sure would subject them to the same Law and Punishment, which they must be conscious they now equally deserved; impending Law, which never let them sleep well, unless when drunk. (1724b, 229 [210])

Sister? Whore? Quite likely neither: yet another account of Kennedy, *Lives of the Most Remarkable Criminals*, published in 1734, does not seem to draw at all on the narratives of the *General History*, but instead confirms the details printed in the *Weekly Journal* account. This story mentions that Kennedy "had not long been in Town [i.e., London] before he was observ'd by some whose Vessels had been taken by the Crew with whom he sailed; they caused him to be Apprehended, and after lying a considerable time in Prison, he was, as I have said before, tried and convicted."[18] That's all. No family squabble; no bawdy-house; nothing that would suggest anything more interesting than being in the wrong place at the wrong time.

Both the *Weekly Journal* and the *Lives of Remarkable Criminals* note especially that Kennedy, once convicted, was quite ready to go to the gallows. The *Weekly Journal* presents him as a repentant Christian, which Joel Baer has argued was more common among condemned pirates than the popular image of them would suspect.[19] *Remarkable Criminals* provides more details, including some reported speech of Kennedy on his way to Execution Dock, but the suggestion here is that Kennedy, having lost his fortune, and forced to return to London mainly through indigence, fell into a deep depression while awaiting his execution: "he was so much tired with the Miseries and Misfortune which for some Years before he had endured, that Death appeared to him a Thing rather desireable than frightful."[20] The author goes on to note that, even when the man who was condemned with him is reprieved, Kennedy is pleased with his own sentence, since he figures that "'tis highly probable I might be tempted to my old way of Life, and so instead of reforming, add to the number of my Sins."[21] This is a very different Kennedy from the man who appears in the *General History*, who is reviled among his fellow pirates for attempting to free himself by giving evidence against his fellow crew, and is dismissed as "*a sad Dog [who] deserved the Fate he met with*" (1724b, 229 [210]).

The Kennedy account reveals that stories of pirate wealth seemed to have been common enough during the period of the most intense pirate activity. *Lives of the Most Remarkable Criminals* specifically mentions Kennedy's hearing tales "from the Time of *Sir Henry Morgan's* commanding the *Bucchaneers* in *America*, to Capt. *Avery*'s more modern Exploits at *Madagascar*,"[22] although it provides no further details than that. What seems certain is that the stories featured these pirates both enjoying their wealth and assuming a certain degree of political power that had accrued to them from that wealth, but that latter detail was pure fantasy. Even Henry Avery, whose capture of the Mogul flagship *Ganj-i-Sawaj* in 1695 had already passed into legend, never established the autonomous pirate community on Madagascar for which he was also famous. Whatever the tales might have said, few authentic pirate narratives—such as newspaper reports or official trial documents—record pirates living like "petty Princes." Certainly the closest that can be found to match such a reality were the buccaneers who, at the end of the seventeenth century, lived fully autonomous, albeit wretched, hand-to-mouth existences on uninhabited Caribbean islands: likely not the sort of thing Kennedy had in mind.

Despite the grim reality, the lure of political autonomy and vast wealth makes the fantasy hard to abandon. The Caribbean is reduced to a colorful, exotic backdrop for adventure stories and ceases to be what it clearly was during the early decades of the eighteenth century: an important locus of trade, and a site of great political contest. Interestingly, vestiges of the colonial past do linger in the buried-treasure stories, since the central tool of the treasure seeker, the map, is also, as Edward Said reminds us, the central tool of the European colonizer, armed with what Said calls the "*geographical* [*sic*] notation, the theoretical mapping and charting of territory."[23] Buried treasure, therefore, gestures toward *other* buried treasures found in New World colonies: both the commodities derived directly from natural resources and the suitable conditions for establishing plantations in the very islands where these literary pirates roam. The pirate mythos, then, is not simply about wealth, or, as Peter Leeson suggests,[24] even just economics, but with *colonial* economics, the transatlantic exchange of goods. What pirates steal in fiction, and what they stole in reality, both shed light on how eighteenth-century pirate narratives reflect larger concerns about colonial economic activity. While the nineteenth-century fictional pirate may, therefore, have something to say about the work of empire, it is important to remember that this same pirate figure is also fixed within a very narrow historical context—and the pirates of fiction are almost always historicized figures.[25]

Seen in this light, the pirate of fiction appears as an imperfect colonizer, a failed capitalist, who is bold enough to acquire great wealth but too foolish to know what to do with it. For the literary pirate, the purpose of acquiring wealth is to stash it away, to remove it from circulation, usually by burial on an uninhabited island. Acquiring wealth by plunder, of course, violates the terms of exchange that are essential to trade; but *buried* pirate plunder further offends good business practice, because it subverts one of the chief goals of acquired wealth: to reinvest it, preferably in one's own business, to help further growth and, presumably maximize profit. Oddly, too, burying treasure removes the pirate from his natural habitat—the open ocean—and ties him to the land, even if only to tiny islands. Buried wealth may signify ownership of the usually uninhabited island on which it is stored, but this is still far removed from the kind of "command" of space that motivated Walter Kennedy to turn pirate. Thus, the pirate is forever relegated to the margins of the successful empire; within literary space he becomes transformed into a relic of an earlier age, fit only for relatively tame adventures within the pages of popular or children's fiction. The real work of empire—the systematic acquisition of land, goods, and money—had, of course, already passed into the hands of land speculators and developers on one side and nabobs and clerks on the other: all landlocked, desk-bound servants of masters far more avaricious than any pirate crew.

Clearly, the pirate of fiction has been recast to conform to a narrative of trade, commerce, and empire that privileges cooperation between merchants and the state. In that narrative, the pirate is ever the outsider, the dangerous, radical Other who seeks to subvert both commercial and state power. During the time of the last great age of piracy, however, the role of pirates within this new global economy was not quite so well defined. It might seem absurd to talk about "pirate businessmen"—the term has a Pythonesque ring to it[26]—and yet, there is every reason to see actual eighteenth-century piracy as something like a business, and every reason to think that pirates saw themselves as engaging in a form of commerce, a continuation of trade by other means. In actual pirate booty we encounter the products of everyday life that kept the wheels of commerce turning in the eighteenth century. What pirates stole, and what they did with their plunder, can therefore be read against contemporary pirate narratives to redraw the portrait of piracy that later fictions have handed down to us, and to understand more clearly how piracy was an integral part of everyday global commerce in the early eighteenth century. We can, in fact, bring pirates in from the margins their fictional selves have been made to inhabit, and reinstate them as part of a larger conversation about the uses of a global economy which raged within the intellectual landscape of the 1720s. The question at hand, therefore, is: how did pirate "treasure" transform from everyday commodities to fantasy wealth? What purpose did such a transformation serve? And, perhaps most important, how do we read this transformation against an explicitly political agenda to eradicate the model of trade that pirate activity offered colonial settlements in the 1720s?

We do not often think of pirates as participating in everyday objects of exchange or of their being especially interested in everyday commerce, but they certainly did and they certainly were. At the same time, the fact that they were interested in it means that we need to rethink our understanding of what pirates considered "valuable plunder." Eighteenth-century piracy emerges as an important attempt to attain economic agency outside of the hegemony of British commercial structures (in the 1720s particularly—but not limited to—the East India Company and the South Sea Company). The parasitic nature of piracy also throws into question the nature of other, similar agents within a global economic system. How, for example, does the shifting nature of the legality of piracy—the blurred lines between legitimized privateers and illegitimate pirates—fit into this economic reality? Similarly, as pirates themselves were quick to point out, European states involved in colonial activity engaged in the same kind of rapacious plundering as pirate crews, with the exception that states enjoyed the legal protection of statehood. Piracy itself, as some narratives uneasily noted, often imitated the virtues found in successful businesses: ruthlessness, swift elimination of competition, and an eye for the main chance.

As historians of piracy have been at some pains to point out, the pirate booty of literary fantasy also ignores many of the realities of pirate life, some of which can be reconstructed from surviving pirate codes.[27] To begin with, both Bartholomew Roberts's and George Lowther's codes emphasize that any plunder taken belonged not to an individual—certainly not the captain—but was shared equitably among all the crew. Captains and a few senior officers were allowed two shares, but the rest of the crew received one share each: this was in direct contrast to normal merchant shipping practice, which reserved shares of cargo only for shipowners and a few officers. Merchant crews were salaried men whose wages were dismally low when compared with the market value of the cargoes they carried.[28] Furthermore, free spending of plunder was actually advantageous to pirates, who were welcomed and even sheltered as important contributors to the local economies. Finally—and, for our purposes, perhaps most significantly—few pirates were lucky enough to seize vast treasures of the sort that we find in pirate fiction. The very concept of a "pirate treasure" ignores the fact that pirating was a lengthy and often unrewarding activity. Pirates could go for days or weeks without spotting a ship worth seizing. When seized, ships did not always yield any worthwhile commodities, or they provided little more than necessary provisions for ships forced to spend weeks or even months at sea. Pirates did, in fact, seize valuable commodities from the ships they raided; in many cases, the ships themselves were the most valuable prize. But more often than not, what pirates stole consisted either of everyday merchant cargo or necessary items for the pirates' own use: food, carpenter's tools and wood for repairing ships, and other such quotidian supplies. Occasionally, too, pirates encountered a type of "cargo" that would test the limits of their humanity and their business acumen.

BLACK MARGINS

One of Jeffrey Cohen's theses, "The Monster Dwells at the Gates of Difference," articulates the role of geographical space in defining the monster. Marked by difference, the monster is also an embodiment of a geographical Other, a space marked, as the monster's body is marked, by strangeness, by its deviation from what is conceived as a European norm.[29] Depictions of places outside of Europe—indeed, outside of England—serve to remind readers that the work of colonial economy involves incursion into the space of the Other, and, naturally, encounters with and even transformations into the monstrous. It is partly the work of the colonizer to map, to describe, and even to catalog these spaces, to make them knowable, even to dispel their inherent strangeness. Doing so, of course, is itself an act of colonization, since the Europeans' knowledge of the other grants them an expertise even over those who actually inhabit those spaces. Moreover, since the primary purpose of these descriptions and maps is to facilitate trade, the spaces described become, in effect, catalogues of potential commodities—a distinction that even includes the people, either as potential labor or as saleable commodities themselves.

The delineation of colonial spaces, the exotic settings for most of the narratives in *General History*, incorporates the idea of what Julia Kristeva calls the abject, that which must be rejected from the body as impure or even toxic.[30] Rebecca Weaver-Hightower suggests that colonial spaces are themselves abject, because they lack the markers of European civilization. At the same time, however, these abject spaces help to define the boundaries of empire: "Colonized people," she writes, "by living on the social and geographical edges of empire, both challenge and confirm imperial boundaries. The so-called imperial center, then, needs the abject, its colonized people, in order to establish itself."[31] Weaver-Hightower further notes that both the literary pirate and the cannibal also help delineate the limits of empire by acting as two of the monsters that castaway figures such as Robinson Crusoe must overcome in order to return to the civilized center.

The eighteenth-century geographical "description," ostensibly objective, is actually a highly politicized genre. Travel narratives and accounts of places in Africa, the "East Indies," South America, and the Caribbean all are written with the understanding that the reader will assess these spaces according to their colonial utility. In travel narratives, Africa, in particular, appears as both a highly desirable source of commodities and a place of particular savagery and danger. The denigration of African peoples, of course, helped to justify slavery, but it also helped to reinforce the colonial center, the superiority of Europe and, especially, of England. Roxanne Wheeler has noted that much of the disinformation about the African interior came from Africans themselves, who wanted to retain control of trade and keep European confined to coastal factories.[32] Eyewitnesses such as William Snelgrave and John Atkins—both of whom also had direct experience of pirates—used their accounts both to reinforce long-held notions of African savagery, even as they were delighting in the richness and variety of African flora and fauna.

It is important to note, too, as Wheeler also reminds us, that "savagery" and the Othering of Africans in general has relatively little to do with skin color or with physical appearance in general. Definitions of race based on physically quantifiable data would become an obsession in the nineteenth century; at this period, "Christianity still dominated English concepts of self versus Other."[33] By being baptized, Black people could even think of themselves as white.[34] European accounts of Africa, and of Africans, perpetuate a notion of Otherness simply by highlighting the strangeness of the people and their customs alongside the strangeness of the land itself. Everything described is seen through the lens of utility to European interests: description includes accounting for what is familiar, valuable, and useful on the one hand, and what is exotic, unknown, and arguably useless on the other.

Such a view of the White colonial settlers belies the notion that European incursion into colonial spaces is part of a larger agenda of bringing "civilization" to non-European places. The universal improvement of humanity is, of course, the goal of modernity. As has been previously mentioned, pirate historian Marcus Rediker suggests that pirates, in their seemingly egalitarian shipboard management, were protomoderns, whose resistance to hierarchies and class structures allowed them to "civilize" their own vessels. Gay's pirates, however, betray no such enlightened ideals, and reveal themselves to be as concerned with money and power as any aspiring merchant. Moreover, Gay's Creole pirates—closer, incidentally, to the pirates of *General History*—allow us to see the relationship between even the supposed monsters of commerce and the actual victims of commerce, the slaves and others whose chief purpose is only to serve the colonies. Paul Gilroy, in *The Black Atlantic*, proposes that "the history and expressive culture of the African diaspora, the practice of racial slavery, or the narratives of European imperial conquest may all require simple periodisations of the modern and the postmodern to be drastically rethought."[35] I would like to take up Gilroy's suggestion and examine how even a seemingly neutral treatment of the realities of the African slave trade in travel and pirate narratives of the 1720s critiques the veracity of the narrative inherent in Habermas's Enlightenment project.

It should be easy to see at this point how the narratives of both piracy and slavery can be contorted to conform to an idea that, as Gilroy puts it, "an all-encompassing modernity affects everyone in a uniform and similar way."[36] It should also be easy to see how a book like *General History*, which speaks to the anxieties of colonial trade through the stories of the monstrous Others who form its main subject, seems to reinscribe the basic principles of the Enlightenment project by presenting maritime trade at its most gruesome and most criminal. However, *General History* is a strange, multifarious book, and within its pages lie at least the beginnings of an alternative narrative that gestures toward what Gilroy wishes to articulate as the Black Atlantic. Although there is little mention of slavery and the slave trade in *General History*, there are some fascinating textual additions in the second edition that point to a world beyond Britain and the North Atlantic colonies as the locus of pirating activities. Two inserted "Descriptions," of the islands of São Tomé e Principe and Anóbon (referred to as "St Thome," "Del Principe," and "Annobono") and of Brazil, shift the reader's attention away from blood and plunder, and ostensibly serve to bolster the reader's success in trade: "I don't doubt," the preface notes, that the "Observations will be found curious and very serviceable to such as Trade to those Parts, besides a Method of Trade is here laid down with the Portuguese, which may prove of great Profit to some of our Countrymen, if followed according to his Plan." The descriptions are attributed to John Atkins, a surgeon aboard the ship that eventually pursued and caught Bartholomew Roberts, based on his own experiences in West Africa and Brazil.

Atkins himself is an intriguing figure. A maverick ship's surgeon who proposed practices, such as triage, that were little used in his own time but that have since become standard medical procedures, Atkins was best known in his own time as the author of *The Navy Surgeon* (1732), which was reprinted throughout the century. Atkins also published *A Voyage to Guinea* (1735), both a personal account of his own time cruising the west coast of Africa and a series of observations similar to (and in some instances derived from) his accounts in *General History*.

Immediately intriguing about these interpolated passages is his choice of places: São Tomé and Brazil. These two spaces are the bookends of the Middle Passage, the starting point of the Black Atlantic, and its logical conclusion in the New World sugar plantations. Atkins begins his description with a nod to the navigational skill of the Portuguese, noting that one Bernard (seemingly a mistake for Fernão) Gomez held exploration rights to the African coast, and was the first European to land on Tomé. Much the same story is told in Howard W. French's 2021 book *Born in Blackness*,[37] except that French is quite explicit about the Portuguese interest in this island chain. Beginning early in the sixteenth century, São Tomé became, first, an important entrepôt for slaves arriving from farther south, in the area of the Congo Basin; it also very quickly became the locus for the experiment of the plantation system: agriculture employing elaborate machinery that required the constant attention of a small army of workers whose labors were parceled out in specific tasks. São Tomé thus became the template for the entire plantation system and, as such, the place where colonial economy was born.

Atkins, by contrast, has only this to say about the slaves:

> The Negroes have yet no hard Duty with them, they are rather Happy in Slavery; for as their Food is chiefly Vegetables, that could no way else be expended, there is no Murmurs bred on that account; and as their Business is Domestick, either in the Services of the House, or in Gardening, Sowing, or Planting, they have no more than what every Man would prefer for Health and Pleasure; the hardest of their Work is the Carriage of their Pateroons, or their Wives, to and from the Plantations; this they do in Hammocks (call'd at *Whydah, Serpentines*) slung cross a Pole, with a Cloath over, to screen the Person, so carried, from Sun and Weather, and the Slaves are at each End; and yet even this, methinks, is better than the specious Liberty a Man has for himself and his Heirs to work in a Coal Mine. (1724b, 202–203 [189–90])

In Atkins's account, slavery coexists with other valuable natural commodities: cotton, yams, manioc, plantains, and corn. Africans, therefore, are a resource, a raw material to be exploited. Those who participate in selling and buying Africans may be free from any moral qualms, because they can convince themselves that these slaves are happy in their captivity. Indeed, as Atkins dryly notes, they can be said to enjoy better working conditions than those found in English coal mines.

Although he is undoubtedly sympathetic to the African peoples he encounters in his voyage, Atkins nevertheless speaks in the idiom of the colonizer. He is precise in his observations, and endeavors to encapsulate something of the culture and even the language of those he describes. But they remain objects of scrutiny, no different from the rest of the flora and fauna of this vast continent. Seemingly without meaning to, Atkins slips into the language of trade and commodity, noting which plants and animals are good for food, which are valuable for trade, and which have already been adapted into commodities by European traders. Moreover, he attempts to distinguish between Africans in their own environment and Africans who have been commodified. But, in the end, it is the commodified African, much like the cash crop transplanted from its wild setting and modified to suit the plantation, who proves most useful and most valuable.

Atkins continues in the same vein in his description of Brazil, inserted rather awkwardly into the already lengthy chapter on Bartholomew Roberts, which may also have been written or revised by Atkins. Atkins's observations on Brazil are even more perfunctory than his description of São Tomé, yet he does take some time to comment on the Portuguese handling of the slave trade:

> From these casual Observations on the Country, the Towns, Coast, and Seas of *Brasil*, it would be an Omission to leave the Subject, without some Essay on an inter loping Slave Trade here, which none of our Countrymen are adventrous enough to pursue, though it very probably, under a prudent Manager, would be attended with Safety and very great Profit; and I admire the more it is not struck at, because Ships from the Southern Coast of *Africa*, don't lengthen the Voyage to the *West-Indies* a great deal, by taking a Part of *Brasil* in their Way. (1724b, 218 [202])

Atkins's message is clear: the Portuguese maintain a monopoly on slaving in Brazil, yet handle the business incompetently. What he wants is not an end to the slave trade but a more efficient slaving system, perhaps run by the English, who could easily introduce "Safety" and "very great Profit" into the business. The problem, then, is not one of a repugnant commodity but of poor management.

Yet another perspective on both slavery and piracy can be found in a book that has intriguing connections with both Atkins's *Voyage* and *General History*: William Snelgrave's *A New Account of Some Parts of Guinea, and the Slave Trade*, published in 1734. Snelgrave (1681–1743) was a slave trader who had made several voyages along the African coast. In 1719, at Gambia Castle, he encountered a trio of pirates, Cocklyn, La Bouse, and Howell Davis. This encounter is obliquely mentioned in *General History*, but Snelgrave is not identified, and the whole incident is presented as tangential to Davis's story, perhaps because Snelgrave was primarily Cocklyn's prisoner. One intriguing detail that emerges from the story is Snelgrave's near-murder at the hands of Cocklyn's boatswain, whom Snelgrave actually calls a "Monster." The boatswain is prevented from executing Snelgrave by members of Snelgrave's own crew, who plead, "For God's sake don't kill our Captain, for we were never with a better Man."[38]

Despite his apparent goodness, however, Snelgrave staunchly defends the slave trade, arguing that the slaves sold to Europeans were generally either prisoners of war, convicted criminals, or already slaves through debt. He asserts that the prisoners would have been otherwise executed, and so a life of slavery is at least a kind of reprieve. He suggests that slaves are, on the whole, quite well treated, "For as the Planters pay a great Price for them, 'tis their interest to take care of them." Finally, he argues that the plantations themselves have been "so much improved" by African labor that he cannot but conclude that "from this Trade proceed Benefits, far outweighing all, either real or pretended Mischiefs and Inconveniencies."[39]

Snelgrave, like Atkins, represents what may be called the mercantile view of Africa; he clearly perceives Africa as primarily a store of resources, but understands Africa only through his own limited experience. In this monstrous continent, the normal rules of center and periphery are reversed: the edges of the coast, especially those places settled by Europeans as slaving ports, are familiar and relatively safe, while it is the interior, the heart of Africa, that is unknowable, frightening, and "savage." Even places relatively familiar to Europeans, as Wheeler reminds us, are fraught with "ritualized business dealings and trade constantly renegotiated because of European breaches of protocol and local power shifts. At the same time, the constraints of the African trade frequently curtail contemporary systems of othering, but they do not revise them significantly; characteristically, they coexist."[40] In these topsy-turvy mercantile outposts, the notion of "business ethics" seems ludicrous. The slaver and the pirate operate with equal authority, but by the time the goods produced from slavery have emerged from the plantations and been repackaged as desirable commodities back in Europe, all traces of their morally dubious origins have been cleansed from them.

The glimpses of a world beyond the Caribbean in *General History* actually serve to illuminate the narrowness of the book's focus. If we hear little about the African slave trade and its relation to piracy, we hear almost nothing about a group of pirates who helped define slavery itself for Britons in the 1720s. *General History* is largely silent about the Barbary Corsairs, the Muslim pirates who routinely enslaved Britons during this period.[41] The idea that Britons could be slaves, Linda Colley suggests, "inflected the British vision of slavery in ways that have scarcely been acknowledged."[42] Colley argues that, acknowledging that "the business of slavery" was not restricted along racial lines meant that, as odious a practice as it was, it was nevertheless a "ubiquitous practice" that had "always existed in some form"—just like "the business of making empires."[43] If Colley is right, the racial demarcation of slavery, and hence the argument that the enslavement of Africans was justifiable because of their inherent inferiority to Europeans, belongs to a period after *General History*, as does the counterargument that Africans and Europeans share a common humanity, and therefore enslavement of either can never be justified. The slave trade, therefore, exists in a morally justifiable space, unlike piracy.

So, where does that leave pirates? It seems clear to me that the intellectual space that pirates occupy in the discourse of the 1720s, that of the universal enemy, the subhuman monster who threatens all commerce, effectively displaces consideration of the slave trade and of slavery itself as the true evil of colonial commerce. Again, as Paul Gilroy argues, to foreground the experience of the Black Atlantic is to destabilize the narrative that had already been established by the 1720s, of the needs of a growing nation/empire set against the dangerous uncertainties of the wider world. While merchant ships fretted over the threat to their cargo from pirates, the free trafficking of human beings across the Atlantic continued unchallenged, except perhaps by those very pirates who threatened more mundane, certainly less evil cargo. From all accounts—as even Linebaugh and Rediker reluctantly acknowledge—pirate ships did not necessarily regard enslaved Africans as fellow victims of the merchant navy: while some runaway slaves were, in fact, welcomed as part of pirate crews, a pirate ship encountering a well-stocked slaver could just as easily see the slaves as valuable cargo, and sell them accordingly.[44] In doing so, ironically, pirates revealed themselves not as their legal designation made them, the enemies of all humanity, but as savvy businessmen who, like their legitimate counterparts in London, kept an eye out for the main chance.

Ultimately, the reader is left to question what, specifically, it is that pirates do to make themselves so thoroughly despised. There is a telling comment found only in 1724a that serves to introduce the otherwise unremarkable pirate Charles Martel.[45] Johnson remarks that piracy increased after the War of the Spanish Succession because:

> In War-Time, there are [no pirates] at all, because so many arm'd Vessels being continually in Commission, and going out against their Enemies, it would render the Business too precarious, as well as hazardous; and

> since in Time of War, any Vessel may obtain Commission from the Governors of Islands, and Provinces, to whom Application is made, to attack, plunder, and destroy, all Ships and Vessels, belonging to the Prince or Country they are at War with, none will be so foolish, as to prey at large upon the Seas, especially in time of Danger, and run the Hazard of their Necks, when they may have a lawful Authority for doing the same Thing, only with some Restrictions. (1724a, 54)

Johnson continues in the following paragraph, noting that, "when the War is over, and they can have no farther Business in the Way of Life they have been used to, they too readily engage in Acts of Pyracy, which being but the same Practice without Commission, they make very little distinction betwixt the Lawfulness of one, and the Unlawfulness of the other" (1724a, 55).

This passage may have seemed far too sympathetic to pirates, or, at least, may have seemed to make a too-uncomfortable observation on the arbitrary legality between privateers and pirates. At any rate, this passage is omitted entirely from 1724b and the following substituted in its place:

> In War Time there is no room for [pirates], because all those of a roving advent'rous Disposition find Employment in Privateers, so there is no Opportunity for Pyrates; like our Mobs in *London*, when they come to any Height, our Superiors order out the Train Bands, and when once they are raised, the others are suppressed of Course; I take the Reason of it to be, that the Mob go into the tame Army, and immediately from notorious Breakers of the Peace, become, by being put into order, solemn Preservers of it. And should our Legislators put some of the Pyrates into Authority, it would not only lessen their Number, but, I imagine, set them upon the rest, and they would be the likeliest People to find them out, according to the Proverb, *set a Thief to catch a Thief.*
>
> To bring this about, there needs no other Encouragement, but to give all the Effects taken aboard a Pyrate Vessel to the Captors; for in Case of Plunder and Gain, they like it as well from Friends, as Enemies, but are not fond, as Things are carry'd, *of ruining poor Fellowes*, say the Creoleans, *with no Advantage to themselves*. (1724b, 64 [63])

Notice the considerable change in focus between these two passages. In the first edition, the pirate is represented as something closer to an agent in a legitimate business: he assesses the risk of a particular enterprise and is willing to submit to "restrictions" in the interest of reducing personal hazard. The result is that, after the war, pirates simply continue their line of business, merely disregarding what seems to them to be an arbitrary point of law. The revision in the second edition removes the agency from pirates altogether, and suggests that pirates, like "our

Mob in *London*," are somehow tamed and awed by their newfound authority, and become "solemn Preservers" of the rule of law. The implication, then, is that those who persist in piracy do so not because of a flaw in the legal system in wartime, which has temporarily declared lawful what in normal circumstances would be unlawful, but because of their inherent disregard for the law itself, regardless of circumstance or temporary shift.[46]

INTERLUDE

4
"PIRATE VICES, PUBLICK BENEFITS"
The Social Ethics of Piracy in the 1720s

THE END OF THE GOLDEN AGE OF PIRACY can perhaps be dated specifically to 12 July 1726, the date of the execution of the pirate William Fly. Fly's story is chronologically the latest of the narratives in *General History*; in Johnson's version he appears very much as the last of a dying breed, stubbornly trying to operate within a culture that had largely been eradicated, thanks to Woodes Rogers's aggressive war on piracy. Fly himself, although defiant and rebellious to the end, is hard to romanticize as a swashbuckling, freedom-loving adventurer. Fly was exceptionally violent, short-tempered, and foul-mouthed (even for a sailor), and his pirate career was brief and mostly undistinguished. What makes him noteworthy is his appearance in a remarkable 1726 pamphlet by Cotton Mather, *The Vial Poured Out Upon the Sea*. In the pamphlet, Mather, already well known as a minister to convicted pirates, engages in a series of conversations with the condemned Fly and his crew. Mather hopes to turn them to true repentance before their sentence is carried out. His concern for the pirates' salvation is genuine. Following his religious principles, Mather believes that the pirates, even at the point of imminent death, can still acknowledge the wrongs they have done and hope for God's grace to be merciful to them. The pirates' submission to a temporal authority that has justly and fairly determined death as the proper punishment for their wrongdoings is to be the first step in their proving themselves worthy to receive God's mercy.

The trick, of course, is getting the pirates to believe in a just and fair authority. To that end, Mather engages Fly in a fascinating debate over the place of forgiveness as a preparation to receive justice. Fly has acknowledged his own failings—though he will not admit to murder—but at the same time he insists that there are people who have wronged him whom he cannot forgive. Mather reminds him, "Our Lord has taught us to pray, *Forgive us as we forgive*. I hope you *pray*, according to that *Prayer*." Fly replies, "*Yes, I do!—But for all that, I cannot Forgive that Man.—GOD Almighty Revenge me on him!—'Tis a Vain thing.—I won't dy with a Lye in my Mouth*."[1] A few days later, Mather again urges Fly to forgive, arguing that a truly repentant soul forgives all wrongs and has made peace with all enemies. However, Fly argues that for him simply to pretend to forgiveness would make him guilty of lying, an even greater sin. Then, he challenges Mather's whole notion of justice:

> *I can't Charge myself,—I shan't own myself Guilty of any Murder,—our Captain and his Mate used us Barbarously. We poor Men can't have Justice done us. There is nothing said to our Commanders, let them never so much abuse us, and use us like Dogs.*[2]

Fly openly declares that the game is rigged, thereby suggesting that Mather's attempts to get him to confess are, in effect, simply attempts to get him to acknowledge that the status quo is right, and that neither he nor the other condemned crew had any justification for their actions.

Fly accurately notes the double standard that existed on ships; he was hardly unique in making that complaint. Part of the motivation for turning pirate involved rejecting a social order that was so manifestly unjust and which offered little hope or comfort beyond that of resigned forbearance. Captains, answerable only to the ships' owners, could indulge in sometimes horrific abuses, especially in the name of discipline. Fly's conversation with Mather, then, becomes a debate about the ethical boundaries of life aboard ship: Are the victims of such abuse expected to submit unquestioningly? Between sadistic captains and bloodthirsty pirates, who, in fact, is guilty of the greater moral wrong? Or, put another way, who actually are the monsters? Intentionally or not, then, Mather's pamphlet highlights the complex relationship between crime, vice, and morality that piracy in the 1720s revealed.

The whole debate over the true nature of forgiveness, penitence, and even justice, takes us a long way from the central, defining feature of pirates: namely, they were sailors who attacked and plundered other ships for personal gain. The monstrous nature of pirates, implied even in Mather's pamphlet, precludes the idea of the pirate's having any legitimate moral or legal position. Unlike Frankenstein's Creature, the pirate cannot successfully assert that "misery made [him] a fiend"; the essential monstrosity of piracy leaves no room for alternate positions. Mather's discourse focuses less on the moral wrong of theft and more on the entire character of pirates themselves, thereby rendering moot the questions considered earlier here about the ethical boundaries of global commerce.

However, as we have seen, the idea of constructing pirates purely as monstrous ignores their essential role in that global commerce that itself was understood to be ethically ambiguous. Even the supposedly venerable figure of the merchant—the central person in the commerce that pirates are invariably seeking to destroy—does not always emerge as estimable or heroic. Merchants themselves are suspect, being neither part of the landed gentry, and therefore of the majority of political power, nor part of the common mob, suppressed by poverty, ignorance, and alcohol-fueled lethargy. Merchants, like pirates, unsettled the social hierarchy, and, as James Raven has noted, could easily be satirized as boorish upstarts, vulgar louts with champagne money but beer taste.[3] Perry Gauci has examined representations in the press of both the merchant figure and commerce itself between 1660 and 1713: he reveals that the image of the merchant as a "patriotic adventurer," willing to undergo great personal risks for the sake of Britain's economic health, is balanced by the image of the merchant as a merely self-interested profit seeker. Any benefits that might accrue to the nation as a whole are thus merely incidental to the merchant's main goal, which is purely profit.[4] As Gauci describes the portrayal of merchants, he delineates some of the anxieties surrounding merchants and overseas commerce that, significantly, also parallel some of the anxieties surrounding pirates. For example, he notes that "the merchant can be distinguished for his essential independence and readiness to take advantage of any opportunity to advance personal interest."[5] This idea is echoed in the words of John Taylor in 1694, which Gauci quotes at the head of his chapter: "I do not pretend to love my country so much better than myself as to encourage a trade which would be to my prejudice." Here, then, is the masterless man once more: the merchant's independence and opportunism single him out as one who may act in the interest of the nation, but only if the interest of the nation is congruent with his own. The question then, is how to encourage merchants to align their primary focus on profit making with the wider political interests of Great Britain. Indeed, the considerable anxiety over ethics and commerce—which became more acute in the 1720s—included piracy within its parameters. As we shall see, the issue was not that the pirates differed from merchants in their behavior, but that they so closely resembled them.[6]

By 1722, the nature of the discourse was beginning to shift into considerations of "greatness," and the unsuitability of that term for the age in which writers found themselves. The broad outlines of the argument can be summed up in Thomas Gordon's "An Essay Upon Heroes," which appeared 8 September 1722 as number 93 of *Cato's Letters*. Gordon reminds his readers of the "brave disinterested men" of former times, who "established and reformed communities, and taught them laws, and punished those who violated justice and law: They destroyed publick robbers and monsters, and the greatest of all publick robbers and monsters, tyrants; and lived the patterns of virtue and useful valour." Contrasted with these heroes, argues Gordon, are the ones of the present day, who are the very "tyrants and monsters as the old heroes had destroyed."[7] While Gordon is most overtly talking about political leaders, the language is vague enough to include any who might be regarded as heroes, including merchants. The previous essay, written by John Trenchard, deals with the directors of the South Sea Company, and those responsible for the South Sea Bubble, which had been the occasion for the series of *Cato's Letters* in the first place.

A shift in emphasis away from the purely economic value of what pirates stole to the moral value of what they stole reflects a shift in the view of pirates themselves after 1713. Margarette Lincoln has noted that, prior to the War of the Spanish Succession, pirates—usually acting as legally sanctioned privateers—enjoyed not only the sanction of the law to plunder as they saw fit, but also sometimes the sanction of aristocratic society, some of whom even supported their expeditions.[8] In colonial settlements, too, pirates were generally welcomed as eager supporters of local economies. Mark Hanna has noted that the influx of cheap commodities to British colonies after the Treaty of Utrecht, and the general improvement of colonial economies that resulted from the expansion of the slave trade, made the pirates' support of maritime communities "unnecessary," and even a threat to this newfound economic stability.[9] At the same time, the early 1720s in Britain were marked by the destabilizing effects of the South Sea Bubble, which raised pertinent questions about the right uses of money, credit, and financial speculation. Within this economic context, the pirate figure could not be normalized as a necessary part of colonial commerce, nor even regarded simply as an occasional nuisance to transatlantic trade. We can see this recasting at work dramatically in *General History*.

PIRATES, COMMERCE, AND MORALITY

By the second decade of the eighteenth century, despite misgivings about the moral character of the merchant, Britain had come to regard the health of its commercial interests as a barometer of the overall health of the nation. Colonial trade, especially, provided an influx of luxury goods as well as considerable profits for the merchants who undertook overseas trade. Lincoln cites William King's *The British Merchant*, published in 1721, as proof that merchants of the day "like to flatter themselves" as being "as essential . . . to the state as blood to the body."[10] Such an important status requires a figure of moral integrity, which explains in part Defoe's desire to establish an ethical base line for individual merchants to follow. Certainly, the antithesis of the ethical merchant is the pirate, whose prosperity is rooted in crime. However, Lincoln notes that, in official discourse at least, the pirate is an especially abstract figure: often discussed, certainly feared, but rarely, if ever, seen. As Peter Linebaugh and Marcus Rediker have explored, the pirate of the early eighteenth century assumes both the position and the radical ideology of the mid-seventeenth-century masterless man. They note, for instance, that "the ship became both an engine of capitalism in the wake of the bourgeois revolution in England *and* a setting of resistance, a place to which and in which the ideas and practices of revolutionaries defeated and repressed by Cromwell and then by King Charles escaped, reformed, circulated, and persisted."[11] While the crimes that pirates commit certainly resemble those of land robbers or murderers, the pirate is a unique category of felon, in that his primary victim is not the individual sailor or the merchant ship owner, but rather commerce itself.

The emergence of the merchant as a new kind of hero necessitates a reconsideration of the kinds of qualities a hero may possess. The triumphs of the merchant are not those of the traditional military hero; the goal is not fame through displays of physical strength or courage, but through the acquisition of wealth, a new marker of greatness than martial or political "great deeds." At the same time, the language of commerce employs military metaphors; the locus of conflict is not the battlefield but the boardroom. For eighteenth-century merchants, the shift in perception of what constitutes greatness also suggested a different model of masculinity: a Great Man doesn't need to have his hands stained with blood to prove his greatness; ink will do just fine.

In the same way, the pirate's connection with global commerce, which, like the merchant, measures success in the acquisition of wealth, suggests a different model of masculinity than the "criminal masculinity" that Erin Mackie analyzes.[12] Interestingly, both the merchant and the pirate are defined by their sole interest in wealth. Mackie acknowledges that the pirate is "most often depicted and understood as violent, always economic, often sociocultural, and utterly outside sexual representation."[13] Mackie notes that the lack of piratical sexuality sets pirates apart from the more "gentlemanly" highwayman and rake, whose erotic prowess is part of the composition of their masculinity, whether or not they actually demonstrate that prowess in reality. Mackie's summary of pirate representation endorses the image of the monstrous pirate presented here: the lack of sexual element in pirate narratives—as she bluntly declares, "there is no pirate sex"[14]—suggests something unnatural and monstrous.

That all makes perfect sense, yet it also gestures toward another way of representing pirates that I will explore in the second half of this book. Mackie locates the Caribbean counterpart of the eighteenth-century pirate in the modern Rastafarians and the rude boys of contemporary Jamaican culture: figures of resistance against White colonial power. She even cites a speech by Peter Tosh in which he specifically invokes "pirates" Henry Morgan and Francis Drake as role models for Jamaican youth. Mackie's insightful connections reveal the continuity between the eighteenth-century pirate and contemporary postcolonial figures of resistance. However, she also deftly sidesteps the vexing question of the hypermasculine pirate as a curiously unerotic figure. Interestingly, this image of the pirate emerges contemporaneously with another masculine figure who is also characterized a rather marked lack of erotic appeal: the overseas merchant.

If Mackie seems "perplexed" by the pirate's lack of sexuality, either homo-, hetero-, or bi-—if she is right that the pirate is "a form of pronounced masculinity outside of sexuality"[15]—what we encounter in the figure of the pirate is a new type of heroic figure, whose masculinity is located not in violent or sexual conquest but in economic conquest: greatness manifested in commercial superiority, masculinity demarcated by fiscal rather than generative prowess. Moreover, economic masculinity focuses purely on the acquisition of wealth, ignoring the "domestic" aspect of economics that is contained within the very word "economics" itself ("eco" derived from οἴκος, "house"). Mercantile apologists, as Margaret Hunt has argued,[16] attempted to direct the merchant's attention to domestic affairs and to promoting domestic virtue, by proposing the domestic sphere, and the merchant's ethical management therein, as a model for the mercantile state itself, a state that promoted ethical business practices and established the "home"—the British—as an ideal of economic and political virtue. Piracy, as both an economic and a state crime, naturally results from the pirate's violation of the οἴκος, of the state that maintains and controls the nation's wealth.

However, that argument is less applicable when commerce takes place outside the οἴκος, beyond the snug confines of the nation. Here colonial economics and piracy begin to blur into one another: the colonial merchant, like the pirate, pursues wealth in a world cut off from the domestic sphere, free from the demands of fatherhood, and able to establish what R. W. Connell and Julian Wood have termed "transnational business masculinity,"[17] whose potency lies in the ability to colonize and to capitalize. Seen in this light, pirates and merchants are two sides of the same imperial coin.[18]

Given the change in perception of pirates, it is perhaps unsurprising that an overview of latter-day piracy should emerge that would attempt to define and articulate a distinct pirate culture. *General History* made pirates knowable to its urban, largely middle-class readership, even to the point where its biases and its errors became incorporated into the general iconography of piracy. Johnson repeatedly shows his awareness of the intellectual conversations in print surrounding vice, luxury, criminality, and the proper use of money and credit, especially in the aftermath of the South Sea Bubble (to which Johnson specifically refers at one point). The pirate, as the monstrous *hostis humani generis*, the perpetual margin walker, is the quintessential antihero, the *doublure* of the Great Man that exposes all the vice, rapacity, and squalor that lies behind that elevated figure. Since the pirate-monster exists mainly in relation to the state, it is the pirate's assault on the state—a form of petty treason—that must occupy the moral focus of arguments against piracy. Part of the issue here is how the law contributes to the formation of virtue. This is not an insignificant question, since the law is the state's exercise of moral authority, especially if the church's exercise of moral authority—namely, the fear of Hell—does not seem to hold much sway with pirates. A sailor who refused to be terrified by the threat of hellfire could be cowed by the promise of the gallows. Except, of course, often they could not.

Richard Frohock suggests that "*General History* enacts a double satire, upholding the pirates' view that mainstream society is structured to privilege the rich and powerful at the expense of the weak and disadvantaged while simultaneously mocking pirates who cannot—and often intend not—to live up their principled claims."[19] Johnson's challenge in *General History* is not necessarily about the souls of his pirates, but the acknowledgement that, despite their monstrosity, pirates have much in common with the so-called Great Men of the age. Even the fact that *General History* enshrines the public lives—and, sometimes, the public deaths—of common pirates suggests an unusual importance in the acts of men and women who would otherwise be considered mere members of the mob. Johnson himself addresses the issue in his preface:

> I presume we need make no Apology for giving the Name of a History to the following Sheets, though they contain nothing but the Actions of a Parcel of Robbers. It is Bravery and Stratagem in War which make Actions worthy of Record; in which Sense the Adventures here related will be thought deserving that Name. (1724b, A4r–A4v [6])

Bestowing the title of "history" on his pirate tales allows Johnson to treat his subjects as something nobler than a "Parcel of Robbers," even if at times he seems to take pirates' "Bravery and Stratagem" ironically. One reason that Fly does appear as such a shabby and uninspiring figure in Johnson is that readers have already seen much more successful—even noteworthy—examples of piracy, such as Henry Avery, Edward "Blackbeard" Teach, and Bartholomew Roberts. While Johnson does not go out of his way to romanticize his pirate subjects, he does acknowledge that pirates can and do display some aspects of "greatness," however perverted it may be.

Johnson's ironic suggestion that pirates may exhibit greatness coincidentally echoes Mather's deep engagement with Fly and his crew. Mather embraces the somewhat radical idea that the so-called lower orders are even worth encouraging to reform. After all, why bother wasting time and energy trying to coerce an eleventh-hour repentance out of a hardened criminal who expects no mercy either in this world or the next? If pirates are truly the "enemies of all humanity," then does their monstrous nature preclude them from genuinely seeking God's grace? Mather, of course, wishes to use Fly and his crew as rhetorical devices, and hopes his readers will see in their example a warning against considering piracy at all. And yet, Mather's allowing Fly a voice and a rational perspective elevates him from simply being a disposable member of the mob into someone whose ultimate destiny actually matters.

PIRACY AND THE "PUBLICK GOOD": JOHNSON AND MANDEVILLE

It is assumed in the moral literature against pirates that merchant ships and merchant sailors act out of sense of public benevolence; indeed, commerce itself is said to be undertaken for the general health of the nation. Pirates, on the other hand, act *only* out of self-interest, since their aim is not to carry on legitimate trade but to take what they want for themselves and to dispose of it as they see fit. Pirates' predation on merchant ships, therefore, is a crime against the public good; everyone suffers from acts of piracy. *General History* acknowledges this view, but also shows it to be problematic, since the idea of what actually constitutes a public benefit is itself problematic. *General History*'s perspective on social ethics clearly has little in common with Cotton Mather's Puritan piety or with the admonitions to sailors to submit to authority, however harsh, that can be found in *The Seaman's Monitor*, a standard vade mecum issued to sailors that even included, in its 1723 edition, "A Kind Admonition to all Seafaring Persons, against Mutiny and Pyracy," a special section warning sailors against considering a life of piracy.[20]

Piracy's relationship to the rest of society, as Johnson demonstrates, is complex and multifaceted; pirates themselves are not easily branded just as deviants, in part because, as he takes great pains to show, pirates themselves both mimic conventional society and yet also deconstruct it. Johnson is fascinated with the codes of conduct that existed on pirate ships, reprinting several lists of rules that were to be followed. He is also fascinated by the collective nature of piracy, that pirates do exist within networks and associations, even as those associations were often unstable. The solidarity implied by the buccaneer term "Brethren of the

Coast" is not really applicable to Johnson's pirates—there is too much distrust and self-interest for these associations to last indefinitely—and yet, there is a high degree of cooperation among the Caribbean pirates. Pirate society, then, is primarily utilitarian, with all pirates understanding that friendship is based on convenience and mutual benefit. This utilitarian model of society, that accepts that self-interest and avarice form the backbone of society, is fully articulated in Bernard Mandeville's notorious *Fable of the Bees*, which, perhaps not insignificantly, become a cause célèbre after it was reprinted in 1723.

James Raven has noted eight responses between 1724 and 1728 to Mandeville's *Fable of the Bees*, which had been published in a slightly expanded third edition in January 1724.[21] Although much of the criticism surrounding the *Fable* relates to its defense of luxury, and its assertion that vice is a necessary element of any commercially successful society, Mandeville also asserts that crime—as a type of vice—is also essential to wealth. Furthermore, crime that results in the acquisition of wealth may also be related to greatness.

The discussion of vice and virtue here is also recalls the *Fable*'s "Enquiry into the Origin of Moral Virtue," which opens the Remarks, and "Remark (G)," which is a gloss on the lines "The Worst of all the Multitude / Did something for the Common Good" (24). Mandeville argues that crimes against property—in particular, the kind of plunder practiced by highwaymen and, by extension, pirates, may actually participate in a kind of benefit, since highwaymen and pirates steal money so that they can spend it—and, given the amounts that successful pirates might win, returning such large sums of money into general circulation must be considered a public benefit. As he argues:

> If an ill-natur'd Miser, who is almost a Plumb, and spends but Fifty Pounds and Year, tho' he has no Relation to inherit his Wealth, should be Robb'd of Five Hundred or a Thousand Guineas, it is certain that as soon as this Money should come to Circulate, the Nation would be the better for the Robbery, and receive the same and as real a Benefit from it, as if an Archbishop had left the same Sum to the Publick; yet Justice and the peace of the Society require that he or they who robb'd the Miser should be hang'd, tho' there were half a dozen of 'em concerned.[22]

Although the *General History* does not quite go to these lengths, it seems clear that these pirate histories do more than simply offer cautionary tales against vice, and consider pirates as morally ambivalent figures in what Mandeville demonstrates is a morally ambivalent age.

In the *Fable*, Mandeville argues for a holistic model of society, as he expresses in his famous analogy in "Remark K" comparing society to a bowl of punch, whose individual elements may seem unpalatable, but together make a pleasing taste. In this analogy, "Avarice" is "a griping Acid that sets our Teeth on edge, and is unpleasant to every Palate that is not debauch'd,"[23] while "Prodigality," which Mandeville calls a "Noble Sin," is "a pleasing Balsam that heals and makes amends for the smart."[24] Mandeville's remarks are clearly based on a radically different conception of "virtue" than the religious moralists. *Fable* is important not only as an iteration of the philosophical debates around the very features of commerce and luxury that also occupied pirates, but as a critique of the social and political forces that, in part, explain the rise of pirates in 1720s. There is a shared feeling in *General History* and *Fable of the Bees* that criminal behavior is endemic to society. The love of gold and material wealth is far too ingrained in us to be driven out so easily, and Johnson's remarks about "Bravery and Stratagem" align the pirate with the celebrated military hero. Moreover—and this is where both texts start to be read politically—when the same behavior is being exhibited by the so-called betters, then we can hardly expect pirates or land criminals to behave any differently. If Mandeville, as F. B. Kaye points out, is working out a utilitarian view of morality, and suggesting that morality is not an absolute concept, then it would stand to reason that the moral arguments against piracy are null and void.[25] In fact, Mandeville suggests that highwaymen (and, by extension, pirates) participate in the public good—something Hanna, throughout *Pirate Nests*, demonstrates was true of colonial ports who benefited from pirate plunder.

So what is the solution for pirates? One option is to enact their own laws, as with Bartholomew Roberts's famous set of rules that Johnson reproduces. They may take issue with the practice of law, the unfairness with which it is applied, or the corruptions of those given authority to uphold the law, as Johnson underlines in the mock trial discussed earlier.[26] Piracy is unsettling because, in Johnson at least, it moved beyond simply living outside the law—Roberts's rules in effect recognized the pirate ship as an autonomous state, to which an alternative moral and legal code could then apply. *General History* reveals the limitations of law in much the same way that Mandeville reveals the limitations of morality.

Johnson's engagement with Mandeville's ideas of self-interest also resonates with two critics of Mandeville who, perhaps not surprisingly, have also been closely associated with *General History*: Daniel Defoe and Nathaniel Mist. In "Mandeville and Defoe,"[27] John Robert Moore considers Defoe's remarks on *Fable of the Bees*. Moore argues that, far from joining in the near-universal condemnation of Mandeville's defense of vice in the *Fable*, Defoe actually shared a good deal of Mandeville's sentiments. Defoe engages with Mandeville's central thesis that what can be called "the public good" depends on encouraging public vices. While Defoe is very much a keen moralist, he appreciates that Mandeville, in the *Fable*, is actively working out a definition of the public good that tries to comprehend the complexity of that term. Defoe himself works out his own definition of the public good both in his pamphlets on the South Sea trade and in his curious handbook for merchants, *The Compleat English Tradesman*, the latter composed and published at the same time as the most intense period of the *Fable of the Bees* controversy and the first two editions of the *General History*.[28]

Defoe, Mandeville, and Johnson all, in various ways, specifically engage the question of how much public benefit depends on private vice. Common to all three writers is the tricky distinction between treating criminal behavior without acknowledging its moral repugnance, while at the same time not appearing to encourage vice. Johnson, in particular, remarks on the viciousness of some individual pirates, while passing up many opportunities to condemn piracy itself. All three writers share the notion that crime is an inevitable part of modern society, which is itself an outward and visible sign of the inherently degraded nature of that society. What we find in Defoe and Mandeville, and also in Mist and Johnson, is a focus on criminality and the public good, on understanding crime not merely as a marker of human depravity but as a distinct and complex social phenomenon, and especially on the ways in which crime and criminal activity affect the public benefits of trade and commerce.

In *Defoe's Review* no. 107 (18 October 1707), Defoe uses the stories of Henry Avery's Madagascar pirates as a way of introducing the subject of business ethics that he will return to in more detail in *The Complete English Tradesman*. Defoe notes that these pirates have petitioned for a pardon, vowing to "return to their own Country, live quietly at home, and ceasing their old Trade, become honest Freeholders," rather in the same way, he snidely remarks, that "others of our *West-India* Pyrates, *Merchants I should have said*, have done before them."[29] Defoe then comes to his main point, that in terms of ethics, there is little to distinguish between the "Litteral" pirates who have established themselves on Madagascar and the "Allegorical" pirates whom Defoe sees as unethical colonial tradesmen:

> the Clandestine Trade Pyrates, who pyrate upon fair Trade at home; the Custom-stealing Pyrates, who pyrate upon the Government; the Owling Pyrates, who rob the Manufactures; the privateering Pyrates, who rob by Law; and because *A* the *French* Man of St. *Maloes* rob'd them, rob *B* of *Marsellies*, that never did them any Hurt; whether we mean the cheating Pyrate, that robs at home, or the Factor Pyrate, that robs abroad, of all sorts, from the *Madagascar* Man to the *Buchaneer*—If all these should be taken off of the *Exchang*, and rendezvous'd, might we not say of them, as one of the Coward Captains of the Fleet,
>
> *Bless Us, what Crowding there'd be when they meet!*[30]

Clearly, Defoe is less interested in pirates as such than in using the term "pirate" to cover a wide range of dishonest business practices among supposedly honest tradesmen. Yet that in itself is noteworthy, since Defoe raises the question of why some criminals, who at least honestly identify themselves as criminals, should be punished for committing the same crimes as those who flock to Exchange Alley daily? Defoe even draws the parallel of colonial merchants who build up great estates in Jamaica, just as the Madagascar pirates have supposedly done, and then bring their wealth home to retire in England.

Defoe's real point in the essay—ostensibly a continuation of the essay in the previous number—is the power of money to obliterate all wrongs. The Madagascar pirates' offer to buy a pardon, though morally outrageous at first sight, is actually the best of all possible options, argues Defoe. The government can set its own price on the pirates' freedom, and use the money they have stolen and return it to the public purse: a clear case of a private vice yielding a public benefit. None of this, of course, condones piracy itself; nor does Defoe much concern himself with the lives of the actual pirates. But he does see piracy as an intrinsic and perhaps even necessary part of global commerce, and as such he sees a direct connection between merchants and pirates—especially colonial merchants who enter into trade primarily to make money, regardless of ethics: "Who would not be a Thief . . . that could live in all manner of Luxury and Wealth for a Time, and then having gotten Money enough to buy his Pardon, turn honest Fellow again." Defoe's point will, with some expansion, form the basis of much of Mandeville's arguments in *Fable of the Bees*, and will lie behind much of *General History*'s perspective on pirates.

Defoe picks up the threads of the argument in his *Essay Upon the South Sea Trade* (1711).[31] While the focus of the essay is undoubtedly the economic viability of the South Sea Company, Defoe is well aware that trade is not an isolated phenomenon, and he is unwilling to separate considerations of trade from their social effects. Indeed, although Defoe wrote extensively and passionately about trade his entire life, although economics and commerce are never far from his thoughts even in his fiction, his entire outlook is driven by his sense of the effects on society as a whole. Or, to put it another way, he is always aware that discussions of human activity—whether politics, economics, or religion—must always place real humans at their center.[32] Therefore, there can be no study of trade without considering its effect on the public good, since all activity within the public sphere must be directed toward that end.

We can see Defoe's focus on the human factor in trade most succinctly in a short work published on 2 April 1724, a month before the first edition of *General History*: "The Great Law of Subordination Consider'd." An essay on the proper behavior of servants—and a surprisingly conservative document for anyone who might have considered Defoe a protoegalitarian—it is also a meditation on the power of law to reaffirm what Defoe sees as a natural social hierarchy. Central to Defoe's argument is a particular definition of "liberty" that qualifies the notion of the free-born Englishman with the restrictions on that freedom demanded by one's place within the social hierarchy. Specifically, Defoe points out the danger of the masterless man in acting rashly or uncivilly. He relates the case of a servant who desired to take a gentleman to court for public swearing (an offence punishable by paying a fine for each instance noted). The master points out that, while the servant is free under the law to pursue his legal action, the master is also free to terminate his servant's employment should he do so. Just because one is free to take an action, Defoe suggests, does not mean that such actions may not have consequences. This, he asserts, is one of the problems an unqualified focus on "liberty" might engender.

Having reworked the notion of liberty, Defoe next considers the place of wages, What Defoe says of the corrupting influence of money on servants may just as easily be applied to pirates:

> *The Error is in their Morals*; the Money prompts their Vice, and their Vice depraves their Manners; so that every Advantage which shou'd encourage them to Diligence, and an humble Behaviour, is the ruin both of their Diligence, and Behaviour. (115)

For Defoe, everything proceeds from the basic principle of lax morals: the hierarchy is unsustainable in a social structure that admits the possibility of a meritocracy. We will consider this point more fully in the next chapter, when we consider the place of civility and politeness within the pirate world. For now, it is enough to reiterate that wealth—and the pursuit of wealth—does not alone make for greatness, although it is much easier for the wealthy to mask their corruption with a veneer of civility.

On 8 August 1724, just a few weeks before the publication of the second edition of *General History*, Nathaniel Mist published an essay in the *Weekly Journal; or, Saturday's Post* attacking Bernard Mandeville's defense of vice.[33] This essay was but the first of several that would appear in the *Weekly Journal* throughout August. Taken as a whole, the papers in August 1724 constitute an extended attack on Mandeville, but, significantly, they also include a curious puff piece for the *General History*. It would not be out of character, then, for Mist to direct readers' attentions toward the revision and reissue of what was clearly for him a major title.

In his attack on Mandeville, Mist echoes the sentiments of publications such as Woodward's "Kind Admonition" mentioned above, warning "young people" against reading such publications as *The Fable of the Bees*: "The loose Ideas they raise, are Temptations to loose Actions, and a strong Provocation to Lewdness is within a Degree of the Thing it self.—I shall not take upon me to dictate to my Superiours, what Course to take with those who draw their Pens against good Manners and Modesty; but tis I know, that Vertue never flourishes more than when Vice is removed out of Sight."

Mist continues his argument in the following week's issue (15 August 1724), which is essentially a defense of the clergy:

> What makes Men despise Government, rob, defraud, oppress, or malign each other, but this want of Veneration to Religion, the Conclusion is right with the Profligate and Irreligious. *Let us eat and drink, for to Morrow we dye.* For why should any Man who is perswaded he has no Interest in another Life, sit down, despair, and starve, while others of the same earthly Original live in Power, Affluence, and Plenty? No, when under no such Restraint, every Man of Spirit only watches more carefully against the Penalty of human Laws. . . . To hazard the Punishment than want always: Hence proceeds our Land and Sea Robbers more numerous amongst us (to the Disgrace of our Nation be it spoken) than in all the other European kingdoms put together, and hence, with those who have more Fear and less Courage, ensue Prisons, Starvings, Suicides.[34]

That Mist should include the piece on 29 August is hardly surprising; it was obviously written to coincide with the publication of the second edition, but it is the nature of that piece that is most remarkable. The essay suggests a political reading of the *General History* that, in fact, ties in with the argument against anticlericalism that Mist has been developing thus far. It includes an imaginary letter from a member of a club of gentlemen in some unnamed country location. The letter describes another club member, a justice of the peace who was formerly a "Fanatick and a Tradesman" in London. This justice, clearly both a dissenting protestant and a Whig—the very sort whom Mist had blamed the previous week for promoting vice and for attacking Anglican clergy—overhears some of the other club members reading Mist's May and June essays aloud; he immediately assumes that Mist is talking about pirates only metaphorically, since "this shim-sham Story of Pyrates is an impudent Libel upon great Men."[35] Mist thus cleverly directs the reader's attention to a particular way of reading *General History*—as a commentary on the present government—and yet at the same time suggests that ardent Whig supporters would find such a reading disgusting. Mist, moreover, does not deny the validity of such a reading, only that it was not apparent to the other club members.

LAST OF THE MONSTERS

The monster-pirate embodied in Johnson's *General History* stands as an incarnation of the anxieties of colonial trade. That pirates could openly flout both civil and moral law, that they could construct protosocieties of their own, organized along radically different lines, all suggested a moral crisis at the heart of the society of the 1720s that events such as the South Sea Bubble seemed only to verify. That pirates could also be successful at what they did, that relatively few of Johnson's narratives end with capture and execution, serves only to highlight that the pirate is offered here as an apt image of the moral bankruptcy of the age.[36]

Lest it seem as though, as the moralists would argue, pirates were entirely without any ethical dimension, we may return to the hapless William Fly, and examine a little more closely his reason for refusing to forgive William Atkinson. As *General History* records, Fly had pressed Atkinson into navigational service, in effect relying on him to bring the pirates out of danger of being captured. Fly, of course, threatens Atkinson with execution if he refuses to comply, but he presents Atkinson's compliance as a moral obligation, rather than a coerced action:

> *Now, Capt. Atkinson, you may do as you please, you may be a Son of a Whore and pilot us wrong, which, G—d d—n ye, would be a rascally Trick by G—d, because you would betray Men who trust in you; but, by the eternal J—s, you shan't live to see us hang'd. I don't love many Words, G—d d—n ye, if you have a Mind to be well used you shall, G—d's B—d; but if you will be a Villain and betray your Trust, may G—d strike me dead, and may I drink a Bowl of Brimstone and Fire with the D—l, if I don't send you headlong to H—ll, G—d d—n me; and so there needs no more Arguments by G—d, for I've told you my Mind, and here's all the Ships Crew for Witnesses, that if I do blow your Brains out, you may blame no Body but your self, G—d d—n ye.* (1728.2, 234 [611])

Fly's refusal to forgive Atkinson, therefore, stems from Atkinson's betrayal of trust, from his "rascally Trick" of pretending to navigate them to safety. Fly's moral sense is consistent with other pirate codes: that, though self-interest is a major part of the pirate ethos, one may also appeal to the larger "public good" of the ship itself. Fly is not without a social ethic, even if that ethic would satisfy neither the authorities who hanged him nor the Puritan minister who attempted to redeem him.

By incorporating pirates into discussions of the public good, Johnson, Defoe, and Mist all reaffirm the anxieties about piracy that permeate discussions of commercial activity—especially colonial commercial activity—and attempt to answer those anxieties. The pirates of Johnson's *General History* already exist within a morally ambiguous universe, and, it is clear, that universe dominated discussions of public and private good throughout the decade. The ideas that a criminal may also be a Great Man, or that "greatness" may be a mask for criminality, and that the wealthy and powerful exhibit the same vices as common sailors, only to escape without punishment, permeate Johnson's accounts of pirate activity, especially since Johnson avoids the kind of overt moralizing against piracy that normally accompanies such narratives. This discussion of the relationship between greatness and vice, the acknowledgment of a double standard under the law for crimes against property, would find its best-known expression in 1728—the same year that volume 2 of the *General History* was published—in John Gay's *Beggar's Opera*, but the parameters of that discussion also get articulated in the pages of Johnson's rogue's gallery book.

GREAT MEN

5

PLUTARCH ON THE SPANISH MAIN

Pirates and "Great Men"

WHEN IS A PIRATE NOT A PIRATE? Perhaps when he sees himself as something else. In volume 2 of *General History*, published in 1728, we find the story of Captain Misson,[1] who spends a good deal of time trying to convince himself, his crew, and—possibly—the readers that, despite plundering ships, he should never be branded with the "ignominious" name of pirate. Instead, he and his eager band of sailors see themselves as men of "Liberty," committed to living life on their own terms, free from external restrictions, and certainly from external labels. Of course, they chase, fire on, and capture ships; of course they plunder those ships; but because they treat their victims with utmost civility, because they do not hack off body parts or pelt captains with broken bottles or indulge in any of the other cruelties recorded in the chapters of *General History*, they do not consider themselves pirates. Such is the wide, wild world of Captain Misson—sailor, philosopher, freethinker, libertarian, unpirate, and possible Great Man—and star of the strange second volume of Johnson's pirate gallery.

The term "civility" above is not used lightly: in the colonial wilds, in the middle of the ocean, along the slave coasts of Africa, the ability to maintain one's civility was, perhaps more than one's reason, a marker of one's full humanity, worthy of joining other humans in the world of the *civitas*. Civility, and its cognates "politeness" and "courtesy," all signify a connection between the city, the court, and refinement or "polish" (the source of the word "polite"). For a pirate to display civility, then, is to challenge the idea of the pirate as Monster, as a thing bred in the social, political, economic, and even geographic margins. Civility, or at least the ability to mimic the discourses and actions of the civil person, is a necessary ingredient of greatness, the thing that sets the successful pirates, the Henry Averys and the Bartholomew Robertses, apart from the common run of pirates who, for their crimes, are remembered only in lists of condemned felons in trial accounts.

Even violent psychopaths, like Blackbeard or Edward Low, occasionally display at least a parodic version of civility, even if only to cover over their brutality with a veneer of Bond-villain distinctiveness: Blackbeard's smoking hat, Low's careful sparing of married men.

Significantly, it is in this measure of civility that pirates and global merchants have a similar problem. Merchants were vilified in satirical literature for pretending to civility: they were often portrayed as oafish, money-grubbing boors, like Ducat in *Polly*, or as tacky, tasteless, status seekers, such as one finds in plays such as *The Nabob* or Frances Burney's *A Busy Day*. These portrayals may seem like Tory satires of Whig merchants, but Markku Peltonen, in his study of dueling, argues that the relationship between civility, politeness, and the rise of commerce was multifaceted and not necessarily divided along partisan lines. He cites *Cato's Letters* and Mandeville, as well as Addison and Steele, to show that the adoption of civility by the rising middle class was not as simple as an assault on social mobility.[2] These commentators wrestled with the implications of the rising middle class's adopting civility—court manners—as a means of continuing commerce. If one adopts the forms of civility and politeness *only* in the service of commerce, then one may be accused of dissembling or hypocrisy, masking one's essential boorishness with empty gestures and phrases that simply mimic one's so-called betters. One must therefore adopt a genuine code of ethics suitable to middle-class values; however, to do so is to rewrite the social rules altogether, and to suggest an alternative social order to the established hierarchy. As with merchants, so with pirates: it is one thing for a pirate or a merchant to make himself a figure of fun by pretending to greatness; it is quite another for them actually to display qualities that might challenge what is understood by greatness.

GREAT MEN AND GREAT CRIMES: THE CRIMINAL AS EXEMPLUM

We may consider the same questions with regard to *General History*. If piracy is the continuation of commerce by other means—and if the pirate is a type of the "new gentleman" that the new global commerce has produced—then the pirate stands in an ironic relationship to the legitimate merchant. The pirate's reputation is built as much on his lack of civility, his rejection of politeness, of flattery or of any of the arts of dissembling that both Mandeville and Cato believe to be essential to a well-functioning commercial society. Pirates are sadistic and blasphemous, and they bow to no one. Like monsters, they respect no authority but their own, and amass great fortune precisely by intimidation and force, not by politeness.

The relatively narrow focus of *General History* is part of its strength as a literary work. More than just a miscellany of crime narratives, the book seems to take its pirate subjects as representative, to construct what might be termed a sociology of piracy. These stories situate the pirate within a context that does, as we have seen, exist mostly on paper. Moreover, *General History* appeared at a time when debates about criminality in all levels of society were especially acute. Julian Hoppit has noted that the years from 1723 to 1727 were, politically, "something of a damp squib";[3] according to Hoppit, there was little in the way of actual controversy, and few pieces of legislation that might stir the nation as a whole. At the same time, those years saw astonishing and vigorous debates on the efficacy of Walpole's ministry in the aftermath of the South Sea Bubble scheme and the Atterbury Plot, most of it carried out in newspapers, pamphlets, and popular books. It is not surprising that the *General History* should have links to publications such as *Mist's Weekly Journal*, the crime pamphlets of Applebee, or even Defoe's journalism and fiction: whether or not these publications can confirm authorship, they certainly confirm that the author of the *General History* was conversant with all of these publications—was, in fact, a significant voice at the table in the midst of these debates.

As we have already seen, the lines between legitimate commerce and piracy were often blurry. Seen in this light, piracy is simply commerce by other means. Peter Leeson, in *The Invisible Hook*, offers a reading of pirate culture from the perspective of an economist, and concludes:

> Pirates didn't use democracy because they were "more democratic" than merchant owners. They didn't torture prisoners because they were more naturally sadistic. And they didn't treat some black sailors as equals because they were less bigoted than their contemporaries. Pirates just acted to maximize profits in the particular, and rather unusual, economic context they confronted.[4]

Leeson touches on an important aspect of pirate culture that was certainly not lost on the author of the *General History*: that pirates operated within what was the first successful global economy, and they quickly learned the rules for success within that economy: expedience, ruthlessness, and an eye for the main chance, just as their more legitimate merchant counterparts did.

The primary issue in the argument against pirates, of course, was the assault on trade. Piracy represented a significant trade risk, added to the natural dangers already present in oceanic trade. That was nothing new in the 1720s, but within the context of other debates on the significance of trade to the overall life—and identity—of Britain, piracy necessarily moves from being a public nuisance to a public crisis. Pirates, therefore, occupy a much more important economic and political position within the public sphere of mid-1720s Britain than that of mere criminals, and the *General History* is well aware of this. In the book, pirates are represented, like other so-called Great Men, as morally ambiguous figures, who have actively exploited the peculiarities of the burgeoning transatlantic economy to further their own ends—but how are they, then, markedly different from any other trader who has seized similar opportunities? The *General History* sometimes makes this point obliquely, as in the Blackbeard narrative, but occasionally the book is more direct. In the Edward England account, the first edition quite clearly sets the pirate narrative within the larger economic concerns in the aftermath of the South Sea Bubble—in fact, it almost goes out of its way to do so. The narrative ends with the crew sailing in the captured vessel, *Cassandra*, to Portobello in Panama. A notice in the *London Journal* (24 August 1723) quotes a letter from Jamaica dated 18 June 1723, reporting on the pardon that Spain has granted to the crew. The writer notes that Spain had sought an amnesty agreement with France, Portugal, and the Netherlands, but these nations had not, at time of writing, ratified any such agreement. Therefore, the writer notes, "I cannot see on what Pretence the Spanish Governour has taken upon him to grant to every Man on Board the Cassandra, a Pardon, who are, as we are informed, all, or most of them, of our own Nation." His primary concern is that, if colonial governors take it upon themselves to offer pardons to pirates, "It must necessarily be the occasion of the increase of Pyrates, and the Destruction of all Commerce." He goes on to urge, "This is a Matter which so highly concerns the Merchants of England, as well as the two Trading Companies, that it is to be hoped they will join in representing the Consequences thereof to his Majesty and Ministers."[5]

General History presents the matter rather differently:

> Here [i.e., at Portobello] they sat down to spend the Fruits of their dishonest Industry, dividing the Spoil and Plunder of their Fellow-Creatures among themselves, without the least Compunction or Remorse for what they had done; satisfying their Consciences with this Salvo, that other People would have done the same Things, if they had had equal Courage, and the like Opportunities. And, I can't say, but if that they had known what was doing in *England*, at the same time, by the *South-Sea* Directors, and other Persons, they would certainly have had this Reflection for their Consolation, *viz. That whatever Murthers and Robberies they had committed, they were not the greatest Villains that were then living in the World.* (1724a, 142 [134])

Later editions change the wording slightly, significantly perhaps, removing the phrase "equal Courage." The first edition makes no mention of England's having been marooned on Mauritius because of his leniency toward the captain of the *Cassandra*; nor does it mention what happened to the pardoned crew members. The *History and Lives* volume changes the context of this: rather than the South Sea comment originating from the author/narrator, it is given as a direct quotation. Here the pirates "swear . . . *That whatever Robberies they had committed, they are not the only Rogues in the World*; for that the *South-Sea did more Mischief in one Year, than they are able to do in their whole Lives*." The narrator goes on to note, "Tho' 'tis difficult to compute the Mischief they did in 5 Years; which certainly was more than what they had plunder'd; having sunk or burnt all the Vessels they took, either to prevent their giving Intelligence, or out of Wantonness, or because the Captives had disoblig'd them by making too stout a Resistance" (53). Here, then, a swipe at the greed of the South Sea Company directors becomes watered down into a mendacious claim by the pirates themselves. Far from decrying the pardon as a step towards the ruin of all commerce, the *General History* uses the occasion as a dig at the South Sea Company directors, the South Sea Bubble having taken place around the time that England and his crew were most active.[6]

Whatever Edward England and his crew were actually thinking about when they "sat down to spend the Fruits of their Dishonesty," it is clear that Johnson wants to present them as something a little more than crooks who got away with their crime. Specifically, he wants the reader to consider them in the context of the dire economic landscape of the 1720s; yet the text also points to Captain England and his crew as essential components of that landscape. It is a subtle effect: it does not alter any of the facts of England's crimes, yet it does establish a perspective for reading this life story. Such effects are present throughout *General History*, and they constantly nudge the reader to focus outward from the specifics of pirate activity. By way of example, we can return to the pirate we considered previously in terms of his monstrosity, Edward Teach, better known as Blackbeard.[7] All editions make a particular point of discussing the origins of this nickname after the main narrative of Blackbeard's piracies, because the name—or rather, the beard itself—"did not a little contribute towards making his Name so terrible in these parts" (1724a, 99 [84]). The passage is worth quoting in full:

> *Plutarch*, and other grave Historians, have taken Notice, that several great Men amongst the *Romans*, took their Sir-Names from certain odd Marks in their countenances; as *Cicero*, from a Mark or Vetch on his Nose; so our Heroe, Captain *Thatch*, assumed the Cognomen of *Black-beard*, from

> that large quantity of Hair, which like a frightful Meteor, covered his whole Face, and frightn'd *America*, more than any Comet that has appear'd there a long Time. (1724a, 99 [84])[8]

Blackbeard's "cognomen" puts him in the same company as Cicero—and not, it should be noted, for any record of great deeds but for unusual physical features. Thus, the *General History* dryly remarks, is greatness marked.

We may also note that Blackbeard's distinctive physical attribute is something of a rarity in *General History*: Johnson's pirates, even the most monstrous ones, tend to veer away from the "eye patch and peg leg" stereotypes of popular culture. However, if *General History* fails to provide us with many of the recognizable visual icons of the Treasure Neverland pirates, it nevertheless excels, even in its diversity, in constructing a recognizable, reasonably coherent pirate culture. Johnson achieves this is in part by making his history representative rather than comprehensive: following the model of Plutarch, the pirates whose lives appear in the chapters are presented as exempla. As Johnson notes in the preface, "*When we found the Circumstances of* Roberts*'s Life, and other Pyrates, either as to piratical Articles, or any Thing else, to be the same, we thought it best to give them but once, and chose* Roberts*'s Life for that Purpose, he having made more Noise in the World, than some others*" (1724a, A4r [6]). Johnson thus leaves his readers to infer a great degree of similarity in the lives of these pirates. This strategy, moreover, is not merely accidental, nor is it entirely done, as Johnson suggests, simply to avoid tiresome repetition of similar details. Johnson, like other contemporary writers on pirates, stresses the idea of the pirate as universal enemy, a social aberration, a diseased outgrowth of maritime commerce itself; and yet, as he asserts, "*If the progress of our Pyrates had been equal to their Beginning; had they all united, and settled in some of those Islands, they might, by this Time, have been honoured with the Name of a Commonwealth, and no Power in those Parts of the World could have been able to dispute it with them*" (1724a, A4v [7]). Pirates, then, are enough of a force to have the potential to be a dominant power; some of them may even display qualities that could be considered those of a Great Man. As many of the lives in *General History* reveal, successful pirate captains were often intelligent, resourceful, capable leaders, even if they could also be violent and cruel. They possessed many of the skills of the successful entrepreneur, albeit directed toward personal gain rather than, as Johnson suggests, the "common weal" of an organized state. They are at once admirable and detestable, noble and undignified, attractive and terrifying: in short, as has been articulated before, they are both the Monsters and the Great Men of global maritime commerce.

The ambivalence inherent in *General History*'s view of pirates can be seen in the first biography, that of Henry Avery, which navigates between celebrating his obvious successes and, in the curious—and likely apocryphal—tale of his eventual demise, rounding out his story with a suitably ironic moral twist. Avery, having left his diamonds in the care of some merchants in Bristol, returns, at great risk to himself, to retrieve them. Instead of paying him, however, the merchants "silenced him by threatening to discover him, so that," as the story pointedly concludes, "our Merchants were as good Pyrates at Land as he was at Sea" (1724b, 55–56 [57]). The point is clear: ruthlessness and rapacity in commerce are not restricted to pirates, but neither is it entirely clear who is worse, the honest-plundering pirate or the underhanded merchant.

The story of Avery's untimely end raises a question: What distinguishes a great pirate from a simple scoundrel? There is no doubt that the merchants who dupe Avery are clever and resourceful, outwitting and blindsiding him in a move worthy of any good crime-caper film. But they are not "great" in the way that Avery is great; their role is simply to act as a satisfying resolution to the plot of Avery's life. Lincoln Faller suggests that the criminal appears as great in contrast to the larger darkness surrounding him, that there is something heroic in the criminal's defiant stance against a world that is inherently unjust, corrupt, and squalid. The great criminal does not merely participate in the squalor but acts as social critic.[9] Coupled with this idea is the highwayman's and pirate's pretentions to gentility—a feature not seen in common footpads or simple murderers. Pirates, we often forget, were trained sailors, skilled labor, and as such were escaping a social order that both badly needed their skills and yet treated them extremely shabbily. For a pirate to become great is to fulfill a potential that, in the merchant navy, might never be realized: following Faller's point, it is only in the world of crime that the common sailor can stand out against the general murkiness of colonial expansion, exploitation, slavery, and venality that is the world of eighteenth-century global commerce.

The issue of greatness, and the relationship between greatness and criminality, would take on an even greater relevance after 1724. Although the idea of a great criminal is perhaps most fully treated in the case of Jonathan Wild—both in Defoe's pamphlet and in John Gay's satirical equation of Wild with Robert Walpole in the character of Peachum—Wild's very public execution in 1725 served only to complicate a discussion that had been raging heatedly since the previous year: Does greatness consist only in actions that contribute to the public good? What are we to make of a moral universe that allows people who commit crimes not only to escape justice, but to flourish, to be celebrated public figures, even to become objects of admiration? As Johnson himself admits, the whole point of producing a book about "a Parcel of Robbers" seems to contradict the very purpose of biography, which is, following the example of Plutarch, to choose the lives of men and women whose contribution to the public good is indisputable or who display virtues that act as exempla for readers to follow. The underlying question in *General History* is how one finds contemporary exempla in a morally ambiguous world where obviously corrupt men like Robert Walpole gain significant political power, where Jonathan Wild can lead a double life as a crime boss and as "thief-taker general," and where public disasters like the South Sea Bubble can be allowed to flourish, even endorsed by the royal family itself?

As Faller has already noted, the thief—in which category I also include the pirate—existed in the eighteenth century within a "tangled knot of ambivalences,"[10] moving within a shifting mass of signifiers. For Faller, the thief "resists reduction to absurdity and confusion; there is something about him that remains positive and coherent, that invites consideration."[11] So it is with pirates—with the important distinction that the highwayman of Faller's studies commits crimes against property, to be sure, but crimes directed at individuals. A gun pointed at my chest and a demand for my money is an unambiguous transaction, with one clear victim and one clear transgressor. Piracy operates on a more abstract level of transgression, since it is primarily not directed at the individuals who happen to be on board captured ships, but rather at the mercantile community, at commerce, and, by extension, at the state itself. If I, as a sailor, comply with a pirate's request and hand over my ship's cargo or supplies, my victimhood is much more abstract, and I am likely to be spared personal violence or even any personal loss. Acts of violence, of course, were sometimes directed at individuals, but the *General History* is careful to note that cruel, sadistic pirates were the exception, and were vilified even by their fellow pirates. Edward Low and Blackbeard were especially noteworthy for their sadistic enjoyment of physical cruelty, even in an age that tolerated violence much more than our own. As a rule, though, most pirates were simply interested in booty, and reserved violence for officials, as Edward England did with his former master, Captain Skinner. Violence is a means to an end, a necessary component of doing business on a global scale.

To see violence as simply a commercial tool is again to realize that piracy, far from being an aberration of the mercantile system, is a direct outgrowth of it. Piracy, in its purest form, wrests control of global commerce away from merchant-owners and representatives of the states, and puts it back in the hands of individuals. The same debates about the ethics of commerce that were being discussed in London were being played out in real time in the waters of the Caribbean and Madagascar. *General History* is well aware of this, and situates the debate within a particular ethical framework: if the merchant is the Great Man of the new age, and if we allow that pirates can, like merchants, also be Great Men, then it may be possible to recast pirate biographies as a kind of parodic Plutarch. In fact, Plutarch is invoked on more than one occasion in *General History*. A telling passage occurs in the preface, which serves as a justification for the book itself:

> *Plutarch* is very circumstantial in relating the Actions of Spartacus, the Slave, and makes the Conquest of him one of the greatest Glories of *Marcus Crassus*; and it is probable, had this Slave liv' d a little longer, *Plutarch* would have given us his Life at large. (1724b, A4v [6–7])

It is tempting to read this and other Plutarch references ironically, but that may be an oversimplification. The Spartacus reference above has an echo in Mist's *Weekly Journal* (18 August 1722), in a lengthy attack on the Duke of Marlborough by way of comparison with Alexander the Great, that is worth examining in some detail.

The issue at hand in the *Weekly Journal* article is how much of the truth of the lives of public figures should be recorded, and whether the character of so-called Great Men should include their vices as well as their virtues:

> It is certain, that when *Plutarch* wrote, all the Descendants and Friends of *Alexander* were dead; so that he had nothing to *hope* from the *Favour*, or *fear* from the *Resentment* of any Man: And, therefore, was he at the greater Liberty to pursue Truth without Bias or Prejudice. But we know that, in the worst of Times, Men have been ashamed of appearing publickly in the *Prosecution* of *Truth*. Even under the Reign of *NERO Lucan* writ his *Pharsalia*; the Design of which was to extol the Actions of *Pompey* and the *Republicans*, and lessen the Reputation of those who *chang'd* the *Commonwealth* of *Rome* into a *Monarchy*. . . . We know all the little Arts and Contrivances of *Marcus Crassus* in accumulating of *Wealth*; and his Name is more distinguish'd at *this* Day for his *Avarice*, than for his *overcoming of Spartacus*, and putting an End to the War of the Slaves, a War which made *Rome* tremble, when it was at the top of its Glory and Power. . . . It is the same in all Nations; there is not a Man who has been thought worthy of being taken Notice of in History, but his *Vices*, as well as his *Vertues*, are transmitted to us.[12]

The point here is that, if an admittedly great figure such as Alexander can stand to have his vices exposed, then a much lesser "great figure"—and the context clearly points to the recently disgraced Marlborough as the parallel—should be able to stand the scrutiny of biographers.

More than simply invoking a "favorite author," therefore, the author of the *General History* appears to be consciously using Plutarch as a way of directing reading. Plutarch's *Lives of the Noble Grecians and Romans* embodies the principle that narrative should be primarily for the purpose of, as Brian Stock puts it, "The application of moral thinking into public life."[13] Stock notes that early modern readers of Plutarch would have grasped that the narrative presentation of the events in the lives of the subjects covered is specifically designed to highlight their virtuous actions. In turn, these biographies constitute a guide for right conduct in public life. How, then, can one apply the same principle to pirates? Only by acknowledging that conduct in public life, especially as one gets further away from what is seen to be the center of civilization, necessarily becomes more complicated, and that what constitutes "virtuous conduct" is altered by the introduction of a social determiner—wealth derived from commerce—that Plutarch is never concerned with. In 1724, merchants, and pirates, can represent Great Men as much as statesmen and military leaders.

CAPTAIN MISSON: THE PIRATE AS RULER

Volume 2 continues to explore the issue of the pirate as Great Man in the figure of Captain Misson, whose story gets pride of place in this volume much as Henry Avery's story did in volume 1. Like Avery, Misson is a highly successful pirate, a man of intellectual curiosity and a natural leader. His talents eventually lead him beyond piracy, to establishing a colony on Madagascar, Libertatia, a kind of pirate utopia. At its height, Libertatia enjoys an egalitarian constitution and a protocommunist economic system; the Liberi (the name Misson himself gives to the colonists) even find wives from the nearby island of Johanna,[14] and so mark the beginnings of a permanent, multigenerational settlement. Libertatia, however, does not survive long, since it is attacked and destroyed by the island's native people. Misson, the only survivor, abandons what is left of his settlement and is last seen in a ship battling a storm off the Cape of Good Hope.

Unlike Avery, however, Captain Misson is a fictional creation, a larger-than-life construction of everything one might expect in a successful pirate. Misson is, from the start, an unusual addition to the rogue's gallery. Misson is the son of a wealthy and well-established family; unlike Crusoe, he seems not to have had any difficulty convincing his father to let him follow his dream of going to sea—in fact, if anything, Misson's father is only too happy to set him up in a position where he will not be demanding money. Misson distinguishes himself as a sailor, but soon ends up in Rome, where he encounters a "lewd" priest, Father Caraccioli. If any part of the Misson story resembles any of Defoe's fictions, the friendship between

Misson and Caraccioli reads as something of a parodic version of Captain Singleton's friendship with the shrewd and pragmatic Quaker, William. William is not exactly corrupt, but he does not necessarily condemn Singleton's life of piracy; instead, he systematically persuades Singleton, through rational discourse, that pursuing a life as a legitimate man of business offers just as much wealth, if not more, without the risk of legal retribution that pirates face. William is streetwise and clever, but he is also firmly committed to turning his friend toward a more pious life. Caraccioli, on the contrary, is a rogue from the start—to English readers, of course, an Italian priest living in the Vatican puts him at the very center of corruption and vice, and Misson quickly falls under Caraccioli's spell. Caraccioli not only urges Misson into a life of piracy, he reveals himself to be "as ambitious as he was irreligious" (1728.2, 8 [388]). He eventually converts Misson to deism, which the author equates with a kind of atheism. The pair set off on a series of pirating adventures, engaging in moral and theological discussions even as they plunder ships.

Faller reads the Captain Misson story as a kind of "'sport,' an instance of freewheeling utopian *and* dystopian imagining from a single powerful premise."[15] In Faller's reading, the Misson story is a fantasia exploring what a life truly free from European hierarchies would actually look like: and it's not a promising picture. We may go further and suggest that the rise and fall of Libertatia demonstrates the inevitable progress of the masterless men or, perhaps, Libertatia is a kind of idealized Whig establishment, run along the lines of liberty, justice, and an eye for main chance, but ultimately doomed to fail as it has left itself vulnerable. Libertatia is the well-meaning but ultimately unsustainable eighteenth-century version of the hippie communes of the 1960s and 1970s, committed to a way of life beyond commerce, beyond social norms, and closer to an ideal state of nature, yet ultimately doomed to dissolve as its members eventually find their way back to Establishment life. There is an element of satire in all this: for all their high-minded social intentions, including the outlawing of slavery, the Liberi practice capital punishment and coerce the women of the island of Johanna to follow them back to Madagascar. Much is made of Misson's civility, his philosophical leanings, and his desire for an ideal system of government based on individual merit rather than family connection, and yet, the fledgling colony fails to defend itself, and everything ends in dissolution and squalor. As Henry Avery ended his days in poverty, duped by the very merchants he trusted and tried to emulate, so Misson ends his days lost at sea, with all trace of his grand experiment now obliterated. Misson's seeming greatness, and his sophisticated distinction between the man of liberty and the pirate, seems undermined by the inclusion of his story in a collection of pirate narratives. If the monster isn't caught, he may eventually be tamed. To be a successful pirate means having to reckon with one's own version of greatness.

BARTHOLOMEW ROBERTS: THE PIRATE AS LAWMAKER

If Henry Avery is the archetypal "successful pirate," he also embodies many of the qualities that help to define the *hostis humani generis.* Avery's career is about freedom—from national and natural laws, from national borders, even from material wealth itself. Johnson's unique anecdote about how Avery was defrauded of his wealth by English merchants more rapacious even than the great pirate himself somewhat misses the point: Avery died a free man, never caught by authorities—no small part of his mythology or his success.

However, as the arrangement of the chapters in 1724a demonstrates, Avery belongs to a different age from the rest of the pirates in *General History.* The archetypal successful pirate of the 1720s must surely be Bartholomew Roberts, whose success is measured in purely material terms. Moreover, Roberts himself was no anarchist; if anything, the pirates under his captaincy were subject to a strict, albeit more equitable, set of rules. Roberts's pirate code is perhaps his greatest legacy: the code is proof that piracy actually attempted to construct a more democratic society. It is also an inspiration for the fanciful "Pirate Code" of "Morgan and Bartholomew" in the third *Pirates of the Caribbean* film, there depicted as an actual set of written laws contained in an ancient oversized book. Yet there is more to Roberts's code than simply a set of rules: *General History* carefully constructs Roberts as the archetypal colonial entrepreneur, who conducts his business both among the sugar plantations of the Caribbean and in the heart of the slave trade, at the port of Cape Corso. Roberts is shown not simply plundering but negotiating with various merchant captains, being careful to seize the best prizes but willing to let less interesting prey go, if the captains will provide them with what they need. He and his crew undergo periods of great hardship, but are rewarded for their diligence with bigger and better prizes. Finally, Roberts himself is depicted in *General History* as the "gentleman of fortune" he claims himself to be: a fold-out engraving shows him, splendidly dressed, posed in front of his fleet of ships, flying his own flags. More than any other pirate in *General History,* Roberts engages the full range of transatlantic trade. No wonder Johnson devotes more than three times as much space in the book to his narrative.

We may focus our attention here on Bartholomew Roberts, certainly the pirate whose life and career are most thoroughly chronicled in the *General History.*

Roberts is the subject of the largest and most elaborate of the three engravings in *General History*, a fold-out page captioned "*Captain* Bartho. Roberts *with the two Ships, Viz the* Royal Fortune *and* Ranger, *takes 11 Sail in* Whydah *Road on the Coast of* Guiney, *January 11.th 172½*." The image is a triumphant spectacle, the moment of Roberts's greatest victory, surpassing even Avery's capture of the Moghul flagship. Roberts himself is posed and dressed as a gentleman. More to the point, he is posed as an owner of property. The ships behind him are his possessions: two versions of his flag are clearly visible on the foreground ships.[16]

Roberts's triumph as a victor over the eleven captured ships is presented as theatrically as any military leader's triumph. Interestingly, none of the depictions of pirates in *General History* show them as condemned criminals, even though such depictions were certainly common. Such a depiction does occur within the text, in the reprint of the trial account, but the theatricality of law depicted in that text is mirrored here by the theatricality of the pirate-hero Roberts. In fact, both the chapter devoted to Roberts and its addendum, the chapter on Thomas Anstis, are marked by theatricality and spectacle. It is here that the idea of the pirate as spectacular hero reaches its fullest form.

General History's ambivalent relationship with the law is most noticeable when we compare the original version of the Roberts chapter with its revised version in 1724b. As with many of the revised chapters in *General History*, the rewrites in the Roberts chapter are not consistent throughout. The bulk of the revision occurs in the early part of the chapter, with much being made of Roberts's election to the captaincy.[17] Some of the major revisions to this chapter in 1724b center on Roberts's early life as a man with "an honest Employ" (he was second mate aboard the *Princess* in 1719), and with an initial aversion to pirating. However, after his capture at the hands of Howel Davis, "He changed his Principles, as many besides him have done upon another Element, and perhaps for the same Reason too, *viz.* Preferment,—and what he did not like as a private Man he could reconcile to his Conscience as a Commander" (1724b, 208 [194]). The mildly sardonic view of the double standard of power carries through many of the comments of Roberts's command, culminating in the well-known mock trial that appears in the chapter on Thomas Anstis. Both the mock trial and Roberts's famous code of conduct are—read within the context of the larger story of Roberts's rise and fall, deeply problematic texts—less enlightening as genuine historical documents than as commentaries on the place of law in its performative and ritualistic aspects within pirate culture. In fact, one might even say that in Johnson's account of Roberts and, in what is essentially an ancillary chapter to Roberts, the account of Anstis, we can trace the construction of a pirate culture in its relationship to the law.

The story of Roberts's election in 1724b includes an interesting discourse on the nature of leadership. The entire scene, in fact, sets up some of the larger questions about power and greatness, to which we shall turn in chapter 6:

> There appear'd two or three Candidates among the select Part of them, that were distinguish'd by the Title of Lords, such were *Sympson, Ashplant, Anstis,* &c. and on canvassing this Matter, how shatter'd and weak a Condition their Government must be without a Head, since *Davis* had been remov'd, in the manner beforemention'd, my Lord *Dennis* propos'd, its said, over a Bowl to this Purpose.
>
> *That it was not of any great Signification who was dignify'd with Title; for really and in Truth, all good Governments had (like theirs) the supream Power lodged with the Community, who might doubtless depute and revoke as suited Interest or Humour. We are the Original of this Claim* (says he) *and should a Captain be so sawcy as to exceed Prescription at any time,* why down with Him! *it will be a Caution after he is dead to his Successors, of what fatal Consequence any sort of assuming may be. However, it is my Advice, that, while we are sober, we pitch upon a Man of Courage, and skill'd in Navigation, one, who by his Council and Bravery seems best able to defend this Commonwealth, and ward us from the Dangers and Tempests of an instable Element, and the fatal Consequences of Anarchy; and such a one I take* Roberts *to be. A Fellow! I think, in all Respects, worthy your Esteem and Favour.*
>
> This Speech was loudly applauded by all but Lord *Sympson,* who had secret Expectations himself, but on this Disappointment, grew sullen, and left them, swearing, *he did not care who they chose Captain, so it was not a Papist, for against them he had conceiv'd an irreconcileable Hatred, for that his Father had been a Sufferer in* Monmouth'*s Rebellion.* (1724b, 208–209 [194–195]).

For his part, Roberts immediately set about establishing order on his ships. Roberts's code—found only in the *General History*—has been reprinted many times, but it is worth reviewing in full here, especially as it is not always reprinted with Johnson's comments that precede and follow it.

> But to go back to Roberts, whom we left on the Coast of Caiana, in a grievous Passion at what Kennedy and the Crew had done; and who was now projecting new Adventures with his small Company in the Sloop; but finding hitherto they had been but as a Rope of Sand, they formed a Set of Articles, to be signed and sworn to, for the better Conservation of their Society, and doing Justice to one another; excluding all *Irish* Men from the Benefit of it, to whom they had an implacable Aversion upon the Account of Kennedy. How indeed Roberts could think that an Oath would be obligatory, where Defiance had been given to the Laws of God

and Man, I can't tell, but he thought their greatest Security lay in this, *That it was in their Interest to observe them while they kept in that abominable Combination.*[18]

The following, is the Substance of the Articles, as taken from the Pyrates own Informations.

I.

Every Man has a Vote in Affairs of Moment; has equal Title to the fresh Provisions, or strong Liquors, at any Time seized, and use them at pleasure, unless a Scarcity (no uncommon Thing among them) *make it necessary, for the good of all, to vote a Retrenchment.*

II.

Every Man to be called fairly in turn, by List, on Board of Prizes, because, (over and above their proper Share,) they were on these Occasions allowed a Shift of Cloaths: But if they defrauded the Company to the Value of a Dollar, in Plate, Jewels, or Money, MAROONING *was their Punishment.* This was a Barbarous Custom of putting the Offender on Shore, on some desolate or uninhabited Cape or Island, with a Gun, a few Shot, a Bottle of Water, and a Bottle of Powder, to subsist with, or starve. *If the Robbery was only between one another, they contented themselves with slitting the Ears and Nose of him that was Guilty, and set him on Shore, not in an uninhabited Place, but somewhere, where he was sure to encounter Hardships.*

III.

No Person to Game at Cards or Dice, for Money.

IV.

The Lights and Candles to be put out at eight o'Clock at Night: If any of the Crew, after that Hour, still remained inclined for Drinking, they were to do it on the open Deck; which *Roberts* believed would give a Check to their Debauches, for he was a sober Man himself, but found at length, that all his Endeavours to put an End to this Debauch, proved ineffectual.

V.

To keep their Piece, Pistols, and Cutlash clean, and fit for Service: In this they were extravagantly nice, endeavouring to outdoe one another, in the Beauty and Richness of their Arms, giving sometimes at an Auction (at the Mast,) 30 or 40 l. a Pair, for Pistols. These were slung in Time of Service, with different coloured Ribbands, over their Shoulders, in a Way peculiar to these Fellows, in which they took great Delight.

VI.

No Boy or Woman to be allowed amongst them. If any Man were sound seducing any of the latter Sex, and carried her to Sea, disguised, he was to suffer Death; so that when any fell into their Hands, as it chanced in the *Onslow*, they put a Centinel immediately over her to prevent ill Consequences from so dangerous an Instrument of Division and Quarrel; but then here lies the Roguery; they contend who shall be Centinel, which happens generally to one of the greatest Bullies, who, to secure the Lady's Virtue, will let none lye with her but himself.

VII.

To Desert the Ship, or their Quarters in Battle, was punished with Death, or Marooning.

VIII.

No striking one another on Board, but every Man's Quarrels to be ended on Shore, at Sword and Pistol, Thus; The Quarter-Master of the Ship, when the Parties will not come to any Reconciliation, accompanies them on Shore with what Assistance he thinks proper, and turns the Disputants Back to Back, at so many Paces Distance: At the Word of Command, they turn and fire immediately, (or else the Piece is knocked out of their Hands:) If both miss, they come to their Cutlashes, and then he is declared Victor who draws the first Blood.

IX.

No Man to talk of breaking up their Way of Living, till each had shared a 1000 l. If in order to this, any Man should lose a Limb, or become a Cripple in their Service, he was to have 800 Dollars, out of the publick Stock, and for lesser Hurts, proportionably.

X.

The Captain and Quarter-Master to receive two Shares of a Prize; the Master, Boatswain, and Gunner, one Share and a half, and other Officers, one and a Quarter.

XI.

> *The Musicians to have Rest on the Sabbath Day, but the other six Days and Nights, none without special Favour.*]
> These, we are assured, were some of *Roberts*'s Articles, but as they had taken Care to throw over-board the Original they had sign'd and sworn to, there is a great deal of Room to suspect, the remainder contained something too horrid to be disclosed to any, except such as were willing to be Sharers in the Iniquity of them; let them be what they will, they were together the Test of all new Comers, who were initiated by an Oath [taken on a Bible, reserv'd for that Purpose only,] and were subscrib'd to in Presence of the worshipful Mr. *Roberts*. And in Case any Doubt should arise concerning the Construction of these Laws, and it should remain a Dispute whether the Party had infring'd them or no, a Jury is appointed to explain them, and bring in a Verdict upon the Case in Doubt. (1724a, 169–172; passages in brackets are found only in 1724b, 230–233 [210–213])

While this purports to be an authentic document, Johnson is careful to note that there is no original available for comparison. Certainly, no such list of regulations can be found in the published trial account. A similar, though considerably shorter, list can be found in the chapter on George Lowther, although this list appears to have derived from one originally ascribed to Edward Low. Philip Ashton mentions articles to which he was required to subscribe on Low's ship. Refusal to sign these articles could be used as a legal defense against piracy: one who refused to assent to the articles might forfeit any of the material benefits of the pirates, but they also were likely to escape punishment, since they could claim themselves to be hostages, or unwilling participants in acts of piracy.

We see an example of this code in action in an astonishing scene some pages later. Having anchored in a secluded bay in the northern part of Hispaniola, Roberts's crew commenced to enjoy "their usual Debaucheries" to the extent that "Sobriety brought a Man under a Suspicion of being in a Plot against the Common-Wealth, and in their Sense, he was looked upon to be a Villain that would not be drunk" (1724a, 184–185 [222])—a somewhat astonishing assertion, given that Roberts himself is earlier described as "a sober Man" who had explicitly tried to curb his crew's drinking habits. Suspicion certainly fell on one Harry Glasby, Master of the *Royal Fortune*, whom Johnson describes as a "reserved sober Man." Glasby and two others are accused of attempting to desert the ship, whereupon an immediate trial is ordered. Johnson remarks about this pirate court:

> Here was the Form of Justice kept up, which is as much as can be said of several other Courts, that have more lawful Commissions for what they

> do.—Here was no feeling of Council, and bribing of Witnesses was a Custom not known among them; no packing of Juries, no torturing and wresting the Sense of the Law, for bye Ends and Purposes, no puzzling or perplexing the Cause, with unintelligible canting Terms, and useless Distinctions; nor was their Sessions burthen'd with numberless Officers, the Ministers of Rapine, and Extortion, with ill boding Aspects, enough to fright *Astrea* from the Court. (1724a, 185 [222])

Johnson delights in the irony of a serious—and inherently more honest—court set up to condemn a man for deserting a company of drunk pirates. At the same time, however, he makes it clear that this court, whatever its legitimacy, establishes its own authority through its own ritual and spectacle: a bowl of punch, along with pipes and tobacco, are set out for the judges. Articles of indictment are read against the accused, "upon a Statute of their own making," and sentence is pronounced swiftly, "the Letter of the Law being strong against them, and the Fact plainly proved." The punishment for desertion is, of course, death.

One more dramatic moment follows. One of the judges, the colorfully named Valentine Ashplant, argues clemency for Glasby. His motion is at first challenged, but, as Johnson describes the scene, Ashplant makes "another pathetical Speech": "*G—d—n ye Gentlemen, I am as good a Man as the best of you; d—n my S—l if ever I turned my Back to any Man in my Life, or ever will, by G—;* Glasby *is an honest Fellow, notwithstanding this Misfortune, and I love him; D—l d—n me if I don't: I hope he'll live and repent of what he has done; but d—n me if he must dye, I will dye along with him*" (1724a, 186 [223]). To make his point, Ashplant pulls out a pair of pistols, at which point his argument is deemed "well supported." The judges "thought it reasonable that *Glasby* should be acquitted; and so they all came over to his Opinion, and allowed it to be Law." During the actual pirate trials in March and April 1722, Glasby's escape attempts, his reluctance toward leading a pirate life, and his general civility would be key factors in his acquittal. Ashplant, for his part, was found guilty and hanged.

The wry commentary obscures what is, in fact, a serious, even somber, ritual enacted by a group of supposedly anarchic outlaws. Desertion—specifically mentioned as a capital offense in Roberts's own code of conduct—is clearly taken seriously, and the solemnity of the occasion is fittingly marked with a homemade "form of justice." Whereas the trial account in Anstis is clearly parodic, a spoof on the "form of justice" that routinely condemns all pirates to death, the trial here is deadly serious. Johnson's commentary even suggests that this trial, because it is not conducted by so-called legitimate courts, is free of the corruptions of the actual legal system: no witness tampering, no bribes, no obscuring legal cant—just a need to redress a legal wrong.[19]

Whether or not this trial is an authentic record of an event that actually took place aboard one of Roberts's ships, its presence in *General History* underlines the difference between Roberts's conduct toward both his crew and his captaincy and that of other pirate captains. Moreover, it reminds us that, freedom-loving and outside of the law though they may have been, pirates were not really anarchists—indeed, as Roberts's fleet grew and became more powerful, some need for a legal process revealed itself. In the final chapter, we will examine how the public spectacle of law helped construct the public celebrity of pirates. We will also look at how that status further contributed to the idea of pirate greatness. To steal a fortune and escape justice is certainly one kind of greatness; to give one's body over to the law to be transformed into a warning, a display of power, and a symbol of defiance all at once: that may be a more fitting kind of greatness for the pirate.

6

"THEIR CRIMES CONSPIR'D TO MAKE 'EM GREAT"

Piracy and the Spectacle of Law

THE HISTORY OF PIRACY is also the history of the failure by governments and law enforcement agencies to suppress piracy completely. For Cohen, the failure to eradicate monsters signifies a recurrence of the forces that have produced the monster to begin with: "The anxiety that condenses like green vapor into the form of the vampire can be dispersed temporarily, but the revenant by definition returns."[1] While some of the individuals whose stories are told in *General History* were arrested and tried, many escaped. The pirate is equally likely to vanish and slip into obscurity, like Edward Low, or to survive into the category of legend, like Henry Avery. Narratives themselves contradict each other, even for pirates who are caught: Walter Kennedy's capture, as we have seen, is attributed to betrayal by his sister, by a prostitute seeking revenge, or simply by his being in the wrong place at the wrong time. The details of John Gow's capture, told in narratives published within days of each other, may never be satisfactorily resolved. Many of the stories told in *General History* are ambiguous, subject to extensive revision between editions, fraught with questions, and ultimately untrustworthy as demonstrations of the ultimate triumph of law over lawlessness. Unlike the pirated Midwinter volume, *General History* does not pretend to be a celebration of the power of law and the futility of crime. As we shall see later, *General History* even challenges the spectacle of legal power itself, both by not showing executed pirates (as do other editions) and by including in its own text commentaries and parodies on the legal process itself. Escaped pirates, successful pirates, pirates whose stories are still "unfinished" because they are still at large, all feature just as prominently as those whose narratives are brought to the expected conclusion at the end of a gallows rope.

The idea that the pirate "always" escapes is not, of course, meant to be literally true of all pirates. Pirates were caught and did hang, but the larger drama that plays out, especially in the pages of *General History*, is that of the spectacle of law trying desperately to assert its authority in the face of a criminal element that cannot be entirely suppressed. Even the introduction to *General History*, designed to provide a sweeping overview of the rise of piracy in the Caribbean, ends inconclusively with narratives of Spanish pirates who "escape unmolested."

One of the most iconic and dramatic images of the fate that awaited pirates is that of Captain William Kidd, hanged at Execution Dock, Wapping, London, on 23 May, 1701. Kidd's death was spectacular in itself: the rope is said to have snapped the first time, and Kidd was forced to be hanged a second time. After his death, his body was encased in iron bands and suspended on a gibbet for three years, as a warning to sailors who would consider a life of piracy. The primary image we have of Kidd's suspended body can be found in a rather crude engraving that shows the unsurprisingly glum-looking pirate, still wearing sailor's garb, staring directly at the viewer as a cautionary icon, a visual counterpart to popular ballads and chapbook tales of punished criminals, urging its audience to reconsider following his example before it is too late (Figure 6.1).

The image itself is a rather belated addition to the Kidd legend. It derives from *The Pirates' Own Book* (1837), a broad-ranging compendium of pirate stories compiled by Charles Ellms. Ellms was a Philadelphia-based stationer with a keen interest in maritime tales: in addition to *The Pirates' Own Book*, Ellms published two collections of shipwreck stories. While Ellms's pirate tales range from "Danish and Norman" to Malay to early nineteenth-century Caribbean pirates—and is thus, in many ways, more of a general history of pirates than *General History* itself—the book, naturally, includes generous selections from Johnson. In many cases, Ellms has only lightly rewritten the same text found in either *General History* or *History and Lives*; the primary addition to these familiar texts is a copious supply of illustrations, including the one of the gibbeted body of Kidd.[2]

The image of Kidd in chains gestures toward a kind of authority that appears only intermittently in the *General History* and even then is portrayed ambiguously. Of the nineteen pirate narratives in 1724b, only eight conclude with a trial and execution.[3] Edward England, Edward Low, and Francis Spriggs were still at large in 1724, while others met their ends at the hands of their own crew, as was the case with John Evans, or even by their own hand, as was the case with the marooned George Lowther. And, of course, the legendary Henry Avery escaped legal punishment altogether, although in Johnson's account he does suffer what we might call karmic retribution. The law, we are to infer, is not necessarily all-powerful. At the same time, the image of the bodies of executed pirates dangling in groups from gallows became the enduring icon of the power of maritime justice: ghastly, brutal, and easy to comprehend.[4]

Capt. Kidd hanging in chains. p. 178.

Figure 6.1 "Capt. Kidd Hanging in Chains," from Ellms, *Pirates' Own Book* (1837). HathiTrust.

This idea is not surprising: as Douglas Hay has noted, the law asserted its authority in part through public spectacle, particularly the spectacle of the assizes. Processions, elaborate costumes, lengthy eloquent speeches, and—as a fitting climax—public executions: the assizes were, as Hay remarks, "the visible and elaborate manifestation of state power to be seen in the countryside, apart from the presence of a regiment."[5] At the same time, Hay points out, the spectacle of law was not always successful in its attempts to impress. The gap between the spectacle of justice and the actual exercise of justice seems to have been more acutely felt after the passage of the Waltham Black Act in 1723, when even judges began to balk at the wide range of new capital crimes. Ambivalence toward the spectacle of law is, of course, a common trope in satire, and the satirical depiction of law finds its way into the *General History*.

The gap between the reality of pirate life and its representation in *General History* opens up a larger discussion about why pirates embodied the anxieties of a nation dependent on transatlantic trade, and why the spectacle of law is portrayed so ambivalently in Johnson. We are used to seeing in popular culture the relationship between criminals and the state portrayed as a kind of cops-and-robbers binary, good guys versus bad guys, the forces of law and order actively fighting on behalf of the supposedly law-abiding majority to protect communities from the anarchic forces that threaten to undermine society itself. The criminal, in this paradigm, is a social deviant, outside and ultimately scornful of the laws that supposedly keep the social fabric intact. That paradigm, however, does not fit well with the way either citizens or pirates were actually perceived in the 1720s.

In the early eighteenth-century colonies, as scholars such as Mark Hanna and Rebecca A. Simon have pointed out, such a simple binary seriously misrepresents the relationship between pirates and colonists. As Simon notes, "The leaders of the Caribbean were not innocent bystanders or victims of piracy; they were often corrupted and proved to be as criminal as pirates before Admiralty Courts were firmly planted in the plantation colonies."[6] Simon cites the example of Read Elding, appointed governor of the Bahamas in 1699, but removed from his office in 1701 after he was charged with piracy. Certainly, before Woodes Rogers assumed governorship of the Bahamas, civil authorities actively collaborated with Caribbean pirates to bolster the colonial economy. In this context, then, the concept of a civil order that is demonstrably separable from crime is nonsense. It is not simply a matter of certain individuals corrupting a theoretically pure office; it is that the office itself, indeed the whole structure, is corrupt, at least by the standards of the colonial center. At the same time, as essays such as *Cato's Letters* and satirical works such as *The Beggar's Opera* make clear, the colonial center itself is rife with corruption, the main exception being that those in power can escape the public humiliation of legal process either by their high social status or, more likely, by simple bribery. The colonizer's law was used as a means of establishing and maintaining state power, and did not necessarily act in the best interest of the colonized. Pirates became irrelevant at the end of the 1720s not because of the state's "war on pirates," but because the colonies themselves began to enjoy more benefits from legitimate trade than they did from piracy. The legal spectacle, however, remained in place as a reminder of the presence of state power.

As we have seen, part of the strategy of eliminating piracy includes recasting the pirate as an anarchic monster, inimical to all laws and acting only in self-interest. Some of that image certainly pervades the *General History* narratives, but the image is offset by the strict control that is maintained aboard pirate ships. Defying official authority is one thing, but full-blown anarchy is a poor strategy for running even a pirate ship. The best and most successful pirates established their own legal codes, and are therefore not anarchists. Pirates are, in effect, a law unto themselves, which perhaps accords better with the mutable and uncertain status of masterless sailors: a pirate may operate legally as a privateer one day, only to discover the next that the letter of marque that sanctioned him has been voided. *General History* is well aware of this legal mutability, and participates in a critique of the legal system itself, with its cumbersome, seemingly arbitrary, mechanics.

That being said, the image of the pirate-as-monster cannot be entirely abandoned, and piracy, at least nominally, still needs to be portrayed as a heinous crime. One strategy is not to consider piracy as simply the unlawful taking of goods, but to see the unlawful taking of goods as a sign of a much more concerted rebellion against all authority. Thus, pirates who overpower their own captain and seize control of a ship are guilty primarily of mutiny, and therefore a form of petty treason; but their plundering of the ship's goods is also directly connected with their usurping of authority. Piracy is a crime against the state—against *all* states, in fact, which is how acts of piracy committed in international waters were able to fall under the jurisdiction of the British Admiralty.

The complex relationship between pirates and the legal system cannot be fully captured in the imagery employed by state authority. In fact, the iconic image of the gibbeted pirate distorts the reality of piracy, likely so as to fit pirate narratives into the existing genres of criminal narrative, which focus on individual highwaymen, housebreakers, or murderers. For example, *General History* seemingly highlights individual pirate captains, as if captaincy of a ship is the most important organizing feature of a pirate ship. However, unlike land-based criminals, pirates never worked alone, since the very nature of maritime life depended on collective action. A pirate ship, like other ships, cannot be sailed by a single individual. Solidarity and identification with one's ship, therefore, were paramount to pirate success. Sailors on captured ships were often invited—sometimes at the point of a sword—to join a pirate crew: the implication, of course, is that pirates stand together with able sailors against officers and ships' owners.

Rediker and Linebaugh have argued, as we have seen, that pirate ships were more egalitarian than merchant or naval vessels, even overlooking differences of race, language, or country of origin: an able hand was an able hand, and could expect much better treatment aboard a pirate vessel. Captains were elected democratically, or acclaimed by the crew, and their power was explicitly proscribed in the surviving articles, a few of which appear in the *General History*. All pirate captains knew that they could be deposed at any time, and one of the most striking features of the pirate community is how often new captains were made simply by having one pirate take command of a captured vessel, and either sail with his original crew or decide to go his own way. Splitting of crews no doubt saved more bloody mutinies, and pirate captains knew this as well.

Unlike its closest counterpart, Alexander Smith's *History of the Lives of the Most Noted Highway-Men* (1714, many times reprinted), or even the various pamphlet pirate narratives that sometimes provided Johnson with source material, *General History* hints at an attitude toward the law that is consistent with common satirical tropes of the day. While Johnson believes—and assumes his readers also believe—that robbery and murder are themselves unquestionably immoral acts, he is not concerned in *General History* with providing a moral narrative overlay to the lives he relates, except insofar as the definition of piracy as an illegal practice carries with it a certain moral focus. He can assert that pirates who have been captured and hanged have been brought to justice, but justice, for him, is not an act of divine retribution but an exercise in civil authority. Where pirates end up after they are hanged is really of no concern to him; what matters is that, once caught, pirates largely expect to be hanged. This perspective is consistent with what Douglas Hay identifies as a shift during the Hanoverian period in the center of moral authority from religion and the divine right of kings to the apparatus of the legal system: "With Stuarts plotting in Europe, Jacobitism suspected everywhere at home, and a lumpily unattractive German prince on the throne, English justice became a more important focus of beliefs about the nation and the social order."[7] Not surprisingly, then, laws, forms of legal authority, and reflections on the pragmatic imperative to suppress piracy and the need to punish pirates under the law, all feature prominently in the *General History*, certainly in the various editions of volume 1.

The movement from religious to legal morality has a political dimension, as we shall see, but it is useful for the moment to concentrate on how *General History* treats its subjects as constructions of law. One of the more remarkable features of the *General History* is the appended "Abstract of the Civil Law, and Statute Law now in Force, relating to Pyracy" (1724a, 317–320 [377–379]). This document sets out the terms by which one may be properly termed a pirate, and accordingly cites the various statutes that have been enforced since the time of Henry VIII designed to control piracy. While there is little that is surprising about the definitions of and punishments for piracy, the fact that such a document needs to be included in the *General History* at all merits some consideration. Even a casual reader of the book can glean the basic definitions of piracy from the various chapters. The point, however, is not to tell readers what pirates are, but to remind readers that piracy is a *legal* construction; that one becomes a pirate as a consequence of law. That may seem obvious to a modern reader, but, as Lincoln Faller has suggested, establishing what he calls "an etiology of crime" in the early eighteenth century was a difficult matter.[8] It seems to have been especially complicated in the matter of pirates, since it was not always clear against whom the offence had actually occurred: ship captains and crew were not owners of cargoes; in many cases, individuals were left unmolested even as their ships were plundered. The intensity of the need to eliminate these universal enemies is justified by the argument that pirates are primarily enemies to all trade—but while crimes against persons can be easily understood and quantified, and crimes against property be assessed on the basis of market value, how exactly does one evaluate transgressions against abstract concepts like trade and commerce?

GENERAL HISTORY AND THE THEATRICS OF LAW

The title page of the first edition of *General History* promises an account of "robberies and murders," but also "their policies, discipline, and government." There is much to unpack in those five nouns: taken together, they form a method for reading *General History* as a commentary on the legal system and the alternatives to British law that pirates embody. Significantly, "robbery" is conjoined with "murder," both crimes understood to be capital offenses. Attacks on property, whether in the form of personal articles or commercial goods, are attacks on the common good, and therefore require the very public punishment of execution. Unlike other pirate narratives—such as Charles Ellms's *Pirates' Own Book*—Johnson does not indulge in the details of the execution of his pirates. In fact, Johnson's presentation of the legal process is quite ambivalent. He takes the time reproduce the lengthy trial of Bartholomew Roberts and his crew, yet he also demonstrates the pirates' own satirical version of the criminal trial. Furthermore, in showing the "policies, discipline, and government" of pirate crews, Johnson suggests that piracy is a more complex phenomenon than simple robbery and murder:

pirates flout the laws of society, but they also develop their own laws, and even their own legal processes. The law, Johnson suggests, is not an infallible institution.

A similarly ambivalent reading of the law can be found in William Hogarth's *Industry and Idleness* series, which appeared two decades after *General History*, in 1747. Sean Shesgreen has noted that, behind the obviously didactic message in the narrative of "Industrious 'Prentice" Francis Goodchild's rise and "Idle 'Prentice" Tom Idle's fall lies a complex social commentary, that "represents the conditions of labor as oppressive, discouraging, and sometimes leading to compensatory conduct o disastrous consequences. It further suggests that success of a meteoric and spectacular nature is rare and not achieved on the basis of individual merit alone."[9] Goodchild succeeds because he negotiates a strategic marriage with his master's daughter; Tom Idle fails because seeks escape from the intolerable drudgery of his apprenticeship in alcohol, gambling, and, eventually, in robbery and murder. Idle is actually condemned by his former fellow apprentice—a fitting comment on the legal power that has come with Goodchild's material success. Finally, the ultimate fates of both apprentices are displayed in public spectacles—execution at Tyburn for Idle, the Lord Mayor's procession for Goodchild: the Industrious 'Prentice in his triumph as the symbol of order; the Idle 'Prentice in his notoriety as a condemned criminal. What is significant, however, is the similarity of the spectacle: the mob surrounding Goodchild's carriage seems indistinguishable from the mob that turned out to witness Idle's execution; there is an equal amount of chaos in both prints—curiously, the shadowy, almost subhuman figures that occupy the foreground of plate 12 in the series (Figure 6.2) draw attention away from the spectacle of order in behind. Note, too, that Tom Idle—or at least the narrative version of him—interpenetrates Goodchild's scene: in the lower right corner, a squat man is reading "A Full and True Account of ye Ghost of Thos Idle," a cheap pamphlet clearly designed to cash in on Idle's celebrity, a companion to the obligatory "Last Dying Speech & Confession" pamphlet the woman is hawking in the foreground of plate 11 (Figure 6.3).

Hogarth's prints are about the spectacle of law. In simple moral terms, the final processions of both Goodchild and Idle are visible markers of the rewards of industry and idleness. What matters is not so much that Idle is hanged as that he is hanged publicly, and the attendant rituals of the execution (Idle's public ride to Tyburn, his last-minute penitence, the printing and selling of a final confession, the release of the bird which will carry a message of confirmation of the execution, even the relative disorder of the crowd) are as much a part of the spectacle of law as the carriage, honor guard, sword of state, and dazzling clothing that are part of Goodchild's procession. However, that spectacle cannot disguise, and certainly cannot relieve, the squalor and the desperation of the masses of

Figure 6.2 “The Idle ’Prentice Executed at Tyburn,” William Hogarth, from *Industry and Idleness* (1747). British Museum.

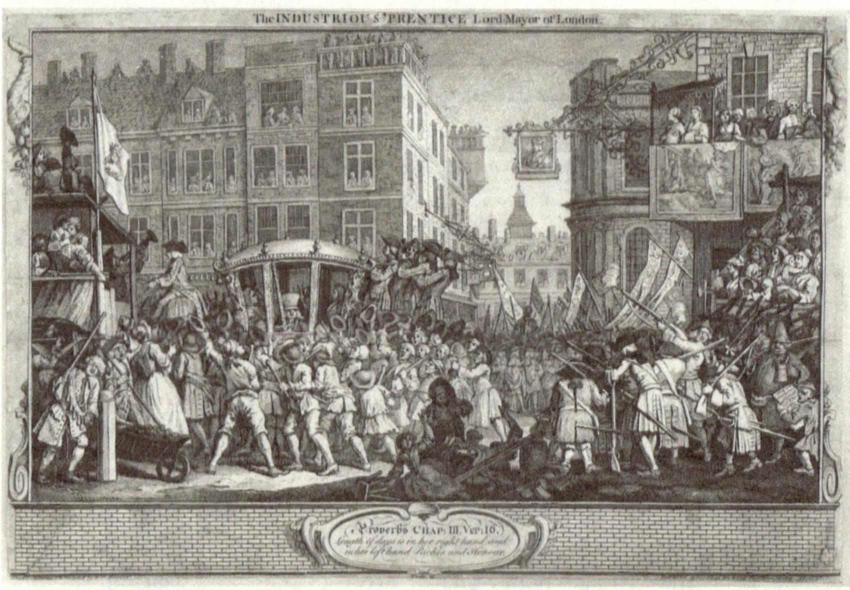

Figure 6.3 “The Industrious ’Prentice Lord Mayor of London,” William Hogarth, from *Industry and Idleness* (1747). British Museum.

workers who are the audience for the spectacle, both of the processions in the prints and the whole print series itself.

A similar ambivalence is at work in *General History*—especially in its view of law. A chapter added to 1724b, concerning Thomas Anstis, contains a remarkable bit of dialogue that purports to be an example of authentic pirate entertainment. This Anstis chapter itself is quite short—twelve pages in 1724b—and is curiously constructed. The opening and closing three pages provide the general narrative framework; one page is entirely devoted to the petition to King George for pardon; two pages comprise a description of the unnamed island where Anstis and his crew had taken refuge; and three pages comprise the text of the mock trial. The Anstis chapter shows the pirates both appropriating the language of legal discourse (in their sincere petition for pardon for having deserted Roberts), and parodying the form of law in the mock trial.

> They pass'd their Time here in Dancing, and other Diversions, agreeable to these sort of Folks; and among the rest, they appointed a Mock Court of Judicature to try one another for Pyracy, and he that was a Criminal one Day was made Judge another.—I had an Account given me of one of these merry Tryals, and as it appeared diverting, I shall give the Readers a short Account of it.
>
> The Court and Criminals being both appointed, as also Council to plead, the Judge got up in a Tree, and had a dirty Taurpaulin hung over his Shoulders; this was done by Way of Robe, with a Thrum Cap on his Head, and a large Pair of Spectacles upon his Nose: Thus equipp'd, he settled himself in his Place, and abundance of Officers attending him below, with Crows, Handspikes, &c. instead of Wands, Tipstaves, and such like.—The Criminals were brought out, making a thousand four Faces; and one who acted as Attorney-General opened the Charge against them; their Speeches were very laconick, and their whole Proceedings concise. We shall give it by Way of Dialogue.
>
> *Attorn. Gen.* An't please your Lordship, and you Gentlemen of the Jury, here is a Fellow before you that is a sad Dog, a sad sad Dog; and I humbly hope your Lordship will order him to be hang'd out of the Way immediately.—He has committed Pyracy upon the High Seas, and we shall prove, an't please your Lordship, that this Fellow, this sad Dog before you, has escap'd a thousand Storms, nay, has got safe ashore when the Ship has been cast away, which was a certain Sign he was not born to be drown'd; yet not having the Fear of hanging before his Eyes, he went on robbing and ravishing Man, Woman and Child, plundering Ships Cargoes fore and aft, burning and sinking Ship, Bark and Boat, as if the Devil had been in him. But this is not all, my Lord, he has committed worse Villanies than all these, for we shall prove, that he has been guilty of drinking Small-Beer; and your Lordship knows, there never was a sober Fellow but

> what was a Rogue.—My Lord, I should have spoke much finer than I do now, but that, as your Lordship knows our Rum is all out, and how should a Man speak good Law that has not drank a Dram.—However, I hope, your Lordship will order the Fellow to be hang'd.
>
> *Judge*.—Hearkee me, Sirrah,—you lousy, pittiful, ill-look'd Dog; what have you to say why you should not be tuck'd up immediately, and set a Sun-drying like a Scare-crow?—Are you guilty, or not guilty?
>
> *Pris.* Not guilty, an't please your Worship.
>
> *Judge.* Not guilty! say so again, Sirrah, and I'll have you hang'd without any Tryal.
>
> *Pris.* An't please your Worship's Honour, my Lord, I am as honest a poor Fellow as ever went between Stem and Stern of a Ship, and can hand, reef, steer, and clap two Ends of a Rope together, as well as e'er a He that ever cross'd salt Water; but I was taken by one George Bradley [the Name of him that sat as Judge,] a notorious Pyrate, a sad Rogue as ever was unhang'd, and he forc'd me, an't please your Honour.
>
> *Judge.* Answer me, Sirrah,—How will you be try'd?
>
> *Pris.* By G—and my Country.
>
> *Judge.* The Devil you will.—Why then, Gentlemen of the Jury, I think we have nothing to do but to proceed to Judgment.
>
> *Attor.* Gen. Right, my Lord; for if the Fellow should be suffer'd to speak, he may clear himself, and that's an Affront to the Court.
>
> *Pris.* Pray, my Lord, I hope your Lordship will consider—
>
> *Judge.* Consider!—How dare you talk of considering?—Sirrah, Sirrah, I never consider'd in all my Life.—I'll make it Treason to consider.
>
> *Pris.* But, I hope, your Lordship will hear some Reason.
>
> *Judge.* D'ye hear how the Scoundrel prates?—What have we to do with Reason?—I'd have you to know, Raskal, we don't sit here to hear Reason;—we go according to Law.—Is our Dinner ready?
>
> *Attor.* Gen. Yes, my Lord.
>
> *Judge.* Then heark'ee, you Raskal at the Bar; hear me, Sirrah, hear me.—You must suffer, for three Reasons; first, because it is not fit I should sit here as Judge, and no Body be hang'd.—Secondly, you must be hang'd, because you have a damn'd hanging Look:—And thirdly, you must be hang'd, because I am hungry; for know, Sirrah, that 'tis a Custom, that whenever the Judge's Dinner is ready before the Tryal is over, the Prisoner is to be hang'd of Course.—There's Law for you, ye Dog.—So take him away Goaler.
>
> This is the Tryal just as it was related to me; the Design of my setting it down, is only to shew how these Fellows can jest upon Things, the Fear and Dread of which, should make them tremble. (1724b, 335–338 [292–294])

This is delightful satire. It's easy to imagine a group of ragged, rum-sodden pirates laughing uproariously at the gallows humor and reveling in the ability to thumb their noses at an authority they had cause to fear, but could never respect. At the same time, the whole piece seems a little too well contrived to be truly authentic. It incorporates many familiar satirical tropes, such as the variation on the maritime proverb, "He that is born to be hanged need not fear drowning," and the assertion that the accused must hang because the trial is interfering with the judge's dinner—a grim joke echoed in Pope's lines, "The hungry Judges soon the Sentence sign, / And Wretches hang, that Jury-men may dine."[10] At the same time, the mock-trial forms a fitting counterpart to the serious shipboard trial of Harry Glasby and his associates, and the genuine trial recorded at length in the Roberts chapter (1724a, 185 [222]), as seen in chapter 5.

A good deal of the social history of the early eighteenth century has focused on the relationship between land-based criminals and the law. The remarkable rise of capital offenses centered on theft of or damage to property has been the subject of a considerable number of important studies that, collectively, present a thorough, nuanced picture of crime and punishment during this period.[11] Hay notes that conviction for a capital crime against property did not always mean a death sentence: in many cases, if the convicted criminal could successfully plead for mercy, judges were often willing to grant pardons, especially if they could demonstrate respectability of character or could show they had come from a "good family."[12] Executions did, of course, occur with great regularity, but the demonstration of benevolence and mercy was, Hay argues, as much an effective instrument of maintaining class stability and state power as was the gruesome spectacle of public hanging.

The tendency toward mercy and leniency for "respectable" criminals did not, however, extend to pirates, who were, by definition, outside any class or social structure and, therefore, never respectable. We can see a clear example of this in the unusual case of Stede Bonnet. Unlike many pirates of this period, who had taken to piracy as a means of escaping the unenviable life of a simple tar, Bonnet "was a Gentleman of good Reputation," was "Master of a plentiful Fortune," and "had the Advantage of a liberal Education" (1724a, 60 [95]). Bonnet was, therefore, the kind of criminal to whom what Hay calls "the magic word"—"respectable"—could be applied, which in many cases was enough to secure a pardon.[13] At the same time, Bonnet's respectability should have been enough to forestall his inevitably fatal attraction to a life of crime. Bonnet, Johnson speculates, must have been suffering some kind of mental disorder for him to consider piracy if not driven by necessity; the second edition further adds the suggestion that this "Disorder . . . is said to have been occasioned by some Discomforts he found in a married State" (1724b, 91 [95]), but otherwise attempts no deeper understanding of why the educated and financially secure Bonnet should have become a pirate.

Bonnet was, according to Johnson, a remarkably inept pirate—or at least, an inept pirate captain. Having no prior naval experience, he failed to gain the respect of his crew, and quickly lost his command to Blackbeard.[14] Even when he was in charge of his own ship, his quartermaster seems to have had more actual power in the daily running of the ship. In keeping with what Linebaugh and Rediker in *The Many-Headed Hydra* refer to as the "hydrarchy" of the eighteenth-century pirate ship, both Bonnet's failure to command, and his crew's rejection of his inherent right to lead based on birth, education, or wealth, suggest that what was most dangerous about pirate ships was not their attacks upon trade but their inversion of the social order. Bonnet's relatively elevated status, however, was not enough to secure him a reprieve from the gallows, either: he was hanged on 10 December 1718.

The Stede Bonnet chapter offers us our first taste of legal spectacle in *General History*, in the form of a summary of the opening proceedings of the trial of 28 October 1718, and the judge's lengthy speech to Bonnet before he passes sentence. These passages, along with the bulk of the material concerning Colonel Thomas Rhett, are essentially lifted verbatim from *The Tryals of Major Stede Bonnet and Other Pirates* (1719), a published account of the trial. While these passages may have been included out of expediency—Johnson had them at hand and decided to pad out his chapter with them—they also offer a glimpse into the inherent theatricality of the criminal trial. The names of the members of the court and the prisoners are all printed at the outside, like dramatis personae; testimonies and cross-examinations are recorded as dramatic dialogue; even the court's actions are painstakingly detailed, as stage directions. While Johnson provides a much fuller trial transcript in the Bartholomew Roberts chapter, the excerpts of Bonnet's trial are enough to suggest the dramatic parallels.

The gruesome image of Stede Bonnet dangling from the gallows never appeared in any of the English editions of *General History*: the image is the product of a Dutch artist's imagination, and in that we may find some useful or interesting readings (Figure 6.4). Unlike Hogarth's well-assembled morality play, the Bonnet print in *Die Engelsche Zee-Rovers* shows little regard for any commentary beyond the spectacle of the hanging itself. In fact, what is most striking about this image is its *un*ceremoniousness. We see Bonnet just at the moment when the cart supporting him is driving off, leaving his body to dangle a few feet above the ground. The small crowd gathered around the gibbet seems both orderly and curiously disengaged: the figure directly behind Bonnet watches with what appears to be an expression of amusement; one woman turns away slightly, but not with any apparent horror. No bleachers, no last-confession hawker, no puppies tossed into

Figure 6.4 Stede Bonnet's execution, from *Historie der Engelsche Zee-Rovers* (1725). KB Nationale Bibliotheek, Da Haag.

the crowd, no bird messenger: the focus is squarely on the punishment, on the raw display of power.

Like all crime narratives, the story of Bonnet's transgressions and his eventual punishment conforms to a pattern that glosses over the more complex relationship between criminals and the law that existed in the first decades of the eighteenth century. Since most pirates were, unlike Bonnet, from the bottom of the social scale, their particular relationship to property, money, and civil authority must be understood if we are to understand fully how Johnson presents them in the *General History*. At the same time, it is essential to understand that the law itself, its formal expression, and its universal applicability were the subjects of considerable debate during the decade in which *General History* first appeared, fueled in no small part (as we have seen) by the fallout from the South Sea Bubble and by the controversy stirred up by the 1723 republication of Bernard Mandeville's *Fable of the Bees*, as discussed in chapter 4.

One lasting effect of the spectacle of law was perhaps the opposite of what lawmakers intended: condemned and publicly hanged criminals were forever removed from the anonymity that pervaded working-class life. Law-abiding sailors could toil for years in absolute obscurity; able seamen were little more than replaceable parts that were needed to sail merchant ships. In fact, as Rediker has suggested, it is the sailor's very lack of skill, their lack of membership in any guild, and their essential masterlessness that made them attractive to the merchant navy: they were, he offers, a kind of forerunner of the proletarian factory-laborer of later in the century.[15] We will never know the names or the stories of the thousands of sailors—Rediker estimates between "25,000 and 40,000 at any one time between 1700 and 1740"[16]—who offered their bodies and their lives to the merchant service. We do, however, thanks to the spectacle of law, know quite a few pirates: their names, their ages, even their towns of residence, appear frequently in trial accounts; their images grace the pages of pamphlets, broadside ballads, and other popular publications of the time. Their notoriety was parlayed into a kind of celebrity—a new type of public image related to, but not quite consistent with, the older idea of Fame.

Almost inevitably, then, the elevation of the pirate into a celebrated public figure—a celebrity—drew comments from moralists on the degradation of fame in the 1720s, and the rise of the morally corrupt as a new kind of role model. Among Tory writers, the key figure was, of course, Robert Walpole. However, as we shall see, the suggestion that the morally corrupt could aspire to be Great Men, and that Great Men now may include the morally corrupt, was part of a larger discourse in the 1720s that did not necessarily include Walpole or the nascent "Robinocracy." Certainly, the discourse reaches its literary peak in John Gay's

The Beggar's Opera, but Gay, wittingly or unwittingly, is drawing on tropes that had already been established in *General History*. Gay even draws parallels between so-called Great Men, piracy, and colonialism: in the *Beggar's Opera* sequel, *Polly* (1729), a group of pirates—Macheath's new gang—are discussing their future and their larger ambitions. One pirate, Culverin, notes that "Our Chief, *Morano* [Macheath's disguise as a Black pirate], had never been the Man he is, had he not been train'd up in *England*. He has told me, that from his Infancy he was the favourite Page of a Lady. He had a Genius, too, above Service; and like us, ran into higher Life: And, indeed, tho' he is black, no body has more the air of a great man."[17] However, the pirates lament that Morano/Macheath has abandoned his own "greatness" by taking up with Jenny Diver, who thwarts his larger ambitions. Their plan, then, is to get rid of Jenny by whatever means necessary, and then the gang can proceed on its imperial goals.

Those goals include dividing up parts of the world for their possession, as if they were playing a real-life game of *Risk*: Hacker and Capstan debate over which of them should possess Mexico, while Laguerre wishes to keep Cuba. Culverin notes that "Captain *Morano* to be sure will chuse *Peru*; that's the Country of Gold, and all your great Men love Gold."[18] The parody of the empire builder is clear: the pirates aim to become landowners and men of status rather than simply wealthy pirates; Macheath, as a Great Man, has ambitions for both. Moreover, the shape of empires, the delineations of borders and the formation of states, is created in an abstract setting: a group of men staring at a map and drawing convenient lines, with regard only to what each wants from his parcel of land. Although the pirates mimic the colonizers in this scene, they also unwittingly draw attention to the fact that, for both pirates and sailors, these lands are not simply lines on a map, but actual places which they have seen. They have experienced empire in a way that no London-based merchant has. The spaces that become for readers Treasure Neverland are not simply collections of resources, but spaces inhabited by people, by cultures, languages, traditions, and mythologies that demand to be acknowledged, if not always valued or respected.

The pirates' mimicking of European heads of state fussing over territories is a variation of the great man idea that Gay had explored with Macheath in *The Beggar's Opera*. Macheath's criminal "greatness" imitates those of legitimate statesmen, especially Robert Walpole. Here, the pirates display their own colonial and political ambitions, the same ambitions we saw attributed to Walter Kennedy earlier. At the same time, the pirates mistake political opportunity in the colonies for genuine status: by the reckoning of British merchants, colonial governors and even plantation owners could never be more than "Creoles," by which they meant men who profited from colonial trade, who got their hands dirty on colonial soil in the process. The Creole, like the pirate, dwells within the margins of civilization, and may be equally monstrous.

The pirates' division of the map is a geopolitical grotesque, as the sight of Macheath engaging in formal dancing with the prostitutes in *The Beggar's Opera* is a social grotesque, and for the same reason: it is an appropriation of upper-class privilege by the lower classes, as outrageous as an illiterate sailor taking on the title of Captain, or a pirate captain daring to sail under his own authority and his own flag. Such grotesques bring us into the realm of the monstrous, but also remind us that colonialism, especially in its creation of the "global citizen" and its distinction between citizenship in the center and at the peripheries ("Briton" versus "Creole"), reveals what Roy Osamu Kamada calls "the capricious and haphazard logics animating the economic and juridical distinction of citizenship and belonging."[19] For pirates, mapping and owning colonial spaces bring together aspects of both the Great Man and the Monster.

The transition from Monster to Great Man is one of the central points of *General History*, and is itself a commentary on the perversity of the decade in which the book was published. Like Macheath, like other criminals celebrated in print, the successful pirate exhibits qualities usually associated with classical exempla of "greatness," the noble figures whom all schoolboys would have encountered in Plutarch's *Lives*. However, the law—itself an uncertain, sometimes monstrous entity at this time—ultimately reasserts piratical monstrosity in the public sphere, both by trial and, more demonstrably, by the very public spectacle of execution. While *General History* strives to construct a nuanced, multifaceted view of piracy and pirates, in the world of law, the pirate must and can only ever be *hostis humani generis*, because, as so many were quick to point out in the 1720s, the law only eliminates Monsters, it never touches Great Men.

CONCLUSION

IN 2003, A TRIO OF SWEDES LAUNCHED a file-sharing website that allowed users to download music, films, computer games, and other large collections of files for free, bypassing copyright and, in effect, allowing users to steal content off the Internet. This website, the Pirate Bay, has been shut down several times by various government authorities, but the sheer number of mirror sites that exist guarantees that the Pirate Bay will be available indefinitely in one form or another; in fact, it bills itself as "the galaxy's most resilient BitTorrent site."

For its logo, the Pirate Bay chose the silhouette of an eighteenth-century sailing ship; one of its sails has emblazoned an image of a cassette tape over crossed bones, an old logo from a 1980s campaign to stamp out home taping and sharing of copyrighted music. Embedded within the Pirate Bay's logo is a capsule history of views of piracy: the cassette-and-crossbones image signifies home taping as monstrous activity, a threat to legitimate commerce, since the caption that ran with the image, printed on vinyl album covers in the 1980s, read, "Home taping is killing music. And it's illegal." However, the Pirate Bay wittily repositions the symbol—both of piracy and of the "death" of the music industry—to signify its defiance of such claims. To emblazon the image on a ship in full sail adds an air of adventure, of gallant defiance, emblematic of another time and place—of a measure of greatness in making downloaded files free for everyone to share.

In effect, the Pirate Bay embodies many of the features of piracy I have outlined in the previous chapters, the features Charles Johnson highlights in his *General History*. The site earnestly embraces its status as the enfant terrible of commerce, offering free content to users in the hard-to-police waters of the Internet; its appropriation of the anti-home-taping logo gestures toward the fear articulated in pirate trials, that piracy is a genuine threat to commerce itself. Its resilience recalls the monstrous aspects of piracy: the adversary that cannot be killed, forever dwelling on the margins of legitimate commerce, boldly flaunting its success and its survival in the face of numerous attempts to obliterate it altogether. In reality, the three men who launched the Pirate Bay have all been arrested and have been fined or even sentenced to jail time, but their rogue website persists as a reminder that, even in the twenty-first century, piracy has a place in the world, and is still capable of causing even the same kind of anxiety it generated in the 1720s.

The spirit of pirate rebelliousness, along with the curious mixture of admiration and ambivalence, continues to feed our fascination with pirates. Pirates are almost always brash, larger-than-life figures, flamboyantly dressed, with exotic speech patterns and more than a suggestion of having done unspeakable things in the name of acquiring gold. They are, at once, monstrous and magnificent. At the same time, that image of pirates derives from a specific historical period—the early decades of the Georgian era—when there was considerable ambivalence about the long-term social and political effects of both the Financial Revolution and colonial expansion. Britain's place on the world stage, its growing empire in both North America and India, and its increasing dependence on the risky and often perilous undertaking of global commerce caused, at least on paper, a critical examination of commerce and empire. The pirate, as we have seen, serves to embody both the dangers and the potential rewards of such undertakings. The pirate is both the monster and the hero of global commerce.

At the same time, as the Pirate Bay example proves, the pirate must always be curtailed, tamed, or otherwise controlled. The most obvious curtailment is in the form of law: piracy is a crime, and criminals must be punished, whether by spectacular public executions, as in the eighteenth century, or by having their website shut down. At the same time, as Jeffrey Jerome Cohen reminds us, "the monster always escapes."[1] Pirates, too, may have their lifeless bodies displayed by the state as a sign of victory and as a warning, but the pirate has never been entirely suppressed, and the pirate returns, even in our own time, to play the same role of the Monster of legitimate commerce.

The initial motivation for this book began with a question: Why do we always associate pirates with the eighteenth century? In one way, the answer is not necessarily complex: one can easily point to the lasting cultural influence of *Treasure Island*, which relied on Johnson's *General History* as a source. That question, however, soon generates a second: How much of Johnson's perspective on pirates have we absorbed into our own contemporary view? Johnson displays a mixture of admiration and ambivalence with his pirate subjects, in effect providing the theoretical lens through which we view them. What is often not noted, however, is that Johnson's lens derives from larger questions about the ethics of colonial commerce, the administration of justice in the early eighteenth century, and Britain's heavy dependence on colonial trade—in particular the slave trade—for its prosperity and its high level of civilization.

What emerges, then, is a view of *General History* as a book that is less about pirates qua pirates, and more a book about ways to read pirates. Charles Johnson—he, she, or they—presents us not with a "history" but with an anatomy, a set of portraits of pirate types, who have in common that they embody anxieties about Britain's identity as a burgeoning world power. Many of the individual stories, taken by themselves, can seem repetitive, even dull: a pirate captain sets out, plunders certain ships, voyages to various places, and is either captured, dies, or vanishes and remains at large. Certain colorful figures do emerge, and are worthy of individual study, but the real impact of *General History* remains its effect in the aggregate: it is the book as a whole that constructs what we understand to be the pirate, both Monster and Great Man.

In this book I have attempted to place Johnson's work in a wider context, to regard it not so much as a quick-sale collection of true-crime stories as a commentary on the new kind of commerce that had developed since the War of the Spanish Succession and the rise of Robert Walpole and the Whigs to political power. By considering *General History* within this larger context, I hope to have demonstrated that Johnson, whoever he or they may have been, understood piracy to be a complex phenomenon, densely intertwined with concerns about colonial commerce, slavery, justice, and political power.

General History emerged at a time when the rise of global commerce also meant the rise of a new kind of heroic figure: the international trader, the overseas merchant, taking considerable risks to bring exotic luxury good to Britain, to expand the influence of Britain into the wider world. Yet the overseas merchant did not always act heroically. Central to the success of overseas trade lay the slave trade, the backbone of the plantation system, which generated massive revenue from sugar, rum, molasses, and other commodities, while at the same time condemning thousands of people to life of disenfranchisement, degradation, endless labor, brutal punishment, and humiliation. We are only beginning to understand how significant the Black Atlantic was to the transformation of Europe into the modern world, to the Enlightenment and its focus on developing the potential of the individual, and even to the flourishing of culture that continues to impress lovers of Baroque and Classical art. Within such a morally ambiguous world, *General History* reads as a mirror held up to the face of heroic commerce. The honest merchant, the slave trader, the plantation owner, and the pirate: all are equal aspects of global commerce, and each has a necessary part to play.

We are, I think, still learning how to come to terms with the effects of global commerce and, specifically, the ethical parameters by which global commerce should operate. The high standard of living enjoyed today by Europe and many former settler colonies masks a global economic disparity that shows no sign of abating. It is worth remembering that, as Europe engaged in global commerce in the eighteenth century, many of the living conditions we associate with "third world" countries were endemic in the supposedly most advanced countries; as Europe modernized, living conditions gradually improved—but the problem of how to sustain vast profitable markets while making overseas goods affordable did not actually get solved. Instead, the same problems simply got offloaded to other countries, including many rarely visited by the people who use the goods they manufactured. The slavery necessary to sustain the eighteenth-century plantation system did not actually disappear; it simply transformed into sweatshops. The idea of "ethical" or "fair trade" commerce as an alternative to mainstream business would have seemed odd to Defoe. In his view, all commerce should be ethical, all trade should be fair—the successful merchant should not resemble the successful pirate.

In its own way, Johnson's *General History* engages with questions of ethical global commerce by engaging with the figures who are supposed to be the merchant's most fearsome adversary. The ambiguities, uncertainties, and mysteries of *General History* become more acute and intriguing the more it is separated into its various incarnations, and compared diligently both with other pirate narratives of the 1720s and with the economic and political writing that emerged from the same literary milieu. Far from being a single-authored, carefully researched source that stands as a definitive account of piracy during the Golden Age, the *General History* reveals a text—or set of texts—struggling to redefine what pirates and piracy might actually mean for its immediate audience. While there was no shortage of newspaper reports of piracy in the early 1720s, and while other essays and tracts on pirates neatly align their subjects with conventional moral wisdom, the *General History* is rarely satisfied with such neat moralizing, and even suggests its own ways of subverting what moral wisdom it does impart.

The moral ambiguity seen in the *General History* parallels the paper debate in the closing years of George I's reign. It is significant, I think, that both Whig (if one sees Defoe's hand) and Jacobite (if we see Mist's) perspectives color these narratives: the *General History*, as a whole, constitutes a snapshot of the state of the global economy at the beginning of the eighteenth century. It provides a commentary on ideals of commerce that had become corrupted and perverted by the rapacity of investors—the same kind of corruption that produced the South Sea Bubble. At the same time, it refuses to admit easy answers or strict moralizing. One need only compare the *General History* with the sermons reprinted in Joel Baer's *British Piracy in the Golden Age* to note the difference in tone.[2] Even other books devoted to the lives of land criminals draw clear moral conclusions from the example of the subjects of these biographies. In his preface to *The History of the Lives of the Most Noted Highway-Men, Foot-Pads, House-Breakers, Shop-lifts and Cheats* (1714), Alexander Smith explicitly states:

> We do not expose the Memory of these Offending Wretches with any design of making them the Sport and Ridicule of vain Idle Fellows, who only laugh at the Misfortunes of such dying Men; but rather revive their manifold Transgressions for a Mean to instruct and convert the wicked and prophane Persons of this licentious Age. (iv–v)

In the same way, the author of the volume that mostly plagiarized the *General History*, the anonymous *History and Lives of all the Most Notorious Pirates* (1725), explicitly states in the preface that the book is designed

> to caution the unwary Mariner against the Temptations he may meet with at Sea, as also to shew the Merchant what Perils poor Sailors daily undergo to make them Rich and Great, being not only every Moment liable to the Dangers of the Seas; but what is worse, to the Cruelty and inhuman Treatment of savage and unrelenting Pirates: Who are a sort of Wretches that defy Providence in all his Works, altho' they are in a more peculiar manner preserved by it. (v)

The *General History*, more in spirit with fictions than with sermons, largely avoids such didactic purposes. Instead, perhaps already aware that the Golden Age of Piracy has passed, volume 2 lets this remark, from Horace's *Ars Poetica* (343), stand as its final advice: "Omne tulit punctum, qui miscuit utile dulci"—"The one who combines profit with pleasure wins every vote." Profit and pleasure: the goal of every successful person of business as well as every successful pirate. Horace's advice to writers thus becomes a classical echo of Bartholomew Roberts's own motto: "A merry life and a short one."

General History ultimately assumes its place within a larger debate about global commerce and ethics. Its central concern, displayed in the pirate's double role as Monster and Great Man, is how global commercial activity can retain its moral integrity and how global merchants can embody the principles of civility and politeness within a sphere that values ruthlessness, dissembling, and winning at all costs. While Defoe, Mandeville, and others debated the implications of "profit and pleasure" as the ideals of *Homo economicus*, and agonized over the morality of material success, it is to the credit of *General History* that it does not shy away from showing us how those ideals play out in a less respectable, but far more fascinating form.

APPENDIX

Editions of *General History*

Note: "Gosse" refers to the relevant entries in Philip Gosse, *A Bibliography of the Works of Capt. Charles Johnson.*

First Edition (1724a) (Gosse 1)

London: Charles Rivington, 1724
Available:

New York: Garland, 1972 (Foundations of the Novel series)
Eighteenth-Century Collections Online (ECCO)

Second Edition (1724b) (Gosse 2)

London: Thomas Warner, 1724
Available:

ECCO
Internet Archive (two copies):
https://archive.org/details/generalhistoryof00john (Wetmore Collection)
https://archive.org/details/generalhistoryof00defo (Boston Public Library)
East Carolina University:
https://digital.lib.ecu.edu/17001

Third Edition (1725) (Gosse 3)

London, Thomas Warner, 1725
Available:

ECCO

Fourth Edition (1728) (Gosse 7)

London, Thomas Woodward, 1728
Available:

Volume 1
Google Books (University of Chicago)
Volume 2
East Carolina University (https://digital.lib.ecu.edu/17002)

Highwaymen (1734) (Gosse 9)

London, J. Janeway
Available:

ECCO

Highwaymen (1742) (Gosse 12)

Birmingham: R. Walker
Available:

Internet Archive
https://archive.org/details/generaltruehisto00defo

Highwaymen (1772) (Gosse 16)

Portsmouth: R. Carr
Available:

Google Books (partial)

NOTES

PREFACE

1. Stevenson to William Ernest Henley, August 1881, in *Letters of Robert Louis Stevenson*, ed. Sidney Colvin (New York: Charles Scribner's Sons, 1911), 2:60.
2. Stevenson, *Letters*, 2:261.
3. It is unclear which edition of the *General History* Stevenson would have seen: very likely it was not an exact reprint of any of the editions of 1724–1728. More likely, Stevenson used either one of the editions that combined *General History* with biographies of land criminals (one such was published by Thomas Johnson in 1850), or one of the many editions which appeared throughout the eighteenth and nineteenth centuries that selected and edited Johnson's original text.
4. Stevenson, *Letters*, 2:260.
5. Arne Bialuschewski, "Daniel Defoe, Nathaniel Mist, and the *General History of the Pyrates*," *Papers of the Bibliographic Society of America* 98, no. 1 (2004): 31.

INTRODUCTION

1. The language-learning app Mango Languages features a course in "Pirate," which is essentially a course in Hollywood-style maritime slang spoken with a Robert Newton–inspired West Country accent. "Arrr," of course, features prominently.
2. Neil Rennie, *Treasure Neverland: Real and Imaginary Pirates* (Oxford: Oxford University Press, 2014). The Golden Age of Piracy technically extends from about 1680, with the rise of the buccaneers in the Caribbean, to about 1730. Within this time span, however, were several waves of pirate activity, the last running from about 1713, at the end of the War of the Spanish Succession, to 1730: this is the period Johnson covers, and is the period understood here by the term "golden age."
3. This title, which will be referred to as *General History* throughout, appeared under slightly different titles in each of its four main editions from 1724 to 1728. The first edition reads *A General History of the Robberies and Murders of the Most Notorious Pyrates*; this was shortened in the second and third editions to simply *A General History of the Pyrates*. The fourth edition reduced the title still further, and made an important change of article: *The History of the Pyrates*. In each of these changes, the book moves away from a salacious collection of lurid crime stories and moves closer to establishing itself as an "official" history.
4. Hans Turley, *Rum, Sodomy, and the Lash: Piracy, Sexuality, and Masculine Identity* (New York: New York University Press, 1999).
5. Nancy Armstrong, *Desire and Domestic Fiction: A Political History of the Novel* (New York: Oxford University Press, 1987), 59.
6. Joel H. Baer, writing on Defoe's use of pirates, suggests that Defoe found piracy "unique, complex, and ambiguous as well as hateful." Baer, writing before P. N. Furbank and W. R. Owens's deattribution (in *The Canonisation of Daniel Defoe* [New Haven: Yale University Press, 1988]), accepts *General History* as part of the Defoe canon. See Baer, "'The

Complicated Plot of Piracy': Aspects of English Criminal Law and the Pirate in Defoe," *Eighteenth Century* 23, no. 1 (1982): 4.

7. Clement Hawes, *The British Eighteenth Century and Global Critique* (New York: Palgrave, 2005), 102.
8. See John Gay, *Dramatic Works*, ed. John Fuller, 2 vols. (Oxford: Clarendon, 1983).
9. Julian Hoppit, *A Land of Liberty? England 1689–1727* (Oxford: Clarendon, 2000), 47–49.
10. Jack P. Greene, *Evaluating Empire and Confronting Colonialism in Eighteenth-Century Britain* (Cambridge: Cambridge University Press, 2013), 21.
11. Edward Said, *Culture and Imperialism* (New York: Vintage, 1993).
12. Christohper Hill, "Radical Pirates?," in *The Collected Essays of Christopher Hill*, vol. 3, *People and Ideas in Seventeenth-Century England*, 161–187 (Amherst: University of Massachusetts Press, 1981).
13. Arne Bialuschewski, "Jacobite Pirates?," *Histoire sociale / Social History* 44, no. 87 (2011): 147–164.
14. Voltaire, *Candide, ou l'Optimisme* (n.p., 1759), 167.
15. Jürgen Habermas and Seyla Ben-Habib, "Modernity versus Postmodernity," *New German Critique*, no. 22 (1981): 3–14, https://doi.org/10.2307/487859.
16. See Mark G. Hanna, *Pirate Nests and the Rise of the British Empire* (Chapel Hill: University of North Carolina Press, 2015), for a fuller discussion of privateers.
17. See Tim Beattie, *Privateers of the Early Eighteenth Century* (Cambridge: Cambridge University Press, 2015).
18. Hanna, *Pirate Nests*, 366.
19. Hanna, *Pirate Nests*, 366.
20. *Buccaneers of America* has been remarkably ill-served in its English translations. Originally published in Dutch as *De Americaensche Zee-Roovers*, it was quickly translated into other European languages, particularly French, German, and Spanish. The Spanish translation made considerable alterations to the original text, but it is this version which formed the basis of the English *Buccaneers of America* in 1685. There has never, as far as I know, been a proper English version of the original Dutch text.
21. See Marcus Rediker, *Between the Devil and the Deep Blue Sea: Merchant Seamen, Pirates, and the Anglo-American Maritime World, 1700–1750* (Cambridge: Cambridge University Press, 1987), 256.
22. Even that most recognizable of pirate symbols, the Jolly Roger, was not as universal as *General History* may make it seem. No example of an authentic Jolly Roger flag from the early eighteenth century has survived. Our knowledge of various pirate captains' flags, therefore, comes from secondary sources. There is no doubt that the flag was used, but a ship did not need a distinct pirate flag to be a pirate ship.
23. The story of Thomas Green does merit a brief digression in the chapter on John Bowen in volume 2 (1728.2, 54–58 [454–459]), but certainly nothing like the full chapter he probably deserves. See the official account, *The Tryal of Captain Thomas Green and his Crew* (Edinburgh, 1705), and the anonymous *Remarks Upon the Tryal of Thomas Green* (London, 1705), a harsh condemnation of the justice system that convicted Green, and *The Case of Capt. Thomas Green* (London, 1705), a painstaking collection of legal statements and depositions designed to refute the charges against Green and his crew.
24. See N. A. M. Rodger, *The Wooden World: An Anatomy of the Georgian Navy* (Glasgow: Fontana, 1988), 252–346, for a comprehensive account of what constituted a naval officer in the Georgian period. The assumption that captains must also be educated gentlemen, devoted to intellectual pursuits and occupying a position of social respectability on land, is especially noteworthy, since the pirate challenges ideals of masculinity, including the powerful ideal that a man must possess intellectual as well as physical and intestinal fortitude.

25. John Robert Moore, *Defoe in the Pillory and Other Studies* (New York: Octagon, 1973; originally published in 1939 by Indiana University Press, Bloomington).
26. John Richetti, *Popular Fiction before Richardson*, rev. ed. (Oxford: Clarendon, 1992), 65.
27. Richard Frohock, "Satire and Civil Governance in *General History of the Pyrates*," *Eighteenth Century* 56, no. 4 (2015): 468.
28. Turley, *Rum, Sodomy, and the Lash*, 74.
29. For example, a recent book on Henry Avery (Sean Kingsley and Rex Cowan, *The Pirate King: The Strange Adventures of Henry Avery and the Birth of the Golden Age of Piracy* [New York: Simon and Schuster, 2024]) uses a woodcut from the edition by Edward Midwinter but declares it to be from Johnson. This book also seems to believe that volume 2 appeared in 1724, not 1728, and that the various editions of the book are of little significance. This may be simply sloppy scholarship, but such errors occur frequently enough to suggest that greater awareness needs to be raised concerning the book's publication history.
30. Jeffrey Jerome Cohen, ed., *Monster Theory: Reading Culture* (Minneapolis: University of Minnesota Press, 1996).

CHAPTER 1 — A GENERAL HISTORY OF *GENERAL HISTORY*

1. Marcus Rediker, *Villains of All Nations: Atlantic Pirates in the Golden Age* (Boston: Beacon, 2004), 80, provides a useful schematic and suggests two major "genealogies": one beginning with Benjamin Hornigold, which lasted until 1724, and the other tracing back to George Lowther, which ended around 1726. It is useful to consider the idea of pirate networks in assessing the parallels between piracy and legitimate commerce during the period.
2. Arne Bialuschewski, "Blackbeard: The Creation of a Legend," *Topic: The Washington & Jefferson College Review* 58 (2012): 39–43.
3. In his *History of Piracy* (London: Longman, 1932), Philip Gosse feels compelled to include Misson's story, even though he acknowledges that "no evidence so far has been found to corroborate [Johnson's] account of the amazing Misson" (Philip Gosse, *The History of Piracy* [London: Longman, 1932], 194). Gosse seems to suspect that the Misson story is fictional, but he includes it as an example of an "amazing," even "unique" pirate: the lure of a good story here outweighs its accuracy.
4. Spelled "Libertalia" in 1728, although reprints of the Misson story invariably spell it "Libertatia." "Libertalia" is possibly a misprint in a badly printed volume, although Schonhorn adopts it in his edition. It seems reasonable to prefer the majority spelling.
5. The play ran for four consecutive nights (Saturday 8 November, and Monday to Wednesday 10–12 November 1712), and was revived for a benefit night for Johnson on 16 December of the same year. Any new play that ran for three consecutive nights could be considered a success, since the author received the profits from the box office take on the third night. Its success, however, was limited, since it was revived only once after its premiere, and seems to have been forgotten after 1712.

   A recent book on Henry Avery, Kingsley and Cowan's *The Pirate King*, rather bizarrely suggests that this Charles Johnson is also a pseudonym, since "no Charles Johnson, playwright of *The Successful Pyrate*, is known to have written scripts in London" (189). This assertion comes as a surprise to theater historians, since Charles Johnson was a fairly active playwright in the first few decades of the eighteenth century: the *London Stage* lists several plays by Johnson that were performed and published, such as *The Force of Friendship* and *The Wife's Relief.* The *London Stage* also notes that Johnson's play *The Cobler of Preston*, in rehearsal at Drury Lane for an opening on 3 February 1716, was undercut by Christopher Bullock's quickly writing and rehearsing his own version at Lincoln's Inn Fields at the end of January of the same year. These and other details hardly suggest a shadowy, unknown playwright. Kingsley and Cowan, for their part, posit that *The Successful Pyrate* is actually a collaboration between Defoe and Henry Avery himself, since the two had apparently been close friends since the 1690s, and that Defoe was somehow harboring the fugitive Avery. Such obvious nonsense keeps the waters of pirate history unhelpfully muddy.

6. John Robert Moore, "Defoe, Selkirk, and John Atkins," *Notes and Queries* 179, no. 25 (1940): 436–438. The association of Crusoe with Selkirk had been questioned as early as 1861. An article in the literary magazine owned and edited by Charles Dickens, *All the Year Round*, for 13 April 1861 points out that Crusoe's island is definitely not Juan Fernández, the island on which Selkirk was marooned; moreover, the details of Selkirk's marooning differ so considerably as to disqualify him as a significant source for Defoe. The author of this anonymous piece considers the case of Peter Serrano as a much more likely model for Crusoe. One can forgive Moore for missing what is admittedly an obscure item in a defunct journal, but the article itself shows that the Crusoe/Selkirk connection was already a shaky proposition when Moore used it to bolster his claim of Defoe's authorship. See "Robinson Crusoe's Island," *All the Year Round* 103 (13 April 1861), 64–67.
7. Moore, "Defoe, Selkirk, and John Atkins," 437.
8. The possibility that Atkins might have contributed substantially to *General History* beyond the interpolations noted seems not to have occurred to Moore. There is even no reason that Atkins could not be Johnson himself, since he fits the criteria of being an educated, literary man with maritime experience, who even had actual encounters with pirates. While I cannot pursue the question of Atkins's authorship further without more substantial evidence, the case for his authorship is at least as compelling—albeit just as circumstantial—as anything marshaled for Defoe.
9. For an example of evidence not considered, see the complicated relationship between *General History*'s account of John Gow and the pamphlet version of Gow's life, *Conduct and Proceedings*, which contains information contradictory to *General History*'s account, even though the two works were written almost simultaneously. I have surveyed the various conflicting versions of the Gow story in Noel Chevalier, "Creative Accounting: Alternative Facts in the Narrative of the Pirate, John Gow," *Humanities* 9, no. 2 (2020): 43, https://www.mdpi.com/2076-0787/9/2/43. Defoe could have written one or the other, but not both, yet Moore uses *Conduct and Proceedings* as evidence of Defoe's authorship of *General History*. For an example of the overlooked new evidence, Furbank and Owens cite the "Description of Magadoxa" in volume 2, which Moore suggests is an entirely fictional work of Defoe's (Furbank and Owens, *Canonisation*, 106). Furbank and Owens point out that an independent manuscript version of the "Description" exists in the British Library (Sloane MS 2992) that clearly invalidates the notion that Defoe invented the description out of his own imagination.
10. Furbank and Owens, not surprisingly, even question the certainty that Johnson the playwright could not be Johnson the author of *General History*: in demolishing Moore's assertion that allusions to Romulus, the cofounder of Rome, are a favorite device of Defoe's—and hence evidence of Defoe's authorship of *General History*—they note that "for other uses of the allusion in the early eighteenth century, we need look no further than the play *The Successful Pyrate* by Charles Johnson—an author whom, despite his name, Moore has specifically told us it would be absurd to associate with the *History*" (*Canonisation*, 107). If, indeed, we have only Moore's word that there is no connection between *The Successful Pyrate* and *General History*, then perhaps this issue bears further investigation.
11. Manuel Schonhorn, private email correspondence, 16 January 2016.
12. Henry Elking, *The Interest of Great Britain, Consider'd; or, The Herring Fishery Propos'd, as the Most Rational Expedient for Paying Our National Debts* (London: Eman Matthews, 1723),

5. Elking may be drawing on some national pride of his own here. While little about him is known, his obituary in 1740 notes that he is to be buried in the Dutch Church, Austin Friars, London. Elking may well have immigrated to England from the Netherlands during the reign of William III.

13. It may be worth noting that Elking's pamphlet was once attributed to Defoe by one of his Victorian bibliographers, James Crossley. See Furbank and Owens, *Canonisation*, 186.

14. Arne Bialuschewski has used this piece, and one published a week earlier, as evidence of Mist's authorship of *General History*. While I remain skeptical of Mist's sole authorship, I certainly concur that this, and the large number of advertisements for various editions of *General History* that appeared in *Mist's Weekly Journal*, indicates that Mist had more than a passing interest in the book's success. Pat Rogers has noted how Mist's legal difficulties persisted in the 1720s ("Nathaniel Mist, Daniel Defoe, and the Perils of Publishing," *The Library*, 7th ser., 10, no. 3 [2009]: 301–302). It is tempting to speculate that some of the sympathetic treatment the pirate subjects receive in *General History* may stem from an author/editor who was himself no friend of the legal system.

15. I am indebted to Bialuschewski, "Daniel Defoe, Nathaniel Mist, and *General History*," for his survey of the publication history of *General History*, and for his compelling argument for Mist's authorship.

16. Bialuschewski, "Daniel Defoe, Nathaniel Mist, and *General History*," 24–25.

17. Maximillian E. Novak, *Daniel Defoe: Master of Fictions* (Oxford: Oxford University Press, 2001), 642.

18. Hal Gladfelder, *Criminality and Narrative in Eighteenth-Century England: Beyond the Law* (Baltimore: Johns Hopkins University Press, 2001), 98.

19. Gladfelder, *Criminality and Narrative*, 98.

20. See Lincoln B. Faller, *Turned to Account: The Forms and Functions of Criminal Biography in Late Seventeenth- and Early Eighteenth-Century England* (Cambridge: Cambridge University Press, 1987), 203–208, for a discussion of the market for crime literature.

21. Bialuschewski notes that, true to form, John Robert Moore attributed these pieces to Defoe, but that "these attributions lack any satisfactory evidence to support them" ("Daniel Defoe, Nathaniel Mist, and *General History*," 34).

22. That the third edition is mostly composed of unsold second-edition sheets can be proven by the identical ornaments that conclude some of the chapters and the same misnumbered pages in both.

23. The same issue—in fact, the preceding entry—notes the trial of two men who were part of Thomas Anstis's crew, with the direction to the reader to "See the *History of the Pyrates*" for further information on Anstis.

24. At this same time—on 7 August—Edward Midwinter is advertising his rival *History and Lives*; the *Daily Post* advertisement is careful to note that the volume covers pirates up to Gow, whose recent execution on 11 June is also noted.

25. This publication was evidently popular enough to be reprinted by Jonathan Cape in 1921, and again a year later in an American edition by Robert M. McBride & Company. An electronic version, complete with Fraser's foreword, is available from Skyhorse Publishing, copyrighted in 2015. This version bears Johnson's name on the title page, so it is listed there in the bibliography.

26. Page 161 is on signature L1r, while page 273 is on S1r—it may or may not be significant that the interpolated "Description of Magadoxa" begins on page 144 (K8v): could this be evidence of how clumsily and hurriedly the volume was assembled?

27. The capitalization of "Great" here is unique to Johnson—and may possibly be a hint of anti-Walpolean sentiment.

CHAPTER 2 — "LET US MAKE A HELL OF OUR OWN"

1. Peter Earle, *The Pirate Wars* (London: Methuen, 2003).
2. Rediker, *Villains of All Nations*, 174–175.
3. Earle, *Pirate Wars*, 9.
4. Rennie, *Treasure Neverland*.
5. Margarette Lincoln, *British Pirates and Society, 1680–1730* (Farnham: Ashgate, 2014).
6. Frederick Burwick and Manushag N. Powell, *British Pirates in Print and Performance* (New York: Palgrave, 2015).
7. Hanna, *Pirate Nests*.
8. Hanna, *Pirate Nests*, 367.
9. Mark Neocleous, *The Universal Adversary: Security, Capital, and the "Enemies of All Mankind"* (London: Routledge, 2016), 6.
10. Carlo Galli, "On War and the Enemy," *CR: The New Centennial Review* 9, no. 2 (2009): 203.
11. This trope finds its way into *Treasure Island*, as Long John Silver plans to retire from his life of piracy and run an inn with his wife; Robert Louis Stevenson, *Treasure Island*, ed. John Sutherland (Peterborough, ON: Broadview, 2011; originally published in 1883 by Cassell, London). An ironic reversal of the trope appears in Rafael Sabatini's novel *Captain Blood: His Odyssey* (Boston: Houghton Mifflin, 1922), and Douglas Fairbanks's 1926 film *The Black Pirate*, in that both title characters disguise their upper-class origins to assume the role of pirate.
12. Neocleous, *Universal Adversary*, 108.
13. Christopher Hill, *The World Turned Upside Down: Radical Ideas During the English Revolution* (London: Penguin, 1975), 40.
14. Hill, *World Turned Upside Down*, 48.
15. See Rediker, *Between the Devil and the Deep Blue Sea*, 77–82, for a discussion of the sailor as part of a labor market. Rediker also refers to the vast number of "masterless men" as a contributing factor to the surfeit of cheap labor available to the merchant navy.
16. Captain Kidd was, to his surprise, convicted of the murder of the gunner, William Moore, who had grumbled against Kidd's authority. Kidd fractured Moore's skull with a bucket after a short verbal altercation, and Moore died of his injuries a day later. According to the testimony of Robert Bradinham, Kidd shrugged off the impending murder charge, saying, "I do not care so much for the Death of my Gunner . . . for I have good Friends in *England*, that will bring me off for that." He was, of course, spectacularly and fatally mistaken. See *The Arraignment, Tryal, and Condemnation of Captain William Kidd, for Murther and Piracy* (London: J. Nutt, 1701), 9.
17. Peter Linebaugh and Marcus Rediker, *The Many-Headed Hydra: Sailors, Slaves, Commoners and the Hidden History of the Revolutionary Atlantic* (Boston: Beacon, 2000), 144–145.
18. Johnson says relatively little about classical piracy in what is supposed to be a historical overview. However, he provides an anecdote about Julius Caesar's capture by pirates that is, perhaps, more significant than it seems at first blush. Caesar is treated well by his pirate captors, but he promises, when he regains his freedom, to eradicate them, a threat that the pirates disregard as mere bravado. True to his word, Caesar brings down the full weight of Roman justice on these pirates (1724a, 18–20 [26–28]).
19. Jeffrey Jerome Cohen, "Monster Culture (Seven Theses)," in *Monster Theory: Reading Culture*, ed. Jeffrey Jerome Cohen (Minneapolis: University of Minnesota Press, 1996), 3–25.
20. The titles of Cohen's theses—axiomatic statements followed by a brief explanation—are as follows:

    I: The Monster's Body is a Cultural Body
    II: The Monster Always Escapes

III: The Monster is the Harbinger of Category Crisis
IV: The Monster Dwells at the Gates of Difference
V: The Monster Polices the Borders of the Possible
VI: Fear of the Monster is Really a Kind of Desire
VII: The Monster Stands at the Threshold . . . Of Becoming

21. Cohen, "Monster Culture," 3
22. Cohen. "Monster Culture," 16.
23. Stephen Pender, "'No Monsters at the Resurrection': Inside Some Conjoined Twins," in Cohen, *Monster Theory*, 150–156.
24. What is not often mentioned in this regard is that a pirate's deformities may not have been incurred solely while engaged in pirate activity. How many digits, limbs, or eyes have been lost in the course of a sailor's exercising his regular duties aboard legitimate maritime vessels? Pirate ships, at least, would offer some monetary compensation for body parts lost in the line of duty—a vast improvement over merchant vessels.
25. Isaac Kamola, "Pirate Capitalism, or the Primitive Accumulation of Capital Itself," *Millennium*, 47, no. 1 (2018): 4.
26. See especially Christopher Hill's seminal essay "Radical Pirates?" and Arne Bialuschewski's "Jacobite Pirates?" for a fuller discussion of this idea. Whether or not pirates formally associated themselves with the Jacobite cause after 1715, it seems clear that they embraced Jacobitism at least as an oppositional ideology to Walpole's Whig government.
27. Cohen, "Monster Culture," 7.
28. Defoe, however, is hardly unique in vilifying stockjobbers. By 1718, the stockjobber had become familiar enough as a type of villain that Susanna Centlivre, in *A Bold Stroke for a Wife*, could depict the stockjobber, Tradelove, as unscrupulous enough not only to engage in insider trading, but to propose "selling" his ward, Anne Lovely, as a payment for a massive debt.
29. Nina Auerbach, *Our Vampires, Ourselves* (Chicago: University of Chicago Press, 1995), 145; Marina Levina and Diem-My T. Bui, "Introduction: Toward a Comprehensive Monster Theory in the 21st Century," in *Monster Culture in the 21st Century: A Reader*, ed. Marina Levina and Diem-My T. Bui, (London: Bloomsbury, 2013), 1. In this respect, perhaps the *Pirates of the Caribbean* films—at least the first three—get it right: piracy and monstrosity are directly linked. The crew of the *Black Pearl* are literally cursed by their theft of Aztec gold (an interesting comment on colonial plunder), and are undead rotted corpses masquerading as men. In the second and third films, the literal monsters—the damned crew of the *Flying Dutchman*—are balanced by a more subtle monster, the cold-blooded villain, Lord Cutler Becket, who embodies the values of the equally cold-blooded East India Company.
30. The *Oxford Dictionary of National Biography* fairly confidently accepts the spelling Teach and the Bristol origin as the most likely, although the entry's author, Peter Wood, acknowledges that there is no certainty about Blackbeard's origins or early life. Baylus Brooks, in 2015, asserted that the 1724a information is more correct, and that the Thache [*sic*] family were prominent Jamaica planters. However, Brooks's proofs have been heavily criticized by historian and filmmaker Kevin P. Duffus. Baylus C. Brooks, "'Born in Jamaica, of Very Creditable Parents' or 'A Bristol Man Born'? Excavating the Real Edward Thache, 'Blackbeard the Pirate,'" *North Carolina Historical Review* 92, no. 3 (2015): 235–277; Kevin P. Duffus, "Rush to Judgement: An Analysis of a New Interpretation of the Pirate Blackbeard's Origins," unpublished manuscript, January 2016.
31. This story may have inspired the mysterious Fedallah in Herman Melville's *Moby-Dick*—an equally shadowy and sinister character secretly smuggled aboard the ship by Ahab himself, and whom the crew suspect to be of diabolical origin.

32. It may be significant that the names of the two female pirates are printed in small type on the title page of 1724a, but in significantly larger type in 1724b. Thomas Warner, perhaps sensing the inherent attractiveness of stories of female pirates, used them as an obvious marketing tool that Rivington had overlooked.
33. Sally O'Driscoll, "The Pirate's Breasts: Criminal Women and Meanings of the Body," *Eighteenth Century* 53, no. 3 (2012): 359.
34. O'Driscoll, "Pirate's Breasts," 359.
35. O'Driscoll, "Pirate's Breasts," 359–360.
36. O'Driscoll, "Pirate's Breasts," 361.
37. *The Tryals of John Rackam and other Pyrates* (Jamaica: Robert Baldwin, 1721), 18.
38. *Tryals of John Rackam*, 18.
39. The *OED* cites the final sentence of this passage as an example of the term "myrmidon" used to mean "a member of a gang or army adhering to a particular leader; a hired ruffian or mercenary" (*Oxford English Dictionary*, s.v. "myrmidon (n.), sense 4," September 2024, https://doi.org/10.1093/OED/1118308163). Johnson's choice of the term, however, serves to emphasize the collective culpability of Low's crew, underlining the inherent monstrosity of all pirates, not just Low.
40. John Barnard, *Ashton's Memorial; or, An Authentick Account of the Strange Adventures and Signal Deliverances of Mr. Philip Ashton* (London, 1726).
41. *The Four Years' Voyage of Captain George Roberts, Written by Himself* (London: A. Bettesworth, 1726). *George Roberts* narrates a lengthy encounter between the title character and Edward Low. Low is portrayed as even-handed and diplomatic, willing to negotiate with Roberts for what he wants, and to avoid bloodshed as long as Roberts shows Low the proper deference. Low's sailing companion, a Portuguese posing as an English captain by the name of John Russel, is actually more of the blustering, easily angered psychotic that Low is presented as in *General History*. In fact, Low frequently has to keep Russel in check to prevent him maiming or killing Roberts or any of his crew. *George Roberts*—naturally, once attributed to Defoe—presents a radically different, and strikingly realistic, image of pirate encounters than one finds in *General History*.
42. Cohen, "Monster Culture," 18.

CHAPTER 3 — THE "BORDERS OF THE POSSIBLE"

1. Cohen, "Monster Culture," 11.
2. Michael Uebel, "Unthinking the Monster: Twelfth-Century Responses to Saracen Alterity," in Cohen, *Monster Theory*, 266.
3. Greene, *Evaluating Empire*, 51.
4. Greene, *Evaluating Empire*, 51.
5. In *City of Capital: Politics and Markets in the English Financial Revolution* (Princeton: Princeton University Press, 1996), Bruce G. Carruthers has remarked on Britain's new status as a world power by the time of Queen Anne. He suggests, however, that Britain's might internationally was not matched by a similar strength in domestic politics. I would argue that domestic strength occurred during the reign of George I, with the consolidation of Whig power under Walpole, but Carruthers's point is relevant here: in the first decades of the eighteenth century, Britain certainly struggled with its own identity.
6. See David A. Hedrich Hirsch, "Liberty, Equality, Monstrosity: Revolutionizing the Family in Mary Shelley's *Frankenstein*," in Cohen, *Monster Theory*, 115–140.
7. Greene cites the popularity of the tragic story of Inkle and Yarico, which had been popularized by Sir Richard Steele's retelling in *The Spectator* 11 (13 March 1711) and by Frances Seymour's poetic treatment of the subject in 1738. We may also mention Aphra Behn's

Oroonoko (1688) as an early attempt to narrate the horrors of slavery. Frances Seymour, *The Story of Inkle and Yarrico. A Most Moving Tale from* The Spectator. *Attempted in Verse by the Countess of* **** (London: J. Cooper, 1738).

8. Greene, *Evaluating Empire*, 52.
9. Much of the history of the East India Company's (EIC) consolidation of power is told in William Dalrymple's *The Anarchy* (London: Bloomsbury, 2019), an extensive history of the EIC itself. Dalrymple notes that, at its beginnings in 1599, the EIC had to work hard to dispel the notion that it was largely a collection of privateers, whose principal function was to prey upon Dutch ships carrying spices from its ports in what is now Indonesia. Until the EIC abandoned its dream of finding its own source of highly lucrative spices, and turned its attention to other valuable commodities readily available in India, there was some truth to the notion that the EIC ships were, in effect, pirate ships.
10. *A Discourse of the Laws Relating to Pirates and Piracies, and of the Marine Affairs of Great Britain* (London: W. Wilkins, 1726), 4.
11. J. L. Anderson, "Piracy and World History: An Economic Perspective on World Predation," *Journal of World History* 6, no. 2 (1995): 193.
12. Leonard Seabrooke and John Hobson, "The Case for an Everyday International Political Economy" (Copenhagen: Department of Business and Politics, Copenhagen Business School, 2006), 15.
13. *The Tryals of Major Stede Bonnet and Other Pirates* (London: Benjamin Cowse, 1719), 8.
14. *Tryals of Stede Bonnet*, 8.
15. *Tryals of Stede Bonnet*, 9.
16. In Joel H. Baer, ed., *British Piracy in the Golden Age: History and Interpretation, 1660–1730* (London: Pickering and Chatto, 2007), 1:299.
17. In Baer, *British Piracy*, 1:300.
18. *Lives of the Most Remarkable Criminals, who have been condemn'd and executed; for murder, highway, house-breakers, Street-Robberies, Coining, or other Offences; from the year 1720, to the present time* (London: John Osborn, 1735), 1:60–61.
19. See, for example, Baer, "Piracy Examined: A Study of Daniel Defoe's *General History of the Pyrates* and Its Milieu" (PhD diss., Princeton University, 1970), 73–74.
20. *Lives of the Most Remarkable Criminals*, 1:61.
21. *Lives of the Most Remarkable Criminals*, 1:61.
22. *Lives of the Most Remarkable Criminals*, 1:54.
23. Said, *Culture and Imperialism*, 58.
24. Peter T. Leeson, *The Invisible Hook: The Hidden Economics of Pirates* (Princeton: Princeton University Press, 2009).
25. Specifically, these pirates are locked in the period at the beginning of empire, generally the period between 1700 and 1730, the so-called Golden Age of Piracy. The action of *Treasure Island*, for example, is roughly determined to be some time after 1760, and Long John Silver specifically claims to have sailed with Bartholomew Roberts in the 1720s. John Sutherland has identified Silver's claims as one of the conundrums of *Treasure Island*, since Silver is said to be around fifty years old during the action of the novel, while the pirates Silver claims to have sailed with were active when Silver would either have been a very young child or even not yet born. Sutherland assumes the action of the novel to take place "in the late 1750s or early 1760s," and blames the odd chronology on Stevenson's having discovered Johnson's *General History of the Pyrates* only after he had started writing *Treasure Island*. See Stevenson, *Treasure Island*, 255–257.
26. Perhaps because something very like that can be seen in "The Crimson Permanent Assurance," the sixteen-minute Terry Gilliam short that precedes *Monty Python's The Meaning of Life* (1983). In the film, an office of staid, elderly insurance clerks literally transform into

pirates and seize control of the company from their oppressive corporate masters. Their London office building becomes a pirate ship, and is "launched upon the high seas of international finance." The connection with pirate films is underscored by extensive use of Erich Korngold's music for Michael Curtiz's *The Sea Hawk* (1940).

27. For accounts of daily life on pirate ships, see especially Rediker, *Villains of All Nations*; David Cordingly, *Under the Black Flag: The Romance and the Reality of Life among the Pirates* (New York: Random House, 1996); and Lincoln, *British Pirates and Society*.
28. For a detailed accounting of sailors' wages between 1700 and 1750, see Rediker, *Between the Devil and the Deep Blue Sea*, 121–124 and 304–305. Common seamen—the type most likely to be attracted to piracy—earned as little as 18 shillings a month and had no shares in the trading profits of the voyage.
29. The most extreme example of this Otherness is perhaps Australia, with its black swans and bark-shedding trees. In some Australian literature, the land itself becomes a kind of monster that envelops and even consumes interlopers—see, for example, Joan Lindsay's novel *Picnic at Hanging Rock* (Melbourne: F. W. Cheshire, 1967), and the 1975 Peter Weir film version.
30. Julia Kristeva, *Powers of Horror: An Essay on Abjection*, trans. Leon S. Roudiez (New York: Columbia University Press, 1982).
31. Rebecca Weaver-Hightower, *Empire Islands: Castaways, Cannibals, and Fantasies of Conquest* (Minneapolis: University of Minnesota Press, 2007), 95.
32. Roxanne Wheeler, "Limited Visions of Africa: Geographies of Savagery and Civility in Early Eighteenth-Century Narratives," in *Writes of Passage: Reading Travel Writing*, ed. James Duncan, and Derek Gregory (London: Taylor and Francis, 1998), 18.
33. Wheeler, "Limited Visions," 22.
34. This interesting color change appears in William Blake's "The Little Black Boy," who is almost invariably depicted as white on the second plate of the poem when he and the European boy stand in the presence of Jesus.
35. Paul Gilroy, *The Black Atlantic: Modernity and Double-Consciousness* (Cambridge, MA: Harvard University Press, 1995), 42.
36. Gilroy, *Black Atlantic*, 46.
37. Howard W. French, *Born in Blackness: Africa, Africans, and the Making of the Modern World, 1471 to the Second World War* (New York: Liveright, 2021).
38. William Snelgrave, *A New Account of Some Parts of Guinea, and the Slave Trade* (London: James, John, and Paul Knapton, 1734), 1:207.
39. Snelgrave, *New Account*, 1:160–161.
40. Wheeler, "Limited Visions," 24–25.
41. The introduction has one anecdote relating to the late fifteenth-century corsair Oruç Reis, known in Europe as "Baba Oruç" or "Barbarossa." The story of Reis's rise to power is included merely as a cautionary tale of what happens when governments do "not take an early Care in suppressing these Sea Banditti, before they gather Strength."
42. Linda Colley, *Captives: Britain, Empire, and the World, 1600–1850* (New York: Anchor, 2002), 63.
43. Colley, *Captives*, 64.
44. Linebaugh and Rediker, *The Many-Headed Hydra*, 165.
45. It may be significant that this chapter is otherwise unchanged between 1724b and 1724a—even the typesetting of the pages is the same between 1724a's D4r–D6r (55–59) and 1724b's E1r–E3r (65–69). The only change is in the ornament that concludes both chapters.
46. An echo this argument occurs in Francis Ford Coppola's film *Apocalypse Now* (1979), when Captain Willard muses in his voiceover that "charging a man with murder in this place is

like handing out speeding tickets at the Indy 500." The arbitrariness—and absurdity—of what constitutes a capital crime in wartime reveals an inherent arbitrariness in all law.

CHAPTER 4 — "PIRATE VICES, PUBLICK BENEFITS"

1. Cotton Mather, *The Vial Poured Out Upon the Sea: A Remarkable Relation of Certain Pirates Brought Unto a Tragical and Untimely End* (Boston: N. Belknap, 1726), 16. "That Man" refers to William Atkinson, first mate aboard the sloop *John and Hannah*, which Fly and his men attacked in June, 1726. Fly released the ship and its captain, named Fulker, but pressed Atkinson into service as a pilot. Atkinson pretended to comply with the pirates, but ultimately betrayed Fly and his crew and was directly responsible for their capture. *General History* features a remarkably oath-strewn speech by Fly countering Atkinson's initial resistance to piloting the pirates' ship.
2. Mather, *Vial Poured Out*, 21.
3. For a comprehensive view of the merchant figure throughout the eighteenth century, see James Raven, *Judging New Wealth: Popular Publishing and Responses to Commerce in England, 1750–1800* (Oxford: Clarendon, 1992). In my introduction to David Garrick and George Colman, *The Clandestine Marriage and Two Short Plays*, ed. Noel Chevalier (Peterborough, ON: Broadview, 1995), I note that Mr. Sterling, the socially mobile merchant father, is a collection of familiar antimercantile tropes: he is frequently derided by the fussy and class-conscious Lord Ogleby for his tacky landscaping and his general social ignorance (such as serving hot rolls and butter in July).
4. Perry Gauci, *The Politics of Trade: The Overseas Merchant in State and Society, 1660–1720* (Oxford: Oxford University Press, 2001); see especially 156–194.
5. Gauci, *Politics of Trade*, 156.
6. Interestingly, Gauci does not include any discussion of the slave trade in his larger commentary on overseas trade. He mentions such important commodities as cloth, fish, sugar, and wine, but not the most problematic—and perhaps the most lucrative—of all commodities: African humans. He does mention the Royal Africa Company a few times, but only as part of a general list of joint-stock companies that existed in the late seventeenth century.
7. John Trenchard and Thomas Gordon, *Cato's Letters*, ed. Ronald Hamowy, 2 vols. (Indianapolis: Liberty Fund, 1995), 2:662.
8. See Lincoln, *British Pirates*, 115–125.
9. Hanna, *Pirate Nests*, 327.
10. Lincoln, *British Pirates*, 82.
11. Linebaugh and Rediker, *Many-Headed Hydra*, 144–145.
12. Erin Mackie, *Rakes, Highwaymen, and Pirates the Making of the Modern Gentleman in the Eighteenth Century* (Baltimore: Johns Hopkins University Press, 2009), 117.
13. Mackie, *Rakes, Highwaymen, and Pirates*, 114.
14. Mackie, *Rakes, Highwaymen, and Pirates*, 115.
15. Mackie, *Rakes, Highwaymen, and Pirates*, 120.
16. See Margaret Hunt, *The Middling Sort: Commerce, Gender, and the Family in England, 1680–1780* (Berkeley: University of California Press, 1996), 193–215.
17. R. W. Connell and Julian Wood, "Globalization and Business Masculinities," *Men and Masculinities* 7, no. 4 (2005): 347–364.
18. I am refraining here from using the term *Homo economicus* or drawing what would seem to be the obvious connection between the merchant-hero and Defoe's *Robinson Crusoe*. Matthew Watson, "Rousseau's Crusoe Myth: The Unlikely Provenance of the Neoclassical *Homo economicus*," *Journal of Cultural Economy* 10, no. 1 (2017): 81–96, argues convincingly

that the reading of Crusoe as an archetype of *Homo economicus* begins not with Defoe but half a century later, with Rousseau.

19. Frohock, "Satire and Civil Governance," 468.
20. Josiah Woodward, "A Seasonable Admonition against Mutiny and Piracy," in *The Seaman's Monitor* (London, 1723). Note that the title page has "A Seasonable Admonition," while the title and running heads of the text have "A Kind Admonition" (67–75).
21. See Bernard Mandeville, *The Fable of the Bees*, ed. F. B. Kaye (Oxford: Clarendon, 1924), 1:xxxivn8, for the dating of the third edition.
22. Mandeville, *Fable of the Bees*, 87.
23. Mandeville, *Fable of the Bees*, 106.
24. Mandeville, *Fable of the Bees*, 106.
25. F. B. Kaye, "Mandeville's Thought," in Mandeville, *Fable of the Bees*, lvi–lxi.
26. See 1724b, 336–338 [292–294].
27. John Robert Moore, "Defoe and Mandeville," in *Mandeville Studies*, ed. Irwin Primer (The Hague: Nijhoff, 1975), 115–125.
28. Daniel Defoe, *The Compleat English Tradesman*, 2 vols., in *The Religious and Didactic Writings of Daniel Defoe*, vols. 7–8, ed. John McVeagh (London: Pickering and Chatto, 2007).
29. Daniel Defoe, *Defoe's Review*, ed. Arthur Wellesley Secord, 22 vols. (New York: Columbia University Press, 1938), 4:425.
30. Defoe, *Review*, 4:425–426.
31. Daniel Defoe, "An Essay on the South Sea Trade" (1711), in *The Political and Economic Writings of Daniel Defoe*, ed. P. N. Furbank and W. R. Owens (London: Pickering and Chatto, 2000), 7:29–56.
32. While this principle is abundantly evident in his fiction, we may also observe it clearly at work in his *Family Instructor* series, in which Defoe takes what could be a series of dry, prescriptive principles for private religious observance, and sets them within a surprisingly fascinating and realistic family drama.
33. "News," *Weekly Journal or Saturday's Post*, 8 August 1724, Seventeenth and Eighteenth Century Burney Newspapers Collection (accessed 17 July 2020), https://link-gale-com.libproxy.uregina.ca/apps/doc/Z2001598965/BBCN?u=ureginalib&sid=BBCN&xid=203b88d2.
34. "News," *Weekly Journal or Saturday's Post*, 15 August 1724, Seventeenth and Eighteenth Century Burney Newspapers Collection (accessed 17 July 2020), https://link-gale-com.libproxy.uregina.ca/apps/doc/Z2001598981/BBCN?u=ureginalib&sid=BBCN&xid=f522feaf.
35. "News," *Weekly Journal or Saturday's Post*, 29 August 1724, Seventeenth and Eighteenth Century Burney Newspapers Collection (accessed 17 July 2020), https://link-gale-com.libproxy.uregina.ca/apps/doc/Z2001599011/BBCN?u=ureginalib&sid=BBCN&xid=933171f3.
36. Margarette Lincoln, drawing on the work of Erin Mackie, notes that the few portraits included in *General History* underline the splendor of some pirate captains, especially Bartholomew Roberts, who was the most successful pirate of his day. Lincoln muddies the waters somewhat by including illustrations from other versions of *General History* (the portrait of Stede Bonnet on p. 136 is taken from an unauthorized abridgement of Johnson, *History and Lives of all the Most Notorious Pyrates* [Edward Midwinter, 1725]), but her point is clear: successful pirates displayed their success in sometimes flamboyant and expensive clothing, a trope which has influenced the image of the pirate-dandy through Captain Hook, the paintings of N. C. Wyeth, and even Johnny Depp's Captain Jack Sparrow. Lincoln, *British Pirates*, 134–139.

CHAPTER 5 — PLUTARCH ON THE SPANISH MAIN

1. Oddly, in *British Pirates*, Lincoln refers to him as "Mission." The book's index even grants him a full name, "James Mission"—an odd name for a French sailor. Lincoln accepts that Libertatia is likely a fiction, but does not suggest that Misson himself is equally fictional. It is perhaps another oddity of *General History* that Misson's own name and that of his colony can have several variants, while scholars also acknowledge *General History* to be the sole authoritative source for this story.
2. Markku Peltonen, *The Duel in Early Modern England: Civility, Politeness and Honour* (Cambridge: Cambridge University Press, 2003), 275–314.
3. Hoppit, *Land of Liberty?*, 413.
4. Leeson, *Invisible Hook*, 195.
5. *London Journal*, 24 August 1723, 4.
6. Interestingly, immediately following the letter in the *London Journal* is a brief report on stock prices, including those of the South Sea Company.
7. The first edition places his biography after that of Stede Bonnet's, presumably because Teach began his pirate career under Bonnet. The second edition has him starting his career under Benjamin Hornigold, then later encountering and sailing with Bonnet. There is evidence of some careful rewriting of the chapters on Bonnet and Blackbeard, although it is debatable which version presents the more coherent chronology.
8. Bialuschewski, "Blackbeard," mistakenly suggests that this passage is found only in the second and subsequent editions, and replaces an earlier, less detailed passage. However, both this and the supposed "earlier" passage—which belongs to the chapter on Stede Bonnet—can be found in all editions of the *General History*.
9. Faller, *Turned to Account*, 185.
10. Faller, *Turned to Account*, 174.
11. Faller, *Turned to Account*, 175.
12. "News," *Weekly Journal or Saturday's Post*, 18 August 1722; Seventeenth and Eighteenth Century Burney Newspapers Collection (accessed 29 April 2024), https://link-gale-com.libproxy.uregina.ca/apps/doc/Z2001596735/BBCN?u=ureginalib&sid=bookmark-BBCN&xid=ad87f06f.
13. Brian Stock, "Reflections on Ancient Narrative and Ethics," *New Literary History* 40, no. 4 (2009): 775, https://doi.org/10.1353/nlh.0.0119. A complete Greek text of Plutarch, with a facing English translation by Bernadotte Perrin, can be found in the Loeb Classical Library edition (trans. Bernadotte Perrin, 11 vols [Cambridge, MA: Harvard University Press, 1914–1926]).
14. Anjouan, or Nzwani as it is now known, is part of the Comoros Islands, and was actually ruled by a female sultan, Alimah III, during the period that the Misson story is set.
15. Lincoln B. Faller, "Captain Misson's Failed Utopia, Crusoe's Failed Colony: Race and Identity in New, Not Quite Imaginable Worlds," *Eighteenth Century* 43, no. 1 (2002): 4.
16. There are two states of this engraving, found in 1724a and 1724b. In 1724a, Roberts's four pistols are slung in a line inside the left side of his coat, while in 1724b, two appear on the left and two on the right. More important, in 1724a, Roberts's ships both show the "later" flag, that of Roberts standing on two skulls, one labeled ABH ("a Barbadian head") and AMH ("a Martinican head"); in 1724b, the ship in the foreground clearly shows Roberts's earlier memento mori flag.
17. It is possible that 1724b's opening paragraph restores some text that was omitted in 1724a. The first edition begins rather abruptly, with "*Davis* being cut off, in the manner before mentioned," as if the Roberts chapter is simply a continuation of the previous chapter on

Howel Davis—the name Roberts, in fact, is presented as if the reader should already know who he is, though he is not mentioned at all in the Davis chapter. The opening of 1724b includes an introductory paragraph much more typical of the other chapters in *General History*. However, the second paragraph is also extensively revised, to set up a longer anecdote about Roberts's election—1724a simply mentions that "he was by a great Majority elected Captain" (161; see also 1724b, 208–209 [194–195]).

18. 1724a, 169. The reading of 1724b (230 [210]) changes the words of Roberts slightly, to "That it was every one's Interest to observe them if they were minded to keep up so abominable a Combination." The suggestion that the pirates themselves have some agency in whether or not they "keep up" their "abominable Combination" may or may not be significant.
19. Glasby is acquitted, but his two co-deserters are condemned and executed on the ship. Glasby later stands trial in London with all of the other pirates of Roberts's ships, and uses his escape attempt as proof of his innocence of and aversion to piracy. He was, in fact, acquitted a second time. Valentine Ashplant, however, was condemned, along with the bulk of Roberts's crew.

CHAPTER 6 — "THEIR CRIMES CONSPIR'D TO MAKE 'EM GREAT"

1. Cohen, "Monster Culture," 5.
2. Charles Ellms, *The Pirates' Own Book; Or, Authentic Narratives of the Lives, Exploits, and Executions of the Most Celebrated Sea Robbers* (Portland, ME: Sanborn and Carter, 1837). Ellms curiously refers to Kidd as "Robert" throughout his account; an 1834 version of the 1728 edition printed in Hartford, Connecticut, gives Kidd's name as Robert. The majority of the chapter on Kidd is lifted from the 1728 edition, possibly by way of the Hartford text, except that Ellms has inserted some editorial details not found in either 1728 or Hartford, such as the report of Kidd's burying his Bible in Plymouth sound before setting out with his privateering commission, "its divine precepts being so at variance with his wicked course of life, that he did not choose to keep a book which condemned him in his lawless career" (168). Ellms also includes the detail of Kidd's needing to be hanged twice, another addition to the account in 1728 also absent in Hartford.
3. The eight are Stede Bonnet, Charles Vane, John Rackam, Mary Read, Anne Bonny, Bartholomew Roberts, John Philips, and John Gow. Some of the crew members of other pirate captains faced trial, but the captains themselves either escaped or were killed before capture.
4. The image even makes its appearance in the *Pirates of the Caribbean* films, when we are first introduced to Jack Sparrow. Sparrow sails by a group of skeletons of hanged pirates, and he salutes them as he passes: this brief moment serves to underline the harshness of British justice and to signal Sparrow's own solidarity with his pirate brethren.
5. See Douglas Hay, "Property, Authority, and Criminal Law," in Douglas Hay et al., *Albion's Fatal Tree: Crime and Society in Eighteenth-Century England* (New York: Pantheon, 1975), 27.
6. Rebecca A. Simon, "The Problem and Potential of Piracy: Legal Changes and Emerging Ideas of Colonial Autonomy in the Early Modern British Atlantic, 1670–1730," *Journal for Maritime Research* 18, no. 2 (2016): 130.
7. Hay, "Property, Authority, and Criminal Law," 59.
8. Faller, *Turned to Account*, 52–71.
9. Sean Shesgreen. "Hogarth's *Industry and Idleness*: A Reading." *Eighteenth-Century Studies* 9, no. 4 (1976): 589, https://doi.org/10.2307/2737796.
10. Alexander Pope, "The Rape of the Lock," 3.21–22; *The Poems of Alexander Pope*, ed. John Butt (New Haven: Yale University Press, 1963), 223.

11. See especially E. P. Thompson, *Whigs and Hunters: The Origin of the Black Act* (New York: Pantheon, 1975); Hay et al., *Albion's Fatal Tree*; and Peter Linebaugh, *The London Hanged: Crime and Civil Society in the Eighteenth Century* (Cambridge: Cambridge University Press, 1992). These books have also heavily influenced the work of Marcus Rediker on pirates, especially *Between the Devil and the Deep Blue Sea* (1987); Rediker and Linebaugh have collaborated on a study of the maritime working class, *The Many-Headed Hydra* (2000).
12. Hay, "Property, Authority, and Criminal Law, 22–24.
13. Hay, "Property, Authority, and Criminal Law," 44.
14. Bonnet's incompetence as a pirate, and his eventual friendship with Blackbeard, form the basis of the comedy series *Our Flag Means Death*, which ran for two seasons on HBO Max from 2022 to 2023. It is worth mentioning that the series, while playing very fast and loose with the facts of both Bonnet's and Blackbeard's lives, also subverts many common pirate tropes, and features a diverse crew composed of numerous LGBTQ+ characters and characters of color; the central relationship between Bonnet and Blackbeard is understood to be openly romantic by the end of the series.
15. For a fuller discussion of the collective nature of maritime labor, see Rediker, *Between the Devil and the Deep Blue Sea*, 77–115.
16. Rediker, *Between the Devil and the Deep Blue Sea*, 78.
17. John Gay, *Polly, an Opera* (1729), in *Dramatic Works*, 2:103.
18. Gay, *Polly*, *Dramatic Works*, 2:104.
19. Roy Osamu Kamada, "Monstrous Citizenships: Coercion, Submission, and the Possibilities of Resistance in *Never Let Me Go* and *Cloud Atlas*," in Levina and Bui, *Monster Culture*, 164.

CONCLUSION

1. Cohen, "Monster Culture."
2. See especially Cotton Mather, *Useful Remarks: An Essay upon Remarkables in the Way of Wicked Men* (Baer, *British Piracy*, 4:155–206), and Josiah Woodward, *The Seaman's Monitor; or, Advice to Sea-Faring Men* (Baer, *British Piracy*, 4:207–292), both published in 1723.

BIBLIOGRAPHY

PRIMARY SOURCES

An Account of the Conduct and Proceedings of the Late John Gow, alias Smith. London: John Applebee, 1725.

The Arraignment, Tryal, and Condemnation of Captain William Kidd, for Murther and Piracy. London: J. Nutt, 1701.

Aubin, Penelope. *The Life of Charlotta Du Pont*. London, 1723.

Barnard, John. *Ashton's Memorial; or, An Authentick Account of the Strange Adventures and Signal Deliverances of Mr. Philip Ashton*. London, 1726.

Black Sails. Created by Jonathan E. Steinberg and Robert Levine, featuring Toby Stephens, Hannah New, and Luke Arnold. Starz, 2014–2017.

The Case of Capt. Thomas Green. London, 1705.

Chetwood, William. *Voyages, Dangerous Adventures, and Imminent Escapes of Captain Richard Falconer*. London: William Chetwood, 1720.

———. *Voyages and Adventures of Captain Robert Boyle*. London: John Watts, 1726.

Colman, Benjamin. *It is a Fearful Thing to Fall into the Hands of the Living God: A Sermon Preached Before some Miserable Pirates July 10, 1726, On the Lord's Day, Before Their Execution*. Boston: John Philips and Thomas Hancock, 1726.

Defoe, Daniel. *The Compleat English Tradesman*. 2 vols. In *The Religious and Didactic Writings of Daniel Defoe*, vols. 7–8, edited by John McVeagh. London: Pickering and Chatto, 2007.

———. *Defoe's Review*. Edited by Arthur Wellesley Secord. 22 vols. New York: Columbia University Press, 1938.

———. "An Essay on the South Sea Trade." 1711. In *The Political and Economic Writings of Daniel Defoe*, vol. 7, edited by P. N. Furbank and W. R. Owens, 29–56. London: Pickering and Chatto, 2000.

———. "The Great Law of Subordination Consider'd" (1724). In *The Religious and Didactic Writings of Daniel Defoe*, vol. 6, edited by J. A. Downie. London: Pickering and Chatto, 2007.

———. *The Life of Captain Singleton* (1720). Edited by Manushag N. Powell. Peterborough, ON: Broadview, 2022.

A Discourse of the Laws Relating to Pirates and Piracies, and of the Marine Affairs of Great Britain. London: W. Wilkins, 1726.

Elking, Henry. *The Interest of Great Britain, Consider'd; or, The Herring Fishery Propos'd, as the Most Rational Expedient for Paying Our National Debts*. London: Eman Matthews, 1723.

Ellms, Charles. *The Pirates' Own Book; Or, Authentic Narratives of the Lives, Exploits, and Executions of the Most Celebrated Sea Robbers*. Portland, ME: Sanborn and Carter, 1837.

Esquemeling, John [Alexandre Exquemelin]. *Bucaniers of America*. 2nd ed. London: William Crooke, 1684.

An Exact Narrative of the Tryals of the Pyrates, and all the Late Proceedings of the Goal-Delivery of the Admiralty, Held in the Old-Bayly, on Thursday and Saturday, the 7th and 9th of January, 1674/5. London: n.p., 1675.

The Four Years' Voyage of Captain George Roberts, Written by Himself. London: A. Bettesworth, 1726. [Attrib. Defoe.]
Garrick, David, and George Colman. *The Clandestine Marriage and Two Short Plays.* Edited by Noel Chevalier. Peterborough, ON: Broadview, 1995.
Gay, John. *Dramatic Works.* Edited by John Fuller. 2 vols. Oxford: Clarendon, 1983.
Hennebo, Robert, trans. *Historie der Engelsche Zee-Roovers.* By "Captain Charles Johnson." Amsterdam: Hermanus Uytwerf, 1725.
History and Lives of All the Most Notorious Pirates and their Crews. London: Edward Midwinter, 1725.
Hogarth, William, and Ronald Paulson. *Hogarth's Graphic Works.* Rev. ed. New Haven, CT: Yale University Press, 1970.
"Johnson, Capt. Charles" [pseud.]. *A General and True History of the Lives and Actions of the Most Famous Highwaymen, Murderers, Street-Robbers, &c.* Birmingham: Robert Walker, 1742.
———. *A General History of the Pyrates.* Edited by Manuel Schonhorn. London: J. M. Dent, 1972. Revised reprint, New York: Dover, 1999.
———. *A General History of the Robberies and Murders of the Most Notorious Pyrates.* London: Charles Rivington, 1724. (1724a)
———. *A General History of the Pyrates.* 2nd ed. London: Thomas Warner, 1724. (1724b)
———. *A General History of the Pyrates.* 3rd ed. London: Thomas Warner, 1725. (1725)
———. *The History of the Pyrates.* 4th ed. London: Thomas Woodward, 1728. (1728.1)
———. *The History of the Pyrates.* 4th ed., vol. 2. London: Thomas Woodward, 1728. (1728.2)
———. *The History and Lives of the Most Notorious Pirates and Their Crews.* 5th ed. Foreword by C. Lovat Fraser. Delaware: Skyhorse, 2015. Originally published in 1735 by A. Bettesworth and C. Hitch, London.
Johnson, Charles. *The Successful Pyrate, A Play.* 2nd ed. London: Bernard Lintott, 1713.
King, Charles. *The British Merchant; or, Commerce Preserv'd.* London: John Darby, 1721.
Lives of the Most Remarkable Criminals, who have been condemn'd and executed; for murder, highway, house-breakers, Street-Robberies, Coining, or other Offences; from the year 1720, to the present time. London: John Osborn, 1735.
Mandeville, Bernard. *The Fable of the Bees.* Edited by F. B. Kaye. 2 vols. Oxford: Clarendon, 1924.
Mather, Cotton. *The Vial Poured Out Upon the Sea: A Remarkable Relation of Certain Pirates Brought Unto a Tragical and Untimely End.* Boston: N. Belknap, 1726.
Plutarch. *Lives.* Translated by Bernadotte Perrin. 11 vols. Cambridge, MA: Harvard University Press, 1914–1926.
Pope, Alexander. *The Poems of Alexander Pope.* Edited by John Butt. New Haven, CT: Yale University Press, 1963.
Remarks Upon the Tryal of Thomas Green. London, 1705.
Sabatini, Rafael. *Captain Blood: His Odyssey.* Boston: Houghton Mifflin, 1922.
Seymour, Frances. *The Story of Inkle and Yarrico. A Most Moving Tale from* The Spectator. *Attempted in Verse by the Countess of ****.* London: J. Cooper, 1738.
Smith, Adam. *Theory of Moral Sentiments.* Edited by D. D. Rafael and A. D. Macfie. Oxford: Clarendon, 1976.
Smith, Captain Alexander [pseud?]. *The History of the Lives of the Most Noted Highway-Men, Foot-Pads, House-Breakers, Shop-lifts and Cheats, of both Sexes, in and about* London, *and other Places of* Great-Britain, *for above fifty Years last past.* London, 1714.
Snelgrave, William. *A New Account of Some Parts of Guinea, and the Slave Trade.* 2 vols. London: James, John, and Paul Knapton, 1734.
Stevenson, Robert Louis. *Letters of Robert Louis Stevenson.* Edited by Sidney Colvin. 4 vols. New York: Charles Scribner's Sons, 1911.

———. *Treasure Island*. Edited by John Sutherland. Peterborough, ON: Broadview, 2011. Originally published in 1883 by Cassell, London.

Trenchard, John, and Thomas Gordon. *Cato's Letters*. Edited by Ronald Hamowy. 2 vols. Indianapolis: Liberty Fund, 1995.

A True and Genuine Account of the Last Confession and Dying Words of John Gow, alias Smith. London: Thomas Warner, 1725.

The Tryal of Captain Thomas Green and his Crew. Edinburgh, 1705.

The Tryals of Captain John Rackam and other Pyrates. Jamaica: Robert Baldwin, 1721.

The Tryals of Major Stede Bonnet and Other Pirates. London: Benjamin Cowse, 1719.

Voltaire, *Candide, ou l'Optimisme*. N.p., 1759.

Woodward, Josiah. "A Seasonable [*sic*] Admonition against Mutiny and Pyracy," in *The Seaman's Monitor*. London, 1723.

SECONDARY SOURCES

Anderson, J. L. "Piracy and World History: An Economic Perspective on World Predation." *Journal of World History* 6, no. 2 (1995): 175–199.

Armstrong, Nancy. *Desire and Domestic Fiction: A Political History of the Novel*. New York: Oxford University Press, 1987.

Auerbach, Nina. *Our Vampires, Ourselves*. Chicago: University of Chicago Press, 1995.

Baer, Joel H., ed. *British Piracy in the Golden Age: History and Interpretation, 1660–1730*. 4 vols. London: Pickering and Chatto, 2007.

———. "'The Complicated Plot of Piracy': Aspects of English Criminal Law and the Pirate in Defoe." *Eighteenth Century* 23, no. 1 (1982): 3–26.

———. "Piracy Examined: A Study of Daniel Defoe's *General History of the Pyrates* and Its Milieu." PhD diss., Princeton University, 1970.

Beattie, Tim. *Privateers of the Early Eighteenth Century*. Cambridge: Cambridge University Press, 2015.

Bell, Ian A. *Literature and Crime in Augustan England*. London: Routledge, 1991.

Bialuschewski, Arne. "Blackbeard: The Creation of a Legend." *Topic: The Washington & Jefferson College Review* 58 (2012): 39–43.

———. "Daniel Defoe, Nathaniel Mist, and the *General History of the Pyrates*." *Papers of the Bibliographical Society of America* 98, no. 1 (2004): 21–38.

———. "Jacobite Pirates?" *Histoire sociale / Social History* 44, no. 87 (2011): 147–164.

Black, Jeremy. "An Underrated Journalist: Nathaniel Mist and the Opposition Press During the Whig Ascendency." *Journal for Eighteenth-Century Studies* 10, no. 1 (2008): 27–41. https://doi.org/10.1111/J.1754-0208.1987.TB00003.X.

Brooks, Baylus C. "'Born in Jamaica, of Very Creditable Parents' or 'A Bristol Man Born'? Excavating the Real Edward Thache, 'Blackbeard the Pirate.'" *North Carolina Historical Review* 92, no. 3 (2015): 235–277.

Burwick, Frederick, and Manushag N. Powell. *British Pirates in Print and Performance*. New York: Palgrave, 2015.

Carruthers, Bruce G. *City of Capital: Politics and Markets in the English Financial Revolution*. Princeton, NJ: Princeton University Press, 1996.

Chevalier, Noel. "Creative Accounting: Alternative Facts in the History of the Pirate, John Gow." *Humanities* 9, no. 2 (2020): 43. https://www.mdpi.com/2076-0787/9/2/43.

———. Introduction to *The Clandestine Marriage and Two Short Plays*, by David Garrick and George Colman. Edited by Noel Chevalier. Peterborough, ON: Broadview, 1995.

Cohen, Jeffrey Jerome. "Monster Culture (Seven Theses)." In *Monster Theory: Reading Culture*, edited by Jeffrey Jerome Cohen, 3–25. Minneapolis: University of Minnesota Press, 1996.

———, ed. *Monster Theory: Reading Culture.* Minneapolis: University of Minnesota Press, 1996.

Colley, Linda. *Captives: Britain, Empire, and the World, 1600–1850.* New York: Anchor, 2002.

Connell, R. W., and Julian Wood. "Globalization and Business Masculinities." *Men and Masculinities* 7, no. 4 (2005): 347–364.

Cordingly, David. *Under the Black Flag: The Romance and the Reality of Life among the Pirates.* New York: Random House, 1996.

Dalrymple, William. *The Anarchy: A History of the East India Company.* London: Bloomsbury, 2019.

Dickinson, H. T. "Bernard Mandeville: An Independent Whig." *Studies on Voltaire and the Eighteenth Century* 152 (1976): 559–570.

Dijkstra, Bram. *Defoe and Economics: The Fortunes of "Roxana" in the History of Interpretation.* New York: St. Martin's, 1987.

Earle, Peter. *The Pirate Wars.* London: Methuen, 2003.

Faller, Lincoln B. "Captain Misson's Failed Utopia, Crusoe's Failed Colony: Race and Identity in New, Not Quite Imaginable Worlds." *Eighteenth Century* 43, no.1 (2002): 1–17.

———. *Turned to Account: The Forms and Functions of Criminal Biography in Late Seventeenth- and Early Eighteenth-Century England.* Cambridge: Cambridge University Press, 1987.

French, Howard W. *Born in Blackness: Africa, Africans, and the Making of the Modern World, 1471 to the Second World War.* New York: Liveright, 2021.

Frohock, Richard. "Satire and Civil Governance in *General History of the Pyrates.*" *Eighteenth Century* 56, no. 4 (2015): 467–483.

Furbank, P. N., and W. R. Owens. *The Canonisation of Daniel Defoe.* New Haven, CT: Yale University Press, 1988.

Galli, Carlo. "On War and the Enemy." *CR: The New Centennial Review* 9, no. 2 (2009): 195–220.

Gauci, Perry. *The Politics of Trade: The Overseas Merchant in State and Society, 1660–1720.* Oxford: Oxford University Press, 2001.

Gilroy, Paul. *The Black Atlantic: Modernity and Double-Consciousness.* Cambridge, MA: Harvard University Press, 1995.

Gladfelder, Hal. *Criminality and Narrative in Eighteenth-Century England: Beyond the Law.* Baltimore: Johns Hopkins University Press, 2001.

Gosse, Philip. *A Bibliography of the Works of Capt. Charles Johnson.* New York: Burt Franklin, 1970. Originally published in 1927 by Dulau and Co., London.

———. *The History of Piracy.* London: Longman, 1932.

Grasso, Joshua. "The Providence of Pirates: Defoe and the 'True-Bred Merchant.'" *Digital Defoe: Studies in Defoe and his Contemporaries* 2, no. 1 (2010): 21–40.

Greene, Jack P. *Evaluating Empire and Confronting Colonialism in Eighteenth-Century Britain.* Cambridge: Cambridge University Press, 2013.

Habermas, Jürgen, and Seyla Ben-Habib. "Modernity versus Postmodernity." *New German Critique,* no. 22 (1981): 3–14. https://doi.org/10.2307/487859.

Hanna, Mark G. *Pirate Nests and the Rise of the British Empire, 1570–1740.* Chapel Hill: University of North Carolina Press, 2015.

———. "Well-Behaved Pirates Seldom Make History: A Reevaluation of the Golden Age of English Piracy." In *Governing the Sea in the Early Modern Era: Essays in Honor of Robert C. Ritchie,* edited by Peter C. Mancall and Carole Shammas, 129–170. San Marino, CA: Huntington, 2015.

Hawes, Clement. *The British Eighteenth Century and Global Critique.* New York: Palgrave, 2005.

Hay, Douglas. "Property, Authority, and Criminal Law." In *Albion's Fatal Tree: Crime and Society in Eighteenth-Century England,* by Douglas Hay, Peter Linebaugh, John G. Rule, E. P. Thompson, and Cal Winslow, 17–63. New York: Pantheon, 1975.

Hay, Douglas, Peter Linebaugh, John G. Rule, E. P. Thompson, and Cal Winslow. *Albion's Fatal Tree: Crime and Society in Eighteenth-Century England*. New York: Pantheon, 1975.

Higgins, Ian. "Remarks on *Cato's Letters*." In *"Cultures of Whiggism": New Essays on English Literature and Culture in the Long Eighteenth Century*, edited by David Womersley, 127–146. Newark: University of Delaware Press, 2005.

Hill, Christopher. "Radical Pirates?" In *The Collected Essays of Christopher Hill*. Vol. 3, *People and Ideas in Seventeenth-Century England*, 161–187. Amherst: University of Massachusetts Press, 1981.

———. *The World Turned Upside Down: Radical Ideas During the English Revolution*. London: Penguin, 1975.

Hirsch, David A. Hedrich. "Liberty, Equality, Monstrosity: Revolutionizing the Family in Mary Shelley's *Frankenstein*." In *Monster Theory: Reading Culture*, edited by Jeffrey Jerome Cohen, 115–140. Minneapolis: University of Minnesota Press, 1996.

Hoppit, Julian. *A Land of Liberty? England 1689–1727*. Oxford: Clarendon, 2000.

Hunt, Margaret R. *The Middling Sort: Commerce, Gender, and the Family in England, 1680–1780*. Berkeley: University of California Press, 1996.

Kamada, Roy Osamu. "Monstrous Citizenships: Coercion, Submission, and the Possibilities of Resistance in *Never Let Me Go* and *Cloud Atlas*." In *Monster Culture in the 21st Century: A Reader*, edited by Marina Levina and Diem-My T. Bui, 163–176. London: Bloomsbury, 2013.

Kamola, Isaac. "Pirate Capitalism, or the Primitive Accumulation of Capital Itself." *Millennium* 47, no. 1 (2018): 3–24.

Kingsley, Sean, and Rex Cowan. *The Pirate King: The Strange Adventures of Henry Avery and the Birth of the Golden Age of Piracy*. New York: Simon and Schuster, 2024.

Kristeva, Julia. *Powers of Horror: An Essay on Abjection*. Translated by Leon S. Roudiez. New York: Columbia University Press, 1982.

Lane, Kris E. *Pillaging the Empire: Piracy in the Americas, 1500–1750*. Armonk, NY: Sharpe, 1998.

Leeson, Peter T. *The Invisible Hook: The Hidden Economics of Pirates*. Princeton, NJ: Princeton University Press, 2009.

Levina, Marina, and Diem-My T. Bui. "Introduction: Toward a Comprehensive Monster Theory in the 21st Century." In *Monster Culture in the 21st Century: A Reader*, edited by Marina Levina and Diem-My T. Bui, 1–14. London: Bloomsbury, 2013.

———, eds. *Monster Culture in the 21st Century: A Reader*. London: Bloomsbury, 2013.

Lincoln, Margarette. *British Pirates and Society, 1680–1730*. Farnham: Ashgate, 2014.

———. "Woodes Rogers and the War against Pirates in the Bahamas." In *Governing the Sea in the Early Modern Era: Essays in Honor of Robert C. Ritchie*, edited by Peter C. Mancall and Carole Shammas, 109–127. San Marino, CA: Huntington, 2015.

Lindsay, Joan. *Picnic at Hanging Rock*. Melbourne: F. W. Cheshire, 1967.

Linebaugh, Peter. *The London Hanged: Crime and Civil Society in the Eighteenth Century*. Cambridge: Cambridge University Press, 1992.

Linebaugh, Peter, and Marcus Rediker. *The Many-Headed Hydra: Sailors, Slaves, Commoners and the Hidden History of the Revolutionary Atlantic*. Boston: Beacon, 2000.

Mackie, Erin. *Rakes, Highwaymen, and Pirates: The Making of the Modern Gentleman in the Eighteenth Century*. Baltimore: Johns Hopkins University Press, 2009.

McVeagh, John. *Tradefull Merchants: The Portrayal of the Capitalist in Literature*. London: Routledge, 1981.

Meier, Thomas Keith. *Defoe and the Defense of Commerce*. ELS Monograph Series No. 38. Victoria: University of Victoria, 1987.

Moore, John Robert. "Defoe, Selkirk, and John Atkins." *Notes and Queries* 179, no. 25 (1940): 436–438.

———. *Defoe in the Pillory and Other Studies*. New York: Octagon, 1973. Originally published in 1939 by Indiana University Press, Bloomington.

———. "Mandeville and Defoe." In *Mandeville Studies*, edited by Irwin Primer, 115–125. The Hague: Nijhoff, 1975.

Mulcaire, Terry. "Public Credit; or, The Feminization of Virtue in the Marketplace." *PMLA* 114, no. 5 (1999): 1029–1042.

Neocleous, Mark. *The Universal Adversary: Security, Capital, and the "Enemies of All Mankind."* London: Routledge, 2016.

Nesvet, Rebecca. "Parallel Histories: Dryden's Plutarch and Religious Toleration." *Review of English Studies* 56, no. 225 (2005): 424–437.

Novak, Maximillian E. *Daniel Defoe: Master of Fictions*. Oxford: Oxford University Press, 2001.

O'Driscoll, Sally. "The Pirate's Breasts: Criminal Women and Meanings of the Body." *Eighteenth Century* 53, no. 3 (2012): 357–379.

Peltonen, Markku. *The Duel in Early Modern England: Civility, Politeness and Honour*. Cambridge: Cambridge University Press, 2003.

Pender, Stephen. "'No Monsters at the Resurrection': Inside Some Conjoined Twins." In *Monster Theory: Reading Culture*, edited by Jeffrey Jerome Cohen, 143–167. Minneapolis: University of Minnesota Press, 1996.

Primer, Irwin, ed. *Mandeville Studies*. The Hague: Nijhoff, 1975.

Prior, Charles W. A., ed. *Mandeville and Augustan Ideas*. Victoria: University of Victoria Press, 2000.

Raven, James. *Judging New Wealth: Popular Publishing and Responses to Commerce in England, 1750–1800*. Oxford: Clarendon, 1992.

———. *The Publishing Business in Eighteenth-Century England*. Woodbridge: Boydell, 2014.

Rediker, Marcus. *Between the Devil and the Deep Blue Sea: Merchant Seamen, Pirates, and the Anglo-American Maritime World, 1700–1750*. Cambridge: Cambridge University Press, 1987.

———. *Villains of All Nations: Atlantic Pirates in the Golden Age*. Boston: Beacon, 2004.

Rennie, Neil. *Treasure Neverland: Real and Imaginary Pirates*. Oxford: Oxford University Press, 2014.

Revolti, Matteo. "Bees on Paper: The British Press Reads the *Fable*." *Erasmus Journal for Philosophy and Economics* 9, no. 1 (2016): 124–141.

Richetti, John. *Popular Fiction before Richardson*. Rev. ed. Oxford: Clarendon, 1992.

Rodger, N. A. M. *The Wooden World: An Anatomy of the Georgian Navy*. Glasgow: Fontana, 1988.

Rogers, Pat. "Nathaniel Mist, Daniel Defoe, and the Perils of Publishing." *The Library*, 7th ser., 10, no. 3 (2009): 298–313.

Said, Edward. *Culture and Imperialism*. New York: Vintage, 1993.

Seabrooke, Leonard, and John Hobson. "The Case for an Everyday International Political Economy." Copenhagen: Department of Business and Politics, Copenhagen Business School, 2006.

Shesgreen, Sean. "Hogarth's *Industry and Idleness*: A Reading." *Eighteenth-Century Studies* 9, no. 4 (1976): 569–598. https://doi.org/10.2307/2737796.

Simon, Rebecca A. "The Problem and Potential of Piracy: Legal Changes and Emerging Ideas of Colonial Autonomy in the Early Modern British Atlantic, 1670–1730." *Journal for Maritime Research* 18, no. 2 (2016): 123–137. https://doi.org/10.1080/21533369.2016.1253317.

Stock, Brian. "Reflections on Ancient Narrative and Ethics." *New Literary History* 40, no. 4 (2009): 771–781. https://doi.org/10.1353/nlh.0.0119.

Thompson, E. P. *Whigs and Hunters: The Origin of the Black Act*. New York: Pantheon, 1975.

Turley, Hans. *Rum, Sodomy, and the Lash: Piracy, Sexuality, and Masculine Identity*. New York: New York University Press, 1999.

Uebel, Michael. "Unthinking the Monster: Twelfth-Century Responses to Saracen Alterity." In *Monster Theory: Reading Culture*, edited by Jeffrey Jerome Cohen, 264–291. Minneapolis: University of Minnesota Press, 1996.

Watson, Matthew. "Rousseau's Crusoe Myth: The Unlikely Provenance of the Neoclassical *Homo economicus*." *Journal of Cultural Economy* 10, no. 1 (2017): 81–96. https://doi.org/10.1080/17530350.2016.1233903.

Weaver-Hightower, Rebecca. *Empire Islands: Castaways, Cannibals, and Fantasies of Conquest*. Minneapolis: University of Minnesota Press, 2007.

Weber, Max. *The Protestant Ethic and the Spirit of Capitalism*. Translated by Talcott Parsons. New York: Scribner, 1958.

Wheeler, Roxanne. "Limited Visions of Africa: Geographies of Savagery and Civility in Early Eighteenth-Century Narratives." In *Writes of Passage: Reading Travel Writing*, edited by James Duncan and Derek Gregory, 14–48. London: Taylor and Francis, 1998.

Withey, Alun. *Concerning Beards: Facial Hair, Health and Practice in England, 1650–1900*. London: Bloomsbury Academic, 2021.

Wood, Peter H. "Teach [Thatch], Edward [known as Blackbeard] (d. 1718), Pirate." *Oxford Dictionary of National Biography*. 23 September 2004. https://www.oxforddnb.com/view/10.1093/ref:odnb/9780198614128.001.0001/odnb-9780198614128-e-27097.

INDEX

Page numbers in italics refer to figures.

ABOUT THE AUTHOR

NOEL CHEVALIER teaches English at Luther College, University of Regina, in Regina, Saskatchewan, Canada. As a specialist in eighteenth-century literature, he has published on a wide range of topics: stage comedy, including an edition of David Garrick and George Colman's *The Clandestine Marriage*; the poet, magazine editor, and vaudeville performer Christopher Smart, including *Reading Christopher Smart in the Twenty-first Century: "By Succession of Delight"* (Bucknell University Press), a collection of scholarly essays he coedited with Min Wild; and, of course, pirates. He also maintains a lively roster of teaching interests, including transhumanism and posthumanism in literature, literary responses to the Bible, the poetry and art of William Blake, and an interdisciplinary course on the roots of cultural modernism and its decline.